THE UNTOLD STORY

THE UNTOLD STORY
Missionary Kids Speak From The Ends Of The Earth

DORIS L. WALTERS

CHAPEL HILL
PRESS, INC.

"Hall of Mirrors" reprinted with permission of Adrian Plass

Copyright © 2007 Doris L. Walters

All rights reserved. No part of this book may be used, reproduced or transmitted in any form or by any means, electronic or mechanical, including photograph, recording, or any information storage or retrieval system, without the express written permission of the authors, except where permitted by law.

ISBN- 10: 1-59715-035-5
ISBN- 13: 978-1-59715-035-4
Library of Congress Catalog Number: 2006940666

First Printing

DEDICATION

I dedicate this book to all missionary kids and their families, from the ends of the earth, whom I have met on my life's journey. MKs, you have taught me so much about your countries. You have educated me about so many places I can never visit. Thanks!

I also dedicate this book to the memory of my mother, the late Mary Lou Helms Walters, who passed away on January 6, 2002, at the age of ninety-two. She was one of the best persons I have ever known, now truly one of God's angels. She taught me so many good values that I hold dear today. Thank you, Mother!

CONTENTS

Foreword ix

Preface xi

Acknowledgments xvii

Chapter One — Reentry 1

Chapter Two — Coping 31

Chapter Three — Schooling 63

Chapter Four — Suffering 89

Chapter Five — Family 133

Chapter Six — Octogenarians and More 161

Chapter Seven — Challenges 187

Chapter Eight — Good Enough 207

Chapter Nine — Secrets of the Heart 237

Chapter Ten — Abuse: Sexual and Substance 267

Chapter Eleven — The Uniqueness of MK Marriage 311

Conclusion — Implications 333

Appendix 341

Bibliography 345

About the Author 347

FOREWORD

Doris Walters has carefully pulled together the essence of a lifetime of pastoral work with missionary children. The life stories and case vignettes captured in this book represent a ministry that is not fully recognized even in the missionary world.

In her first book, Doris Walters shared the dynamics and unique challenges of missionary children. In this book, we intimately experience the struggles and unique issues of missionary children, young and old. Vivid and real storytelling by Doris touches hearts and reminds us of overlooked needs.

REVEREND TED DOUGHERTY JR., PH.D.
Pastoral Psychotherapist
Missionary Family Counseling Services
Winston-Salem, North Carolina

~

I do not know of anyone who could understand the challenges and difficulties encountered by missionary families better than someone who served on the mission field. Dr. Doris Walters, a veteran missionary, experienced youth leader, and pastoral counselor possesses keen insight into the reentry issues faced by missionaries and missionary kids.

A pioneer in identifying these issues and having the appropriate therapeutic treatment skills, Dr. Walters shares the experiences of some MKs as well as her own. This collection provides the opportunity for us to share the pain and healing of some missionary kids and to grow in our own knowledge and concern for those who serve on the mission field.

Frances Roper Lamb
Wilmington, North Carolina

~

In the spring of 1993, Doris Walters and I met to discuss the process of developing a unique counseling ministry focusing on missionary kids and their families. It was my privilege to be a part of seeing Doris's dreams realized in what is called Missionary Family Counseling Services Inc. Creating such a ministry required an overwhelming amount of work. With the task at hand, Doris and I shared the workload.

After submitting the Internal Revenue forms, this counseling ministry was granted nonprofit status on September 3, 1993. The fruits of our labor are recognized in the vignettes Doris presents in this book. I have been treasurer of this ministry since 1993.

Thomas Nichols
Retired CPA, Cannon & Company
Winston-Salem, North Carolina

PREFACE

How I Came to Tell These Stories

JAPAN—I could hardly believe I had arrived in the port of Yokohama. It was a clear morning as our ship, the *President Cleveland*, glided into the waters of Japan. The skies were so clear that Mount Fuji could be clearly seen in the distance. It was September 1, 1966. I had been on the high seas for two weeks. Now I was eager to plant my feet on the soil of Japan.

Immigration officers came on our ship to check passports and immigration papers. Before I knew it, I was walking down the gangplank with two other missionaries and their children. As we made our way to claim our baggage, I heard voices all around me, yet not understanding a single word that was being said. As I walked out into the waiting room, there was a missionary along with a delegation of Japanese university students who greeted me and handed me a handwritten message in English. That message actually was a request for me to become the teacher of their English Conversation class, since the missionary who had been teaching them was due to return to the States for furlough.

As I turned around, there was a missionary who greeted me and told me she was there to transport me to my apartment in Tokyo. I would live there for two years while studying the Japanese language. She helped me put my baggage into her car, and we headed for Tokyo. Although it was September 1, it was a very hot and humid day. She had no air conditioner in her car, which at that time would have been too luxurious for a missionary. After all, were missionaries not supposed to suffer "for the Lord"? With all the car windows wide open, we drove toward Tokyo, that monster of a city about which I had read. Now it was about to become a living reality for me.

The streets from Yokohama to Tokyo were crowded with pedestrians, bicycles, motorcycles, and cars, along with lots and lots of people. As the many bicyclists hit their brakes, there was that horrible, bone-chilling screeching sound. Boy, was it noisy! The wind blew through the open windows. It was, of course, hot, hot air. Yokohama is not really far from Tokyo, but due to the heavy traffic and the unpredictable drivers, it took quite some time to arrive at our destination in Ikebukuro, one of the many sections of the city. There were three apartments, which were referred to as the Triplex. One of those apartments, the upstairs one, was mine. The main streets looked narrow to me, but the width of the community streets were even more narrow. Two American cars could never pass each other without scraping the sides of their cars, but the Japanese cars are very small and narrow, built to fit their streets. Those streets were not built to accommodate American vehicles.

Somewhat dazed from the two weeks on the ship, I was happy to finally arrive at the place that would be my home for two years while I attended language school. I just wanted to relax and let my mind catch up with my body. My first assignment was to study the Japanese language at the Naganuma Language School in Shibuya. In order to get to the language school each day, I took the subway from Ikebukuro to Shibuya Station, and then I walked to the language school. I shall never be able to erase from my mind what I saw the first time I was in the subway. I joined the surge of bodies, mostly Japanese businessmen, all dressed in black business suits. Of course, they all had black hair and black eyes. There was a sea of people like I had never seen before. Yes, there was no doubt in my mind.... I was now in Japan!

The market in my community was a most interesting place, where the ladies would go each day to buy fruits and vegetables to prepare the evening meal. I watched as women, with babies strapped securely on their backs, balanced loads of produce and other items. I watched the shopkeepers as they arranged their produce—apples, oranges, bananas, cabbages, onions, broccoli, and other items—in intricate designs. I listened to the various shopkeepers hawking their wares as they yelled out, "Come! Buy from me!" The music and language I heard was unlike any I had ever heard before.

Day by day in Japan, I was bombarded with an incredible barrage of sights and sounds, information and impressions. Folks who go abroad as tourists bring home with them a highly romanticized, very limited understanding of the culture, customs, and life in any other country which they may visit. I was always amazed at people who came to Japan for a couple of weeks, then returned to the States to write a book. But I was no tourist. My first term of service was five years. I returned to the States for one year and then went back there for another four years. Japan was a place where I would ultimately spend the next twenty years of my life.

Even though I did not know the language, I did not hesitate to shop in the local markets. The shopkeepers were so kind. I did a lot of pointing at items I wished to purchase. I also smiled a lot. Children ran to greet me as I walked down the street. They called out in Japanese, "Gaijin, gaijin," which means "Foreigner, foreigner." I felt the helplessness of a young child who could not even talk to the children. I was frustrated. However, out of my frustration, I was really motivated to learn the language.

I found it easy to love the Japanese people. I realized that we might be different in appearance, but that deep down inside we all had some of the same needs. We had some of the same struggles, pains, heartaches, joys, and happiness. If we cut our finger, it would hurt the same. Red blood surges through the veins of us all. Basic needs to love and be loved, to belong, to succeed, to grieve, and to be comforted are the same. And in the end, we will all die.

Yet our two cultures and customs are very different. In fact, I felt at times like I was living in a topsy-turvy world. Japanese and Americans do things so differently. When I arrived, I ate with a knife, fork, and spoon. They ate with chopsticks. I slept on a bed, but most Japanese slept on a mat on the floor, called "futon." In the Japanese language, the verb always comes at the end of the sentence. This way they can always change the verb if they feel a need to agree with someone, even though they may really disagree. They must be polite. Their car's steering wheel is located on the right side of the car, but they drive on the left side of the road. They say "white and black" while Americans say "black and white." Instead of threading a needle, they "needle a thread." Their favorite foods are fish and rice. I am used to eating meat and potatoes. When they die they are cremated, whereas in America, most often we embalm and bury the dead.

In Japan, the main religions are Shinto and Buddhism, claiming many gods. In America our main religions are Protestantism and Catholicism, with the belief in one God. Japanese read books from right to left and from top to bottom. Whether it is the newspaper or a book, they read from back to front. In Japan you take your shoes off at the door. School students go to school six days a week, and they are required to wear school uniforms. In Japan, I lived mostly in an American-style house. The Japanese, until recent years, lived in poorly constructed houses of wood with paper sliding doors inside the house. The floors were made of woven straw.

Japanese psychology and logic are very different from the American way of thinking. The Japanese mode of thinking is greatly influenced by their religions, just as American ways of thinking come largely from Christianity. I set out to learn all I could about their two religions, realizing that when I did that, I would have a better understanding of the people.

Living in Japan for twenty years was an opportunity to live deliberately. There, I seemed to be more in touch with myself, more in touch with the elements of my environment, with a greater appreciation for nature, more in touch with friends, and more in touch with God. The process of falling more in step with the slower pace of living in Japan was, at first, somewhat frustrating. I had left a growing, thriving church in Wilmington, North Carolina, where I was minister of education and youth. We could make plans and implement them right away. In Japan they believed in taking lots of time to begin something. Their language also could be so evasive. Learning the language was no small task. It has been said that the Japanese language is nine times harder than French. The more of their language I learned, the more I began to sense the soul of the people and to understand their visions. Most of all, I learned that their spirit was not so different from my own.

Yes, Japanese faces continued to look different, but they no longer seemed foreign to me. The language was new, but its message was warm and personal. My new friends welcomed me into their homes and taught me their customs. I realized we were all human beings whom God in his wisdom had created to be unique. In such a short time, their customs and culture no longer seemed so different. In fact, I was amazed how commonplace things became in such a short time. It became my way of life. Yes, at first, I did suffer from some culture shock. At times I longed for home in the States, especially when a friend was very sick. I hated missing the weddings, births, and funerals of people I loved. After twenty years in Japan, I must admit that I brought a lot of Japan with me to America. At the same time, I left a part of myself in that country.

I could not help but watch the children of missionaries who were either born there or went there with their parents at a very early age. They had grown up in the Japanese culture. They had known Japan as their "home." Things there, to them, did not seem so different as they did to me as an adult. I knew the day was coming when each of them would graduate from high school, and then they would return to the States to attend some college. As I watched them mature, I could anticipate some of the reentry issues they would face. Many times

I stood in the airport with families and friends to say "goodbye." I could see how much those young people were hurting as they left their country, their families, their Japanese friends, everything that had been so familiar to them. They were going to that foreign country called America to continue their education.

After living and serving as a missionary in education for twenty years, I returned to North Carolina where I had decided to work on my doctoral degree in pastoral counseling. I would write my dissertation on "The Re-Entry Issues of the Children of Missionaries." Upon completion of that degree, I decided to stay in the States, establish a counseling center, and focus my counseling on the children of missionaries, and the children of business and military families who had spent time overseas. At that time, I knew of no such counseling ministry to the children of missionaries. With an outstanding Board of Directors, we started Missionary Family Counseling Services Inc. in Winston-Salem, North Carolina. Our purpose was to provide free counseling to these young people as long as they were in some kind of study program.

Over a period of fourteen years, I had the privilege of counseling over one thousand individuals from seventy-two countries and thirty-six different religious denominations. Upon my retirement in 2003, I decided I would gather the stories of some of the missionary kids with whom I had counseled over those fourteen years. Thus, the idea for this book was born. I am so happy to now share with you, the reader, the joys and sufferings of these MKs (missionary kids), in hopes that as you read it, you will have a better understanding and a greater appreciation for these young people who have made many sacrifices for God's kingdom work.

ACKNOWLEDGMENTS

This book could never have been written if it had not been for the opportunity I had and chose: to establish a special counseling ministry with my focus on the children of missionaries. I began my counseling with these young people in 1989 in Winston-Salem, North Carolina. First, I worked through North Carolina Baptist Hospital Counseling Center for four years, and then organized and developed the ministry of Missionary Family Counseling Services Inc.

To the more than one thousand individuals who trusted me with their stories, from seventy-two countries, and from thirty-six different religious denominations, my appreciation and gratitude are boundless. As each one shared with me their struggles, feelings, thoughts, joys, and experiences, I felt as if I was treading on holy ground. As our spirits met, our relationships grew into not only therapist-client relationships, but also deep friendships. Our mutual connection was made early since they knew I could really understand their predicaments. I had lived and worked in Japan for more than twenty years. They often said to me, "I am so glad to have a counselor who can really understand where I come from. I don't have to go into great detail about that, for you have been there too." Each MK (missionary kid) with whom I have worked will always have a special place in my heart.

I am most grateful to Tom Nichols, a now-retired CPA from Cannon & Company in Winston-Salem, who worked so faithfully in helping me get the counseling ministry off to a good start. He did all the government paperwork that it took to found this special counseling ministry. I am grateful to him for his service of ten years as treasurer of the Board of Directors. He supported me in every way during my service as executive director/therapist. He continues to serve this ministry as treasurer and board member.

Special appreciation is given to Frances Roper Lamb, a longtime friend and confidante from Wilmington, North Carolina. She served on our Board of Directors as president, and as chairperson of several committees. For the ten years she served, she went beyond the call of duty, publishing our quarterly newsletter, and she did an excellent job even sometimes under the pressures of deadlines. Throughout the writing of this book, Mrs. Lamb has always been available when I got stuck with computer problems, helping to get it up and running again. Thank you for your untiring service.

Jane Cauthen, the daughter-in-law of the late Dr. Baker James Cauthen, and the former executive director of the Foreign Mission Board of the Southern Baptist Convention, has given her devotion to making this ministry better in every way. With her excellent organizational skills, she brought committees together and laid out their duties in a timely fashion. She lives with an MK, Ralph, and knows some of the idiosyncratic temperaments of missionary kids. Ralph, upon marrying Jane, told her that she may not always be happy, but she would never be bored. He has been true to his words. Thank you, Jane, for all your contributions and hard work.

Ted Dougherty has been my mentor for many years, first in 1981–82 when I went to the North Carolina Baptist Hospital to do studies in clinical pastoral education. He was the advisor for my master's thesis at Wake Forest University. My thesis title was: "Death and Funeral Practices in Contemporary Japan." Then from 1986 to 1989, Ted was advisor for my doctoral dissertation, "An Assessment of the Re-Entry Issues of the Children of Missionaries from a First-Hand Perspective." This thesis ended up in a book entitled *Missionary Children Caught between Cultures*. Ted has been a strong supporter through the years as well as a good friend. When I learned he had been selected to be my successor as executive director/therapist for Missionary Family

Counseling Services Inc. upon my retirement at the end of February 2003, I could not have been more delighted.

Strong financial support has come from Mrs. Harry O. Parker, Dr. Eugene Linton, MD/MK who grew up in Korea, and Mrs. Ed (Wava) Howard. Without their continuous, faithful support, we would have been quite hampered in what we were able to do for MKs. I am most grateful for them, along with James Fowler, an MK who grew up in Argentina, and who passed away in September 2002. Some years before his passing, he said, "Doris, even a ninety-year-old MK still needs your counsel and support." Mr. Fowler really believed in what we were trying to do for MKs. He made the statement, "I believe in Missionary Family Counseling Services and what it has done and can do for MKs so much that I have made this organization a benefactor in my estate." After his death, we received a rather large gift from his estate. Mr. Fowler died at age ninety-four, but his legacy lives on though this ministry.

I also wish to express my deep gratitude to many churches that gave financial support consistently to Missionary Family Counseling Services. Perhaps our largest donor was First Baptist Church of Winston-Salem. Other churches who donated large gifts throughout the ten years I was director were Starling Avenue Baptist Church, Martinsville, Virginia, and the following churches in North Carolina: Centenary United Methodist Church, Winston-Salem; Emerywood Baptist Church, High Point; First Baptist Church, Elkin; First Baptist Church, Greensboro; First Baptist Church, Raleigh; Winter Park Baptist Church, Wilmington; University Baptist Church, Chapel Hill; First Baptist Church, Newton; Peace Haven Baptist Church, Winston-Salem; First Baptist Church, Kernersville; First Baptist Church, Marshville; First Baptist Church, Morganton; First Baptist Church, Goldsboro; Highland Presbyterian Church, Winston-Salem; Friedberg Moravian Church, Winston-Salem; Bethel Presbyterian Church, Cornelius; and all the other churches who have ever donated to this counseling ministry. Thank you, one and all!

It is also a privilege to recognize the various foundations that donated to this ministry. They are the Culler Foundation; Winston-Salem Foundation; the Stegall Endowment; First Baptist Church Orlando Foundation; Moravian Church of America, Southern Province; Royce and Jane Reynolds Foundation; Western NC Conference of the Methodist Church; the Cooperative Baptist Fellowship; and the Richard J. Reynolds III and Marie Mallow Reynolds Foundation.

I do appreciate having the opportunity to work with some of the finest board members one could select. Some of those are: Rev. Alec Alvord, MK from Africa; Rev. Dr. James Baucom; Attorney Winfield Blackwell; Dr. Ted Blount, MD; Rev. Dr. David Burr; Mrs. Ralph (Jane) Cauthen; Rev. Dr. Ted Dougherty; Mrs. Kathy Frye (MK); Mr. Roger Howard; Rev. Dr. Robert Iobst; Rev. Dr. Michael Jamison; Rev. Dr. Lamar King; Mrs. Frances R. Lamb; Dr. Eugene Linton, MD (MK); Mr. Andrew Linton, MK; Mrs. Joyce McKenzie; Mr. Thomas Nichols, CPA; Rev. Dr. Jack Noffsinger; Rev. Mickie Norman; Mrs. Harry O. Parker; Rev. Dr. Robert Parsons; Rev. Thomas Shelton; Rev. Dr. Derrill Smith; Dr. Jule Spach; Mr. Richard Stockton; Rev. Vicki Tamer; Mr. John Totten Jr., Attorney; Mr. Walter Wiley; the late Dr. Alan Hinman; and Mrs. Alan (Alice) Hinman.

I am most grateful to some special people, friends, and colleagues: Dr. Ted Dougherty, Jane and Ralph Cauthen, Frances Roper Lamb, Mrs. David (Frances) Parker, and Mrs. Frank (Pat) Hawkins for reading this manuscript.

I am grateful to Dr. Clyde Austin, professor in the Department of Psychology at Abilene Christian University for forty-one years (retired), for reading and editing this manuscript. His suggestions have been most valuable to me.

I am grateful to Linda Ford Farrell, retired English teacher from New Hanover High School in Wilmington, North Carolina, who gave careful attention to the English grammar, punctuation, and sentence structure in this manuscript. Linda taught English for seventeen years at New Hanover and seven years elsewhere. Linda and her family have been longtime, cherished friends.

I am indebted to Marolyn A. Schauss, my neighbor and friend, for her profound Microsoft Office knowledge and skills. Without her expertise I would not have been able to present my manuscript to the publisher in such a professional format. Thank you, Marolyn, for the many, many hours you gave to seeing this manuscript completed.

I am grateful for so many who encouraged me over a long period of time to put the stories of some of my MK clients into print. I am grateful to the fifty-three MKs, men and women, whose stories appear in this book and whose privacy I have sought to protect. *MKs Speak from the Ends of the Earth* would not exist today without them. I am grateful for the lives of each one of them. To simply say "Thank you" seems to inadequately express my deepest feelings, but I hope that each of you know how much you mean to me.

Last, but certainly not least, I gratefully acknowledge some special people at Chapel Hill Press in Chapel Hill, North Carolina, who have been so congenial and a delight with whom to do business. Edwina Woodbury, president; Misty Thebeau, publishing manager; Heather Stockel, administrative assistant; Bob Land, editor; and designer Katie Severa.

CHAPTER ONE

Reentry

Culture Shock Is Real

Clay, an eighteen-year-old male Missionary Kid (MK) had returned from his adopted country and had been in the States only a few days. He had graduated from high school in Ecuador and was now to be a freshman in college. Handsome and starting a new life, he was dressed like the perfect "Joe College" student of the sixties. His parents had been sure that he was dressed properly in nice dress slacks and a button-down-collar dress shirt underneath a beautiful cashmere sweater. I met Clay and five MKs at a large retreat center in North Carolina. All were freshmen with only a week until they would find themselves on some college campus. Of all the six MKs, Clay appeared to be the most disoriented. He was walking around like a zombie. I spent time talking with him, as he let me know that being where he was at the moment seemed like a dream. He thought he would wake up and find himself back in Ecuador.

There was no doubt in my mind that all six were suffering from culture shock. One, saying she had no one to talk to who could understand her situation, told me that she would set her big teddy bear on her bed, and then she would talk to the teddy bear about all her feelings. Perhaps that is the best thing she could have done, for the teddy bear had been with her all along, and these Americans could not understand, or so she thought. This was student week at the retreat center. The assembly hall was full of screaming young people. As they met and embraced one another, there were shouts of glee. I could clearly see this kind of behavior with hundreds of young American students was shocking to the MKs. I must admit that I too was completely surprised at the lack of respect for this place of worship.

The contemporary service with lots of loud singing and handclapping was almost more than I could accept. I had been back in the States myself only three years after serving as a missionary to Japan. This was the first time I had attended such a statewide student gathering. It was so completely different from those I had attended even when I was on furlough. I talked with some of the more mature student leaders, who said to me, "Doris, things have changed so much among students on campuses, and thus this is what you see and hear." I personally did not like the change I was witnessing. The MKs and I were identifying as we watched the week unfold. It was a week of entertaining, and I felt no sense of real worship. At times it even bordered on desecration to me. It was clear that the MKs did not feel a part of that noisy, clamoring crowd of college students.

During the week, I met daily with the six MKs. We discussed many issues that they were facing during these first few days back in the States: separation and loss. We spoke about what it was like leaving their families and the country in which they had spent more time than they had in America; at most they had spent only two to three years in America. We discussed their feelings of being different and having different values than their peers in the States. This feeling of being different was one they had faced head-on right here at this retreat, and they were not too happy. The MKs seemed so much more mature. They were reserved young people, while their peers at this retreat seemed so immature and wild. Among other reentry issues that we discussed were alienation and culture shock, which they had not expected. They didn't know what they would be facing when they arrived on their college campus. There were so many mixed feelings filling their minds and hearts. Some were thinking, *If this is what America is all about, I just want to go back to my country and my family.* Some were thinking, *How am I going to survive and fit into this culture?* They were all downright homesick and admitted that they felt like they were living a bad dream, and that they would wake up and find themselves in their own beds that they had left behind.

As the retreat came to an end, and we were saying our goodbyes and each was going our separate ways, I, along with each of them, felt quite a bit of sadness. While we were together for those three days, we really felt like we were with family. Every one of us had tears in our eyes as we gave each other big hugs. I assured them that I would be there for them, and they could call me at my office or at my home day or night.

Clay was the one for whom I had the greatest concern. He was walking away from the Retreat Center just as much in a daze as he had been when he arrived. Interestingly enough, I knew some of the faculty and staff on the campus where he was headed. When I returned to my home, I called one faculty member who was my good friend and asked him to please look out for Clay. My friend made a point of meeting Clay when he arrived on the campus a few days later. He let Clay know that he had a friend on campus, and anytime Clay needed to ask questions or needed help, my friend was only a phone call away.

That fall, the first time I visited Clay on his campus, a small one in comparison to many campuses, I saw a more relaxed young man. As I watched him walking across the campus to meet me at our designated place, he was wearing jeans and a baggy sweatshirt. He had a different hairstyle, and you would never have known he was the MK whom I met when he first returned to the States. I was delighted. He was dealing with issues as they arose, yet he was homesick. I told him about the man who was the college president when I attended that same college many years before him. In my first chapel service where the president spoke to all freshmen, he had said to us, "I wouldn't give a dime for a student who does not get homesick, but I wouldn't give a cent for one who cannot overcome it and dig into his education."

I took Clay out for dinner on my first visit with him on his campus. We had a great time talking, and I was happy to hear all of his gripes. There were things he liked about his college and other things he strongly disliked. He had been eager to fit in with his peers. This wasn't too hard for him as he had a good personality, and he was handsome. These factors entered into his being readily accepted, especially among the girls. Throughout his first two years, I visited Clay several times. Those visits were always uplifting for me as well as for Clay. As I saw him adjust, I was so proud of him.

As Clay neared the end of his second year, he decided to transfer to a larger university that had more to offer him in his chosen field of interest. That summer he returned to his adopted country for summer vacation. He had a great time with his family and felt some reluctance in returning to the States, yet he knew he must go on with his life.

I had not seen Clay on his newly chosen university campus. However, by the middle of his first year, I received a telephone call from him. He began to tell me what was going on in his life. As he described his feelings and other symptoms, I knew Clay was suffering from depression. He had lost all interest in everything. He had lost his appetite, could not concentrate, and was not able to get out of bed to go to his classes. He was failing most of his courses. He saw no way out of this dark hole.

I was able to say to Clay with all my compassion, "Clay, what you are describing to me is depression." I asked him if he would be willing to come to Winston-Salem to see me. We could talk more about it, and I assured him I would get him appropriate help. Clay was more than willing to do that. After talking further with him, I asked him if he would see a good psychiatrist whom I knew personally and who had a special interest in missionaries and their children. He agreed. I made the phone call to my friend and accompanied Clay to his office. Clay liked this doctor, who asked him if he would be willing to take an antidepressant. He agreed. Clay defined himself to Dr. G as never being on time, not being responsible at all, being unable to handle money wisely, not caring for school, not concerning himself about his future, and having no desire to go to church.

That day, as Clay and I left Dr. G's office, he seemed hopeful and encouraged. In the following days and weeks I kept in close touch with Clay. He would return to Winston-Salem for med checks periodically, and we would always meet. Each time I saw him, Clay seemed to be improving rapidly. Then, one day he called me and enthusiastically told me that he had decided to return to the previous college to finish his junior and senior years. He seemed so happy and relieved.

During the fall semester, I visited Clay again on the smaller campus where he had started his education. He was so happy. In his excitement he told me about how old friends had warmly greeted him, happy to see him again. He said, "I feel at home here among friends, and I have so much peace about my decision to return." The faculty also gave him a warm welcome. Those following two years, Clay did exceptionally well and graduated. He got a very good job in research. From there, he went on to even better-paying jobs and ended up going to a large city in a state where he now resides. He was so proud of himself. On one occasion when we talked by phone, he said, "Doris, I am just out of college, and I am making more money than both my parents' salaries put together."

Clay had grown up in a very loving family, but acknowledged that his father's expectations of him had created stress and pressure on him. Being away from his siblings whom he loved dearly was hard on him at first. He always talked to me about missing his sisters especially. In counseling with Clay, he noted that he felt his parents were a bit too serious. In his home they seldom laughed and had fun. There was also the issue of his father's need to control. As a child he heard lots of "should" and "ought," and heard sermons at church that created a lot of unfounded guilt in him. He didn't remember receiving a lot of praise or positive strokes from his father. This, he believed, created a lot of inner conflict. However, Clay was committed to making things better with his father. He was interested in studying philosophy so that he could learn to think for himself. Clay saw his mother as a very caring person who nurtured him a lot, but he believed her to be a bit naive.

Clay was a really intelligent, intuitive, and caring young man. He was a strong introvert and could be happy spending time alone and thinking. He was very creative, and a logical, analytical thinker who could grasp possibilities. He was a perceptive individual, which caused him to sometimes postpone unpleasant jobs although he would get the jobs done at the last minute. When under the pressure of a deadline, he could be very productive and get his work in on time. One problem Clay dealt with was making decisions, never feeling he had enough information. His Myers-Briggs personality test proved him to be an INTP (introvert, intuitive, thinker, perceptive). Thus, he could focus on one thing at a time. He hated routine, yet would get bursts of energy powered by his enthusiasm, but then he would have his slack period. He was aware of new challenges and possibilities. He was a person of genuine warmth.

In counseling, among other things, we talked about self-worth and how, first of all, Clay was a child of God. He began to care less and less about what others might think of him. He had developed pretty good self-esteem in his adopted country of Ecuador, but returning to the States, where no one knew what he had experienced, was difficult. In Ecuador he was liked by everyone. He said, "There I was somebody, but in America I am nobody." At school he was funny and made people laugh. As a caregiver he realized that he was seeking approval, praise, and immediate gratification. He excelled in extracurricular activities, overdid projects for recognition, and belonged to many sports teams.

As Clay reflected on all of his past, he came to realize that, in his eighteen years, he had gone through a lot of changes. At one point he felt he would never find a place of permanency because of his many moves, living here and then there. He talked about the restlessness—needing to stay on the move, go anywhere at any time, taking any kind of transportation. I explained to Clay that this is what I call the MK syndrome, especially among male MKs. To help him understand this syndrome, I explained that MKs, in general, are set up" for this syndrome since they were always saying "hello" and "goodbye" at least every four years when they returned to the States for one-year furloughs. Often, even on the mission field they are continuously moving from place to place. That sense of restlessness seems to stay with MKs for a long time, and with some, forever.

I am happy that I knew Clay. An exceptional young man, I am proud of the way he was able to work through his struggles and difficulties, and now he has become a very successful businessman. I am glad to have had a part in seeing this happen.

A Sense of Belonging

Cam, a seventy-year-old MK, was driving through Winston-Salem with his wife. They were driving their RV camper on vacation from Ohio. They had heard about me and MK counseling services. As they were passing through, they stopped at a pay phone and called my home in the late afternoon. I could readily see that he wanted and needed to talk, so I invited them to come to my house, which was right off the interstate.

Cam shared with me the great difficulties he had had upon his return to the United States more than fifty years earlier. He hastened to tell me, "And you know, I am still having problems, particularly relational. Often my wife, who is not a MK, cannot understand me. My children don't understand me either." Then he confessed that since he was sent away from home to boarding school at a young age, he never knew how to be a father. He did not know his own father since he was seldom around him. There was never that male role model to show him what a man or a father is to be. He said that his two children had grown up and become very successful, but he gave his wife all the credit for their successes.

Cam said to me, "I only wish there had been counselors such as you when I returned to the States." He acknowledged how envious he was of MKs today having available to them such a counseling service. He had grown up in Africa, and at that time furloughs were only every seven years. That meant that he was in the States only once or not more than twice when he came back here to live permanently. America was certainly the foreign country to him. He had never, after all those years, felt that he belonged in the States, and for that matter, anywhere in the world. He felt like a misfit wherever he had been.

Cam, his wife, and I spent about three hours that winter evening talking, and I did a lot of listening to Cam. My heart felt sad and heavy for him as he discussed his struggles. He said, "Here with you, who have been a missionary and who knows MKs, I really feel like you are my family. I feel a sense of belonging, at least for this short time."

It was clear that Cam found it very difficult to leave my home and be on his way to their next vacation RV camp. I felt his strong reluctance to leave. Perhaps all of us have been with a person or persons with whom we felt so much acceptance and understood that we just didn't want the time to end when we would have to say goodbye. Here, Cam was saying one more goodbye added to all the hundreds of times he had done this before. MK lives are filled with hellos and goodbyes. They are either saying goodbye to their parents, or their parents are leaving them as they grow up and are left in the States to fend for themselves. I truly felt sad and had a heavy heart as we hugged each other and they took leave. A part of my mission family was gone. I never saw them again.

Abandonment and Anger

Walter is a thirty-five-year-old male MK born in South America. Thus, he had dual citizenship. His reason for seeking counseling, first at age twenty-four, was to help him deal with an excessive amount of anger as well as with his past.

The first time I talked with Walter was by telephone on a Sunday evening. Since he finally found someone who he felt could understand, I spent two hours just listening to him and occasionally gave a little input. He was so full of anger, mostly toward his parents who had just left to return to their mission field. He was actually glad to see them leave. Now he could be his own man.

Walter's mother, according to his own description, was hypocritical and full of hate, violence, and lies. She was manipulative and one he could not trust. He felt she had treated him unjustly. In fact he told me that he was so happy when he left his parents on the mission field in the country where he had grown up, although it was hard to leave his many friends, mostly the nationals. At eighteen, he returned to the States to enter the college of his parents' choice. He described his parents and siblings as narrow-minded, ultraconservative people. He went further to say that his family was very dysfunctional. He believes his family lived in a world of repressed anger, lying, gossiping, hating, manipulating, and superficiality. He could never understand why his parents went to another country to be missionaries. He said, "I cannot see how they can speak the truth when both parents have lived lives of lies and hypocrisy."

Walter indicated that occasionally when his mother gave him a phone call, she never seemed to care about what he was doing or what his needs might be. She only wanted to tell him about what she/they were doing in their other country. This would make Walter furious, and they would end up in a shouting match on the phone, which was costly. I suggested to him that the next time she called him to just let her talk and talk. When she paused for his response, simply say to her, "Well, Mom, do you have anything else to say?" He found out that this worked, for she would finally wind down. He no longer argued with her, and he realized that this new behavior really did put him in control. He felt good about himself, and she was left speechless. All of this discord really put him into a state of depression, for he had now turned his anger inside and it was eating away at his gut. He was very anxious and could not sit still very long. Finally, I confronted Walter with his depression and asked him if he would be willing to see a great psychiatrist whom I often used with my clients. He agreed, and I went with him on his first visit. He began to take an antidepressant and thus began to deal with his life in a more wholesome way. When asked if he felt "abandoned in the States," he burst into tears. The "dam" was broken, and he thought he would never be able to stop crying. Previously, he had referred to himself as "wound up inside."

His analogy of his predicament was of a blindfolded person running a race to win but unsure where the finish line was. All during his college years and even into the beginning of his work career, he was confronted with multiple deadlines and demands, and until recently he had no clear-cut goals.

As many missionary kids, Walter had learned self-reliance, willingly or forced. Most MKs feel they have no choice as they are left in the States to fend for themselves. However, he had put social activity, fun, and pleasure quite far down on his list of priorities. His feeling of betrayal by his first serious girlfriend, as a sophomore in college, did not help matters. His self-esteem left much to be desired. He was easily threatened and put on the defensive.

Walter was a brilliant young man who was hired by a large import/export company six months before he graduated from college. He had been doing some translation work for them. He knew the Spanish language and could easily get documents from the land of his birth and then translate them into English for this American company. Needless to say, he became a real asset to this company. Even though he was very successful in the business world, he still seemed to be cut off from his peers, mainly because he always put work before play.

Walter often spoke of his anger toward his mother, but the fact remained that he was fearful of his father's temper. His father often provoked Walter to anger and was inconsistent. Walter said he was always verbally fighting with his mother. He said that his mother always ended up apologizing to his dad, but he doesn't remember ever hearing his father apologize to his mother, much less anyone else. He said, "Not once do I remember my father saying, 'I'm sorry.'" Walter had lots of anger toward both parents. He felt so helpless, hopeless, and out of control. He also carried a lot of anger and resentment toward older brothers. It seems that his parents were always trying to triangle one of his brothers into the mix, which made matters worse. Walter said, "You know, when my father was angry, he literally kicked the dog."

At seventeen, Walter had a minor accident in his father's car. His father did not seem to be concerned about whether Walter was injured. He simply responded with outrage that his car had been damaged. Walter worked and paid for the repairs himself.

Walter remembers one of his parents' big fights when he was in the tenth grade. Their arguments were so disruptive. Walter said that sometimes he just had to leave the house in order to study. He remembers once when his mother threw a cup of coffee in his father's face. On his eighteenth birthday, things had gotten so bad, he confronted them, telling them that they were hypocrites, and he could not understand why they were "playing the role of missionaries" when they were the ones who needed the most help.

For Walter's first year of college, his parents made the choice of schools, never asking Walter where he would like to go. Of course, they chose one of the most conservative schools in the States. Not being able to tolerate the fundamentalism at that school, he told his parents he was transferring. His parents agreed for him to make the move, but told him he would have to pay for his own education. Indeed, he did just that.

Walter had gone away to boarding school for his eighth and ninth grades in high school. The boarding school was two thousand miles from his home. However, for whatever reason, which he never knew, they brought him back home for his tenth grade. He said he missed his home and friends but not his parents. The years at boarding school were two of the more peaceful years of his life. Relationships with his parents did not improve. He missed the freedom he had acquired at boarding school. He said, "In all the schools I attended, not once did my parents ask me where I wanted to go."

Once he entered the college of his choice he said, "I learned more about myself." He learned self-discipline and could easily focus on his studies. During his second and third years of college he worked at a bank and provided for all his own needs. It was at this time he realized he was going through an identity crisis. He felt driven and a need to prove himself. The bottom line was that he was outgrowing his family, but he had nothing or no one to put in their place. This created a lot of loneliness for him. He felt the heavy demands of doing well in school and working to pay his own way. Often he was filled with fear and had anxiety attacks. He remembers once asking himself, *What is happening to me?* His mind was racing, and he did not know how to relax. It was at this point when I took him to see a psychiatrist.

After spending time with me in counseling for two years on a regular basis, his anger began to diminish, yet he felt his parents and siblings had no idea who he was and didn't really much care to know. He felt closer to his friends than to any of his family.

With much support and encouragement, Walter really began to move on with his life and accept the things that he could not change. He worked for two very sophisticated companies. He went on to earn two master's degrees and then his doctorate in international law. By this time he had served as an international trade specialist, arbitrator and consultant, import/export compliance specialist, bankruptcy analyst, and a state supreme court arbitrator and mediator.

Some words I would use to describe Walter are: authentic, intelligent, honest, trustworthy, compassionate, warm, caring, responsible, adaptable, and a linguist. Walter is a living example that MKs can work through the past difficulties in their lives and rise to great heights. I could readily be the first to nominate Walter to a who's who among the children of missionaries.

Shattered Vases

Gertrude, upon reentering the United States, found that it took some time for her to figure out just who she was, and the worst part is that she had no one to work with her on this. Perhaps if she had asked for help, help would have arrived immediately. MKs do have a difficult time asking for help because they want so much to feel independent. In America, she heard the people speaking a different, strange language, and she had no clue what they meant by their jargon or clichés. Gertrude thought and asked herself the question, *If I can't understand these people, then how in the world could these people begin to understand me, much less my experience of growing up in Africa as a MK?*

Gertrude said she eventually came to know folks who had visited parts of Africa. She said, "If an American goes to Africa and spends as much as one month there, they can get a pretty good idea what it might be like living there permanently." She felt that those people do seem to have some appreciation for that continent and its culture. She told about an interesting experience she had when she got married. She did not ask her roommate in college to be her bridesmaid nor her best friends in college to be her maids of honor. She said, "Of course, I wanted my MK friends to play those roles because I considered them to be my family, not my USA college friends." At first, Gertrude's college roommate and other college friends thought Gertrude was angry at them or, for some reason, didn't really like them very much. However, when Gertrude explained her motives to them, they completely accepted the fact that they were not included in her wedding party.

After being back in the States for ten years, Gertrude finally went to an MK reunion. She said that being with all those MKs made her feel like she had "gone home." After her first year in college, Gertrude had not seen or talked to an MK anywhere. Needless to say, at that time she did not know what she had been missing. From time to time she had received invitations to attend MK reunions or retreats, often in states far from where she was residing. Being with those MKs created within her a feeling of sadness for all she had missed. Being all alone as a MK for ten years had caused her to feel that she was the only MK going through so many traumatic experiences. She had felt so alone and no sense of belonging where she was living.

I met Gertrude eleven years after she had been back in the States. I spent time listening to her tell about her growing-up years in Africa and about what her life had been like since returning to the States for college. She confessed that those years she had spent in Africa had "made me who I am today." She had not only lived in this different culture but had taken it into her whole being as her own. She did things like they did, and she felt like they did about daily life.

Another thing that was really different was the weather. She was now living in a city in America that always had some snow every winter. It was always warm in Africa, and she had never seen snow there. Christmas in Africa was always warm, but in America, most often it was cold. She told me that she actually did her Christmas shopping in America in the summer because it gave her more of a sense of the Christmas season in Africa. She said that cold Christmases in the States "just do not seem like Christmas to me."

I remember once talking to a seventy-eight-year-old MK who grew up in China. She said, "I still feel more Chinese than I do American."

This is very common with lots of MKs. How often I have heard them make such statements. Some say, "I know I have the American face, but I do not feel American."

After Gertrude attended that MK reunion, she could now be free to put her African trinkets and other items on display in her home. She found that those who visited her home really were interested, and they became an item for discussion. People were interested in her life as an MK and had many questions to ask her. She said, "Now, I feel it is okay for me to be African. I don't feel so weird anymore. Before that reunion, I thought I *had* to be American or everyone would ignore me and think I was strange." The fact is that Gertrude had come to accept herself for who she was and to cherish that part of herself that she had before denied. She was now proud of her heritage, happy to be who she was, and accepted the fact that "being different was okay."

Gertrude had left home and parents to go to boarding school in the first grade. From the age of thirteen until she graduated from high school, she spent only a total of four weeks in her own home with her parents. Often she felt closer to other missionaries, who lived in the same town as the school she attended, than she did with her own parents. She saw them much more often and were in their homes often.

Gertrude said that she believes that separation from her missionary family and the loss of her own home and family was "worse than death." When people in the States asked her, "How are you?" she would always reply, "I'm just fine," but all the time she knew she was not fine. She was feeling a lot of pain, living in denial, and was even sometimes feeling plain numb. In America, the most complex thing for Gertrude was trying to live with those feelings on a daily basis. However, she said that when her parents retired from the mission field, she, for the first time, realized that now she had completely lost her country. She did have the opportunity during college and the ensuing years before her parents' retirement to return to Africa twice. She went just before they retired and was able to bring closure to that long chapter in her life. One sad statement Gertrude made was, "You know, my parents were never really mine. They were owned by the African people whom they served, and by the Mission Board."

When asked about some of the things she missed in Africa the most, she replied, "The smells. American smells, McDonald's smells, are very different from the smells of Africa." In Africa, Gertrude had learned to do "everything." In America she thought that the people seem to choose one big "thing" and then become very proficient in that one thing. Her belief was that here one is not required to be creative like they are in Africa. She said, "Everything here is already made, and the challenge seems to be absent. Life here becomes routine." That reminded me of a missionary family I knew in Japan. The father became ill with cancer. They had to return to the States. The mother told her two boys they could take only one toy or plaything with them on the plane for their return trip to America. To her surprise, one of the boys chose to bring a piece of screen wire which he had used to sift sand or dirt.

When Gertrude first returned to the States to attend college, she said, "Everything changed. My heart, my soul, and my spirit changed. My body was the only thing that did not change." I remember asking Gertrude what she brought back to the States with her. She had brought only her clothes and a few books. If she had to do this all over again, she said she would have brought more of her familiar things. Here, I recalled my own return to the States after living and working in Japan for more than twenty years. I was living and working in the States, had bought a condominium, and all new furniture. My household items from Japan had not yet arrived. Then, I found myself staying later and later at work, not knowing why. However, when my familiar household items and other belongings arrived from Japan, and I placed them in my new condominium, I felt so happy and so much at home. Thus, I can identify with MKs who need their familiar belongings with them upon their return to the States.

On the day of graduation from boarding school, she said that MKs experience a tremendous amount of sadness and grief because "we know we may never see each other again in this world." On that one last night together, they stayed up all night, talking, sharing, and cherishing their memories, never wanting the night to end. One MK described this kind of experience. He said,

> Each class is like a vase which is continually being formed and molded together through our many activities, such as junior/senior prom and banquet, our senior trip with one week together, and all those activities which lead up to and encompasses these. When graduation finally comes, it is like putting on the final glaze or finish. There is great rejoicing. At the same time, it is like taking the vase, the final product, and throwing it to the ground to see it shatter into a hundred pieces or bits. All those bits and pieces represent each person in our class as they go off to find a new vase to begin to mold—another long process and many times without a catalyst or support group.

Gertrude said that she found it hard to form a new vase since it seemed to her that Americans, in general, do not want to be a part of a close-knit group like they had at the boarding school. She believes that "no other experience is as unique as the MK relationship." She does not believe that Americans can even begin to identify with them as MKs. She said that she knew some MKs who like Job "cursed the day they were born."

Some things Gertrude did learn were, first of all, "be myself and like me, and don't try to change to meet others' expectations. If the MK dwells on his/her losses, things will not get better, but they just keep suffering. Move from the confused self to the whole, real self, and accept responsibility. Focus on my own needs, and finally, don't allow the past to control my future." After carrying rebellion for years, she could now move on with her life in a healthy manner.

Gertrude felt really angry at her parents when they left her all alone on her college campus and walked away to return to Africa. She felt completely abandoned. I asked her, "What did that feel like to you, when they walked away and left you?" She said, "Just to hear you say those words causes me to have a real tightness in my chest. I can't deal with that right now." Grief and pain can sometimes make one feel like they are suffocating.

Most MKs suffer from a tremendous amount of grief. When that happens, hopefully, someone will be there to offer support, encouragement, and guidance, and to help see them through their crisis and their own specific grief. One young male MK told me that in counseling, when his therapist asked him if he felt abandoned, he realized that his therapist had said the right word, "abandoned," and he started to weep and thought he would never be able to stop. The therapist did not leave him.

Abandoned but Not Forsaken

It was a cool fall day when I received a telephone call from a minister in a western state. The news was that he had a young missionary couple in his church who had just returned to the States. They were attending his church with their two children. He explained to me that the husband and father had just left the family and had cleaned out their bank account, leaving only about two hundred dollars. There they were, far away from close family members. The pastor was concerned and was making funds available for the wife and her two MKs to fly to North Carolina. He said, "Doris, they are going to need your support and the support of many people." I assured him that I would be available to counsel them and support them in whatever ways were needed. The children were ages nine and six.

When the two MKs arrived with their mother at my office, it was evident that all were in some state of shock. It was revealed that the husband and father of the two children had become involved with one of his students on the mission field that they had just left. He intended to bring this much younger woman to the States and marry her, which he finally did. Financially, they were destitute. They had been abandoned! The mother said to me, "At the time of our appointment for missionary service, an appropriate position was sought for my husband, and his title was 'seminary teacher.' Although I was told that at that time, there was no request from the mission field for a person with my credentials. I would have to accept the title of 'church and home' missionary." Later, her area director assured her that it wasn't important for her to be named to a position since she could do whatever work she chose because music teachers were always needed. She later discovered that there was indeed a need for a voice teacher at the seminary where her husband was teaching. They would be more than happy to make a request for her to be named to that position.

When they had gone to missionary orientation, the wives were not included when financial issues for the families were discussed. Rather, they were required to attend a class on homemaking and how to be a good hostess. Thus, this wife had no understanding about Social Security. The husband would receive an identification number and the wife was identified under her husband's number. Now, she was ignorant about whether or not she could receive Social Security, since she had not been assigned an identification number. To add insult to injury, all mail was addressed to her husband. He was given a car on the mission field and also a budget for his work. The wife was not treated with equal respect.

Now she was confronted with the truth of her situation: no money, no Social Security funds, and no child support from her children's father. She was at the mercy of her own biological family, yet her ex-husband continued to receive the family salary check. When inquiring of the Mission Board about their money situation, she was told that they could not split the salary, half to her ex-husband and half to her, because that would involve legal implications. Therefore, they could not send her half of their usual salary. Her ex-husband had already set up a new bank account in only his name and asked the Mission Board to mail his check to that new account. They did, no questions asked.

He also went to the Board's Credit Union and signed for a significant loan, but they would make his wife liable as well as this man. She was now seeing the lack of concern of the Mission Board Staff toward not only her, but all the other appointed missionary wives. And now she had two MKs to take care of and support all by herself.

Another month passed without any money coming to her from the Mission Board. Friends intervened. They went with her to confront the staff at the mission board. The results were that this wife would now get the salary of a single missionary for a few months. But what about the children?

Her ex-husband, of course, was required to resign from his assignment with the Mission Board. Even though the wife and children wanted to return to their place on the mission field, she was told that she could not return. Divorcees were not allowed to be missionaries under their new jurisdiction. The truth of the matter is, if her husband had died, then she could have continued her missionary work.

This wife and mother stated it so concisely as threefold.

1. *The lack of proper care and attention to a family in crisis.* The children had been told to call the mission board staff and other missionaries "aunt" and "uncle." This was supposed to be their new family. Now, not only had their father abandoned them, but so had their mission family. The children were crying and having heart-rending nightmares. They were, at the same time, trying to figure out what they were doing back here in the States, when this other country had been their home. All their belongings and all that was familiar to them was back in that other country, and everything here in the States was new and confusing. After all, one of them had lived in that other country from the time she was an infant. The other was taken there as a very young child. That's where their hearts were. America was not home for them.

2. *The status of married women missionaries.* The question was, "Are the wives really employees of the Mission Board?"
3. *The issue of a divorcee.* She and the children wanted to continue their mission work but were told, "No, not under this Board."

Here were two young children, MKs, who were brokenhearted right along with their mother, and Mom was being asked to resign from being a missionary. She had been voice professor/coordinator for the 250-member student music department of a theological seminary. Now, it was clear that she had been simply an appendage to her husband.

I worked with this mother and her two MKs in counseling for several months. It was clear that the two children were devastated, yet they did not know how to verbalize their feelings. I asked them to draw pictures of how they were feeling. I must say that those pictures revealed more to me than words ever could. It should be noted that the first words that came from the mouth of the youngest child were not English, but rather Portuguese, the native tongue. Both children were now speaking the language fluently.

Confusion continued for some time. They could not understand how their father could leave them. They couldn't understand how he could desert their mother and leave them penniless, and how he could bring this "other woman" to the States and marry her, this young woman who had been in their home and whom they thought had been their friend. The feeling they portrayed most often was anger, especially the younger child. The older child just looked somewhat numb. In the ensuing years, both children had to be placed on antidepressants.

For months, I saw these children every week. It was good for them to vent their feelings. They were what we may call "displaced persons." They were living with their mother in their grandparents' home. How they longed for a place for just the three of them. One day, the younger child brought me a drawing and gave it to me. Then she started to explain it to me. There was a house with three people standing in front. There were flowers blooming, and the sun was shining brightly. She said, "This is my wish to have a home again and be happy."

We dealt with a number of issues other than their father's abandonment. There was the issue of adapting at their new school and having their own rooms where they could have their own space and a place to do their homework. Making new friends who might understand where they came from was a big one. They dealt with their anger toward their father, and feelings of helplessness and sometimes hopelessness. Culture shock was a big item. Both longed to be back in the country that they called "home." That was the only real home they had known. They missed the housekeeper who cared for them and gave them lots of love and attention.

One day, upon hearing that the mother would need to go back to their adopted country to take care of their household items, I suggested that the children needed to go back with her as well. They needed to see their friends one more time and say goodbye properly. They needed to bring closure to this most important part of their lives. But how would they pay for airline tickets? The Mission Board was to pay for the mother's trip in order for her to take care of shipping her household goods back to the States. I was able to get some people to donate and pay for the two children's trips back. Their grandmother went with them, paying her own way.

Upon returning to the States, both children told me how helpful it was to go "home" again. Of course, it broke their hearts to have to say their final goodbyes and leave the place and people who had been so dear to them. Through the help of a friend, the mother was able to secure a secular job, and today, after many years, she is highly regarded and respected and is near the top in the company.

Perhaps the people most impacted by this crisis experience have been the two children. For them it was a horrible experience. They have done some acting out, feeling that their father did not love them. In fact, at one point, the father was placed in jail for not having paid child support.

Almost always when they did go to see him, they left angry and had had a very unpleasant experience. This experience has left a dark shadow over their lives and changed their lives forever.

Change is always difficult, but for two small children, their world was turned upside down. The children's cousin, who has been a big part of their lives, wrote a poem about change that best describes what change of this magnitude can do to a child.

CHANGE

Change
What is Change?
Change is when someone special leaves.
When your favorite relative dies
When you move and there's nowhere
Left to keep your heart.
It's hard to trust anybody or anything
Somehow they always
Change.
How is it felt?
Change goes straight to the core of the heart and
Burns the soul.
Change takes your emotions and rips them apart.
It is like no other feeling or emotion felt in the
Human spirit.
It is hard to love anybody or anything.
Somehow they always
Change.
What is change?
No one can really say.
All we know is that it hurts.
Somehow that does not
Change.

Used by permission of author: Sandi Hill

Separation and Loss

Separation and loss are painful issues that every MK must confront. This separation and loss include personal relationships—parents, siblings, other missionaries and their children, and their national friends. They are separated from their host country, its culture, its values, and even its environment. As a result of all these losses, MKs must deal with a lot of unresolved grief.

The children of missionaries find that separation and loss are constant forces in their lives. Both are leaving their homes and parents or their parents are leaving them and returning to their mission field. As MKs go through this experience over and over again, they actually go through the stages of grief that ordinary people go through when some loved one dies: shock, denial, anger, depression, and finally acceptance.

The loss of their country and friends is truly an experience of separation and loss that leaves their hearts full of sadness. More than likely, they will never be with their friends again, these people with whom they have spent the developmental years of their lives, yet they have a treasure box full of memories of that part of their lives.

MKs are aware of the fact that a few years later when their parents retire and return to the States, both they and their parents will have changed. The kind of previous relationship they had will also have changed. Now they must learn to relate to each other as adults. Most MKs will struggle to integrate the past and present, the perceived self and the real self. They are forced to examine and question all that has happened to them. When MKs get a clear perspective of who they are and who God is, perhaps they will be able to experience reintegration. MKs are called to self-responsibility. When an MK does take responsibility, he or she will naturally have feelings of self worth. At the same time, they will feel worthwhile to others. An integrated inward life is manifested outwardly to others. They will, no doubt, find themselves at peace.

Values to Live By: Honest and Accountability

One of the main issues that the children of missionaries are forced to confront upon their reentry into the American culture and society is the fact that their values differ greatly from those of their peers in the United States. MKs are often completely shocked at the values or lack of values they find in people in our own universities, in the business world, and even in some of our churches.

Values are cherished beliefs that determine behavior. Values are chosen and give direction to life. To know a person, we must know their values. Each one of us is a composite of the things we value.

Most missionary children place a high value upon family. Because of the stability of their family life on the mission field, some MKs have been astounded at the unstable family life of many of their peers. After reentry, they say, "All my values and beliefs have been or are being tested." Most feel that after having their values tested, their values have proved worth keeping. Some admit that they, at times, have had to put on blinders to many of the destructive values they encounter. On the other hand, they may become entrapped in abusing their own values. At the same time, missionary children place a lot of value not only on family, but also on friendship, justice, education, the dignity of other human beings, and especially on honesty and accountability.

It seems to me that among all other values, there are two particular values that we *all* would do well to revisit. These are two values that never die. They are honesty and accountability. The Psalmist (15:1–2) holds high the value of honesty. "Lord, who shall abide in thy tabernacle? ... He that walketh uprightly ... and speaketh the truth in his heart."

What about the value of honesty? As children, we heard from one source or another that honesty is the best policy. Truly, honesty is the strongest thread in the fabric of a good life. It not only holds together a society but also is essential to decency. In Romans 13:13, Paul teaches us "to walk honestly."

Paul Ekman, in his book *Why Kids Lie*, states clearly that parents *can* encourage truthfulness. The most common reasons children lie are to avoid punishment, to get something they couldn't get otherwise, to win admiration, and to protect their friends. Ekman found that children who lie the most come from homes where parents lie, one way or another, either outright or in a subtle way. Being a good example is therefore the best teacher.

Dishonesty may take form in small ways, such as cheating on one's income tax returns, making up some excuse for being late, not pointing out a missing item on a restaurant bill, or overcharging someone. But sometimes honesty comes at a tremendous sacrifice. Sooner or later in life, we usually learn something about honesty by acting dishonestly and getting caught.

A second basic value that never dies is accountability: knowing what is right and accepting the consequences for wrongdoing, taking responsibility for one's own misbehavior, refusing to blame someone else. Someone once said. "A mistake can neither be forgiven or corrected until it is admitted." "It is my fault" is often the hardest thing for us to say, but it also has its own rewards.

In the last twenty-five years it seems that something has gone badly wrong with the American way of life that we once cherished. When it comes to our values it seems that the value of accountability has faded from the American scene. Without taking responsibility for our decisions and behavior, we cannot truly maintain our integrity.

Without accountability there can be no respect, no trust, no law—ultimately no society. Only internal controls such as guilt, shame, embarrassment, fear of punishment, reluctance to face ostracism, or public condemnation can control people's behavior. To find excuses, to accuse, and to blame others when we are the guilty one are all copouts. Yes, to be honest and accountable may be painful, frustrating, and humiliating, but it is also the most rewarding way of life. It pays to be honest and accountable.

It is only natural that the values of Missionary Kids differ somewhat from those of their American counterparts. Having taken on some of the values of their host cultures, it is also natural that they may have some strong reactions to some values of Americans to which they are exposed. On the other hand, in order to fit in, some MKs feel they must not only accept but adapt to this society, even though they do not like what they see. Sad to say, MKs may often incorporate some of their peers' destructive values into their own thinking and living in order to feel a sense of belonging. As a result, they lose themselves. Some get caught up in lifestyles that have been foreign to them heretofore. Some mess up their lives and suffer a great deal of pain and agony before they find their way back.

MKs, hold on to your values, particularly honesty and accountability!

Dealing with Alienation and Culture Shock

Alienation seems to be one of those deplorable by-products of being children of missionaries, growing up in a culture different from that of their parents, and then being transplanted into the United States, this foreign country.

The word "alienation" itself is an atrocious word that speaks of isolation, rootlessness, not belonging, and loneliness. Symptoms of alienation that the children of missionaries have identified are feelings of discomfort, dissatisfaction, restlessness, and being out of place. At times there appears to be a sense of helplessness. Upon returning there seems to be little or no sense of permanency in their lives. Even those who have had the fewest difficulties in adjusting to the States to some degree still have some or all of these feelings.

Sociologically, most children of missionaries upon reentry feel much like aliens in the States. They say, "I know I have an American face, but I do not feel American." These young people are the products of two cultures. Needless to say, this produces unique human beings.

A sense of alienation, derived from a sense of rootlessness, is perhaps the most difficult issue with which children of missionaries must cope. One missionary child was heard to say, "Mommy, in our class today, our teacher asked me where I am from? I was born in Indonesia. I have lived in Georgia, but you and Daddy are from Tennessee and Florida. Where am I from?" These young people need help from Americans in finding a place for themselves where they can feel they really do belong.

Perhaps these children who claim two countries for themselves share the same feelings as the immigrants described in Malcolm Cowley's book, *Exiles Return*. Their feelings have been expressed as follows:

> If you came back,
> you wanted to leave again:
> If you went away,
> you longed to come back.
> Wherever you were,
> you could hear the call of the
> homeland.
> Like the note of the herdsman's horn
> far away in the hills.
> You had one home out there and one
> over here, and yet you were an alien in
> both places.
> Your true abiding place was the vision
> of something very far off,
> And your soul was like the waves,
> always restless, forever in motion. (134)

For most children of missionaries, cultural dissolution will always remain a live issue.

Culture shock is precipitated by anxiety that naturally results when children of missionaries lose all of their signs, cues, and symbols upon returning to the States. Culture shock may be likened to a kind of disease that affects those who have been suddenly transplanted into some new country.

Cultural relocation tugs at the roots of the missionary child's identity. Upon reentry, these young people lose their familiar props. They often feel frustrated and anxious. As a first reaction to their frustrations and anxieties, children of missionaries may reject the environment and/or culture that causes such pain. They may actually feel that America must be "bad" because its culture and customs make them feel so bad. Whenever they get the chance, MKs get together to grouse and complain about America and Americans. Those who do not have the opportunity to get together with other MKs find relief by contacting them through the Internet. Just to be able to talk to someone who understands brings some amount of relief.

What Can MKs Do to Resolve Culture Shock
1. They can get to know the American people. The sooner, the better, for they will be here for a long time.
2. They can show a genuine interest in their American peers even though they may not really like them.
3. They can be observant and try to understand what is taking place around them instead of simply being critical.
4. They can join in the activities of their American peers even when they may have preconceived notions that certain healthy sports and activities might not be interesting and/or fun.
5. They can talk to some chosen people, open up, and be honest in discussing their culture shock. To do so is not a sign of weakness. Yes, it is to be vulnerable, but at the same time, it is simply being human.

When considering missionary children, we must recognize that their cultural identity is created from two distinct cultural components, the American one plus the culture of the country in which they have spent the developmental years of their lives. This cultural combination causes children of missionaries some identity confusion.

As one might expect, it would be very difficult if not impossible for the children of missionaries to sever the bonds they have with their host countries, for indeed, they are a part of both, and those countries are a real part of who they are. For the rest of their lives, those experiences will be carried deep within them in their highly complicated search for personal and cultural identity. They cannot and they should not forget the warm mutuality they feel toward the people and the country in which they grew up. When they remember, they will continue to feel the intense pain from the severance of the umbilical cord forced upon them when they return to the States for college. For some, it will be a lifelong grief experience that is irretrievable.

The challenges faced by the children of missionaries upon permanent reentry to the States is formidable, since this transition is the biggest they will face in their entire lives. As they prepare to leave their country on the mission field, children and their parents both agonize at the reality of their separation. MKs want to be brave and act mature, but deep down inside they are anxious and afraid.

My final word is for the churches and mission boards. The children of missionaries should receive far more attention, care, support, understanding. and appreciation than they actually receive. MKs, like their parents, have given so much for the cause of missions. Why not give our MKs the same attention that we afford their parents upon their return to the States?

CHAPTER TWO

Coping

How Do I Cope?

A married male MK with his four children called for an appointment and came to my office to discuss some pressing issues. He asked if he could bring his four children with him. Of course, I welcomed the children. The mother had refused to come for counseling. She had refused to seek any type of counseling in the past. This was not the first session I had had with Billy Ray, although it was the first for him and the children together.

For some time, Billy Ray had been deeply concerned about his relationship with his wife. Previously I had written a letter inviting her to talk with me so that I could get a complete picture of what was going on in their relationship. Of course, she refused to make an appointment. Billy Ray truly loved his wife, the mother of his four children. However, Billy Ray declared that he would never divorce his wife. Neither would he go outside the marriage to meet his own needs. He wanted to learn how to be a better husband and father.

In dealing with his children, Billy Ray admitted that, at times, he might have spanked them too hard. He loved his children, and did not want to hurt them in any way. We discussed better ways of disciplining rather than spanking. He learned, and he put these new ways into practice immediately, which also caused him to feel better about himself. Billy Ray also felt he needed to work on some of his own childhood issues.

Growing up in another country under the strict influence of his parents had impacted his life tremendously. He still suffered from some of the disciplinary methods his father had used. His parents expected a lot from Billy Ray. Some of those expectations were unrealistic, and Billy Ray knew they were, even at the time they were being dished out. When Billy Ray came to see me, his father had died only a couple of years earlier, and he was still grieving his father's death. It was too late for him to try to make things right with his father.

Billy Ray and his wife had completely different value systems. Both had been in previous marriages that had failed. There had been no children born to those unions. Billy Ray married at an early age because he was looking for a place to belong. His wife had lived a less than moral life and had more "street" experience. Billy Ray had some other real concerns besides the fear that his wife would divorce him. He was concerned about their financial situation. Both he and his wife had been compulsive spenders and had now maxed out their credit cards. Billy Ray had always heard that God would take care of all his needs, but he was finding out that God needed his cooperation. Now Billy Ray was earnestly trying to get control of his spending habits. Up to this time, he had encouraged his wife to control the purse strings. He did not blame her for his own spending habits.

Billy Ray was most concerned about his wife's inattentiveness to their four children. Both worked. When his wife came home from work, she went straight to her room and stayed there, smoking cigarettes and reading romance books until Billy Ray had prepared and put supper on the table. He not only did most of the cooking, but he took care of most of the children's other needs. He checked to see if they had done their homework. He got them ready for school and saw that they had their homework in hand. He then drove them to school. He also drove them home from school. He took them to their doctors' appointments. He spent time listening to them about their day's activities, their joys, and their disappointments. Of course, he did the laundry and checked to see that the children had clean clothes. Billy Ray nurtured his four children in every way possible.

When Billy Ray brought his children to talk with me, it was very clear that the children loved him very much. Three of them were still quite young, and they wanted to either sit on his lap or right beside him on the sofa.

In my evaluation of Billy Ray, I would say that he was nurturing, responsible, honest, brilliant, an excellent musician, a loving father who felt deeply, a good caretaker, and a spiritual person, and was sound psychologically. Some words and phrases the children used to describe their father were: nice, kind, loving, good listener, understands me, does not yell at me, usually in a good mood, does not smoke, offers us good indoor games and videos, takes us places and sometimes lets us steer his car (pretending to drive). Since Billy Ray was a little overweight, his eldest child said she would like to see her father exercise more.

The things they expressed that they liked about their mother were things like: "She lets me help her cook and sometimes plays cards with us, takes us to the library and the pool occasionally in the summer time." The things their mother did that bothered them were: "she yells at us, she's often in a bad mood, when at home she stays in her room and does not want us to bother her by knocking on her bedroom door; her smoking bothers my allergies until it is hard for me to breathe, but she won't go outside to smoke; she won't let me sit on her lap, and she never takes us to the doctor." They saw their mother as angry and too serious.

During this time, Billy Ray suffered more grief in the sudden loss of his mother, who had been to church for worship and other meetings and came home a little late one afternoon. She sat down in a living room chair and died of a heart attack. She was not alone, but paramedics who arrived shortly said there was nothing they could have done since she died of a massive heart attack. A couple of weeks later, I visited Billy Ray at his mother's house where they were trying to take care of her things. Billy Ray's wife was present, but she seemed uncomfortable in my presence. That was the only time I had ever met his wife. The children were all in school.

Billy Ray shared much with me concerning his own childhood. He remembers his parents as being very religious. He had three siblings. He felt that his father was particularly tough on the two boys. Expectations were unreasonable. Yet they knew they were the children of missionaries, and their parents were eager for their children to make a good impression on the nationals. They felt that their every move was scrutinized. As for discipline, there was lots of yelling and stern talk, which created in Billy Ray, a very sensitive young man, a lot of guilt, shame, resentment, anger, and defiance. He did not know what to do with his feelings because it seemed that his parents did not want to deal with their own feelings. He remembered his father's controlling anger. Billy Ray felt that his parents' way of discipline was very damaging to him as a young man. It created in him lots of insecurities, and low self-esteem, and continued to cause problems for him in his personal relationships. When younger, he was paddled by his father and mother, and then as he grew older, they used a switch. Even as a senior in high school, he was beaten by his father with a belt. He said, "I lived in fear of being beaten with a belt up until the time I returned to the States for college."

When I was counseling with Billy Ray, I could see that he still carried a great amount of anger toward his parents, his first wife, and now his second wife, who was the mother of his four children. He also carried some anger toward one of his siblings, because he felt that sibling was always trying to give him some nonrequested and inappropriate advice.

It seemed to me that Billy Ray was trying hard to be a good husband as well as a good father, yet his wife did not seem interested and continued to withdraw. Then, one night she asked him to leave the house. He called and came to see me. He began to figure out a plan of action. Since the home actually belonged to him, as a gift from his mother, and since the children, all but the oldest, wanted to live with him, his wife saw "the handwriting on the wall" and decided to go out and find herself an apartment. Her oldest child went with her. In a particular court session that I attended, the judge ordered the three children brought from school. He took them into his chambers and asked them if they wanted to live with their mother or their father. They told the judge they definitely wanted to live with their father. The court ended up authorizing joint custody. Billy Ray did discover that his wife had been having an affair with a much older man. Within the year they were divorced.

It was really difficult for Billy Ray to be a mother and a father for his children. However, he continued to take good care of them. Still, he had not learned how best to handle his finances, wanting to buy things for the children in order to make them happy. It is not uncommon for some MKs to be free spenders since many of them have not been taught how to shoulder responsibility when they return to America. Some have shared with me their anger about not having learned how to be more responsible while with their parents. Those who have been taught how to take on all kinds of responsibilities do very well once they are back in the States. The hardest part has been not having their parents here to consult with about many things.

Perhaps Billy Ray's weakest point was his lack of good organization in the home, and his lack of discipline contributed to some of his pain. As the youngest of the three became a teenager and did not want to live under her father's rules, she became restless and wanted to live with her mother where she would have few if any rules. Eventually, the second and then the last child went to live with their mother. Billy Ray was really feeling a lot of rejection and became more and more depressed. However, after taking an antidepressant, he felt much better about his situation.

Even before the three girls went to live with their mother, Billy Ray had met a very nice lady and had fallen in love. Eventually they were married. Billy Ray's ex-wife was still not what we might call a "good mother." One day the youngest child called her dad and asked if she could return home and live with him and his new wife. Needless to say, Billy Ray was no longer depressed. He was very happy with his new wife, and now he had his youngest child back home with him.

It must be clear to the reader that MKs have a lot of struggles, learning about Americans and America. They struggle to adjust, to reintegrate into this culture, in order to live with some amount of satisfaction, to find a place for themselves, and to find the soul mate with whom they can be happy, and with whom they can spend the rest of their lives. Many male MKs have told me about how hard it was to ask for dates and even to know how to act on a date with young American women. At the same time, female MKs are perhaps too naive and trusting of men. Dating people who are so different and who sometimes have such different values can be most difficult and sometimes confusing. As a result, there are many divorces of MKs married to non-MKs.

Resignation and Grief

Vanna, a twenty-six-year-old married MK, and I met outside my office for a session. Vanna came to tell me her story. She was taken to the mission field by her parents when she was only eighteen months old. One of her earliest memories was when she was about two and one-half years old, and she was playing outside with some friends in front of her house. One of her friends told Vanna that she "talked funny." She went into her house and found her father reading. When she told him about the friend telling her she "talked funny," her father gave her a satisfying answer, saying, "What you are doing is mixing your English and Spanish, and your friend understands only one language, Spanish."

Another memory that is still fresh in Vanna's mind was when she was about three or four years old. Vanna's mother always went to choir rehearsal at the church one night each week. She left Vanna with their maid. She remembers trying to detain her mother because she really did not want to be left with the maid. She would say, "I've got something to tell you." Her mom would answer, "What?" Vanna could not really think of anything to tell her. She realized, after all those years, she was experiencing separation anxiety. She does feel that this was perhaps the root of her insecurities through the years that followed.

Vanna told me about how she was sent off to kindergarten with the national children and how she never felt she fitted in the group. She became aware, at that early age, that she was different. However, one comforting memory she had was sitting with her dad in their bedroom. Often she was crying. At such a time, her mother said to her, "When you are sad and cry, Jesus cries with you." Now, when Vanna cries, she has an image of herself as a child "hugging pillows and crying." When she remembers this, she feels sad even today. Often when her husband sees her sad, and her many tears, he tries to comfort her. She said, "Sometimes he cries with me."

On their first furlough in the States, at age nine, Vanna remembers how scared and insecure she felt on her first day in the new school. Even that early, Vanna liked to think she was superior to her classmates, at least intellectually, but then she thought that on other levels of her life, she might just be inferior. This created some insecure feelings. When in the States, she got really homesick for her "home" back in South America. Even in South America she remembers that they moved a lot and lived in several different houses. Here in the States she remembers feeling lonely and miserable, because she was really not at home. However, when they came back to the States for their second furlough, she was excited about seeing her relatives and receiving many presents from them. At this time, she had grown tired of her school in South America, and she was ready for a change. Here she could make a new start and feel special.

By the time they came on their third furlough, Vanna was thirteen. She said that her six months in school here were miserable and the worst time of her life. First of all, she didn't, for some reason, like being thirteen. Vanna did well academically, but she felt lonely. She consoled herself in thinking that she really was superior. After all, she had lived in another country, and none of her peers knew anything about the country from which she came. However, she never felt a sense of belonging in the States, so she was always eager to return to her home in South America. All the MKs there were always glad to see her return. There she was completely involved in the church activities. Most of her peers were MKs who could understand her and her ways.

Vanna remembered that in growing up she had looked to her father as her role model. Growing up in South America, every day she could see that men were considered superior to women. Therefore she valued masculine traits above feminine traits. She wanted to be seen as equal to the males. She said, "I didn't pay much attention to my feminine traits." Also, she viewed her mother as being very submissive to the point of being passive-aggressive. Her father was considered "head of the house," although that was never verbalized. She said, "I knew my mother had power, but it was rather subtle." Vanna wanted to appear to be self-sufficient even if she did not always feel it.

When Vanna entered college as a freshman, she was learning to survive. As an extrovert she knew she needed people around her, but she did not want to rely on others but rather remain somewhat independent. She said that when they, as a family, traveled by car, her father would waste lots of time and gasoline because he would not stop and ask for directions. This gave her the impression that her dad did not need anyone. Rather he could do everything by himself. Her dad was a nonemotional person. He never expressed feelings, only opinions and ideas. However, on one occasion she did see tears in his eyes. The time had come, for family reasons, that he decided he must resign from their mission board. When her parents told the children that they had decided to leave the mission field and go back to the States to live, she was very sad. This was when Vanna was a senior in high school and she lacked only six months to graduate. She had an older sister already in college in the States. When her grandparents told her sister that her parents would be coming home "for good," her sister "exploded into tears" because she was losing her country.

Now, they were trying to figure out a way for Vanna to stay in South America and graduate with her classmates. Another missionary family told Vanna she could live with them, and the school even gave her a scholarship. However, after graduation, when she had to leave for the last time, she said, "It was like a death." She knew that she was going to see her parents in the States, but at the same time, she was grieving the loss of her country and everything that had been so familiar for so many years. Then she began to think realistically that she would be going back to the States anyway, for now she would be going to college in America, yet it was very difficult to say goodbye to those she would be leaving behind. Vanna did go through a period of depression when she finally left her home in South America.

Her dad was working in the States, but her mom had no job to keep her mind occupied. Much later, she did go to work as a teacher. A younger sister was having educational problems, and nothing seemed to be working out for her. Vanna lived with her parents during her first six months back in the States before going to live in a dorm on a college campus. Upon entering college, Vanna did suffer from culture shock. Her peers on campus seemed immature and "silly." She had two suite mates, and they all got along really well. However, after the first year one of the suite mates transferred to another university. They got a new suite mate. This young lady arrived angry because she had just broken up with her boyfriend. She took most of her anger out on Vanna. Vanna was doing nothing different than she had done before. She was continuing to attend her weekly Bible study group. Her suite mate began coming in late at night completely drunk. She cursed and was erratic. She was inconsistent and unpredictable. She was angry at God, and Vanna also felt she was angry at her. Vanna said that this was not the first time she had been exposed to alcohol and this kind of behavior since some students at her previous school had smoked cigarettes and pot and had drunk alcohol. At the time, Vanna did not realize she was experiencing culture shock, but as she looked back on those days, she recognized it for what it was. During her second year of college she transferred to another college in the same city.

At one point, Vanna had urged her parents to go for therapy. They did go one time but never returned a second time. She saw her mother as an emotional person who "sat on her feelings." Her dad was unemotional. As we talked, she could say that she recognized that her family was, in some ways, dysfunctional. She continued by saying, "But I know that I have choices and am determined to be different." She was still in the process of individualizing and said she had learned much from her own and her family's mistakes.

Vanna indicated that her best experience in being a MK was growing up in another country and culture which gave her a worldview, and she was bilingual. Vanna, along with her family, did have the opportunity to go back to the place they had lived for so many years after all the children had graduated from college. She said, "It was a great feeling! I felt like my real self. I found out I was not considered weird there. I said my final goodbyes and brought closure to that chapter in my life. One other thing I learned was I didn't belong there anymore. And then, I was eager to return to the States, back to the place where my boyfriend was waiting for me."

We can readily see that when missionary parents resign, it does affect each member of the family in different ways. Grief is real, and if the family can work through their grief together, it is much easier than trying to do it alone. Resignation and grief go hand in hand. These missionaries and their family members need understanding and all the support they can get.

The Shock of Being a "Nobody"

Charlie and his parents came from out of state for some therapy. The parents had called me because they were very concerned about their son who "didn't seem like himself." They arrived at my office on a Friday afternoon. We spent three hours together that night, and almost all day on Saturday, except for taking time out for meals. Charlie was a very quiet but gentle college freshman. He was having a difficult time in college and in his everyday life as he tried to adjust to living in the States.

Because of being overwhelmed with everything so different in the States from his "home" country in Honduras, he felt a lot of anger that at times bordered on rage. First, he felt abandoned and rejected by his parents who had left him on a college campus in this strange, new country, and returned to Honduras. He felt so alone. It was hard for him to trust American young people, even his own classmates in college. He had lost his good self-image during the few short months he had been in America. He said, "In my country, I was somebody, but in the States, I am a nobody."

Charlie was suffering from culture shock, big time! He saw all the injustices on his campus. He saw the "stupid" things the students were doing and saw most of them as ignorant and illogical. He knew that his anger had been building over the past few months when he felt so lonely. Perhaps like so many other MKs, Charlie's worst enemy was loneliness. He said that when they were on furlough, and he was in the eighth grade, he saw how badly black kids were treated. This caused him to write a paper on prejudice for one of his classes. Then when he was in the eleventh grade, again on furlough, he didn't like the principal of the school he was attending, and this made him feel "uptight."

There had been times when Charlie had been so lonely since entering college that he found himself dialing 800 numbers just to talk to someone. He had become so depressed. He said, "My nervous system was really messed up." The usual noises caused him a great deal of tension, and he was beginning to feel that he had no control over his life. He was obsessing a lot, which was "driving me crazy."

Charlie began to have thoughts about how he would escape his miserable life. I asked him if he had thought about hurting himself or someone else. He replied, "Yes, many times I have thought of doing something to myself." I asked him if he had considered what and how he would do it. He explained vividly how he had thought of taking his own life. He went to the exercise and weight room at the college gymnasium. He had seriously thought of posturing himself on the floor, underneath the weights just above his head, and he would pull the weights up as far as they would go, and let them fall on his head, crushing his skull. He thought this would be a quick and painless death.

As Charlie talked about all these ideas he had going on in his head, his parents were listening intently. They were in shock at their son's thoughts of suicide. At this point, Charlie's father said, "Son, you are the most important thing in our lives. If we need to leave the mission field and stay home with you, we will. We love you very much." At that point, a big smile came over Charlie's face. This was the first time I had seen him smile since they had been in hours of counseling. Charlie replied, "Dad, I never thought I would ever hear you say that. I thought your mission work was the most important thing in your life. Just to hear you say that you would be willing to do that makes me feel good and that I really am important to you."

Charlie's parents were beginning to understand that their son was dealing with some life and death issues. Charlie was dealing with grief over the loss of his country and his family, his feelings of being different and experiencing culture shock in general. He needed a place to belong. He wanted to love and to be loved.

Charlie and his parents agreed to get in touch with a psychiatrist in the state to which they would return, and get an evaluation on his depression. He also would work on his obsessive-compulsive traits. He would also seek help with his anger because he said, "Often I am scared of my own anger." Charlie was an introvert and a very creative individual. He loved to analyze things and work out problems, but never had he confronted the kind of problems that were plaguing him as a freshman in college. He needed someone to help him get a new perspective on his life and problems and learn how to solve them in a healthy way. Charlie had a tendency also to procrastinate or at least get things done at the last moment, which was also creating a lot of stress and anxiety. He was feeling overwhelmed with not only college life but learning to adapt and face the new demands that he had not anticipated.

The best thing that happened is that Charlie's parents decided to at least take a leave of absence for a few months and then reevaluate whether or not to return to Honduras. The most important thing for Charlie was to know that he really did come first in their lives. Dealing with culture shock is something that every missionary and every missionary kid must face, whether it be in the adopted country or upon returning to the States. Let me tell you from firsthand experience, it is not a good feeling.

Fearful of Growing Up

Anita sent me a letter inquiring about our services at Missionary Family Counseling in Winston-Salem. She lived out of the state of North Carolina. Thus, she had to drive about eight hours to arrive in our city. She had been referred to me for counseling by an acquaintance. Anita had graduated from college and was finding it very difficult to adjust not only to America but also to her new job. Her greatest difficulty was relating to her colleagues. Another issue was her resentment of authority figures. Thus, she was having a hard time working under a supervisor. She was also suffering from depression and was already taking an antidepressant.

She had been in counseling with a lady in her hometown. Since Anita was an MK, and since she knew that I had personally spent more than twenty years in Japan as an education missionary before changing careers to become a therapist, she felt that perhaps I was better equipped to help her. I would be able to understand her life in another country and culture and would be able to empathize with her reentry issues. To put it simply, Anita felt overwhelmed all the time, which caused her to be very unhappy and filled with anxiety. At night, she felt God was loving her, but during the day, she was having such a hard time, and she did not believe God was with her. She said, "My head knows he loves me, but my heart has a hard time feeling his love." This issue of God and feeling overwhelmed by the people around her caused so much anxiety that it was really hard for her to deal with the events of each day. She was tired of being overwhelmed all the time. Her two greatest fears were not having enough money to survive adequately from paycheck to paycheck, and the other fear was of death.

Anita finally decided to come to Winston-Salem for a week of intensive counseling, which meant that we spent two to three hours each day together. She made hotel reservations. I do believe that simply getting away from her job and the frustrations in her office, and also taking a look at her whole life, gave her some significant insight into her problems.

In the first session, we spent time getting to know each other. I learned that Anita had grown up in a very ultraconservative missionary home. She said that when the family had Bible reading and prayer in their home each evening, "it meant nothing to me." Her father was the one who always prayed and did the Bible reading for the family. She remembers that there was seldom any laughter, much less smiling among her family members.

As for her background, Anita's mother had thirteen siblings while her father had only one. She remembers or was told somewhere along the way that among her mother's siblings, several had attempted suicide, and at least one had a nervous breakdown and was hospitalized. Early on, Anita, as a child, was afraid of God. She said, "God was with me when I was in bed and asleep, but during the day, I was afraid to go out because I was afraid I would sin." She had worried and felt overwhelmed much of her life. It was clear that Anita had heard much talk about an angry God but very little about a loving God. She evidently had never experienced God's grace. Then she said, "I am afraid to grow up!" She was afraid of responsibility and of running out of money, and she was so unsure about her future. Also, her parents were "a world away." If she approached them with her fears, she would be told she did not have enough faith. She never felt good enough. She had a childlike innocence and was naïve about the world, and America in particular. She simply did not know how to get along without her family.

At one point, Anita believed that she was possessed by demons, since she did have a problem with epilepsy. She was even told by someone that "demons may be hovering over you." They urged her to seek "sanctification," whatever that meant. At age twelve, she was sent to boarding school some distance from her parents' home. She said, "That was the worst year of my life! I was so afraid and homesick." At this early age she was afraid to deal with her sexual feelings and referred to them as her "shadow side."

Anita felt neglected as a child. Too many missionary parents seem to be too gung-ho about "reaching the lost for Christ" in their assigned mission, and thus they can easily lose sight of their own children and their spiritual needs. At age two, she remembers her dad taking her rag doll to clean up some leaked oil.

Anita had a tonsillectomy at age five. However, she was not informed about going to the hospital and having this medical procedure done until the morning of the day that she was to enter the hospital. She had no idea what was going to happen since no one had explained it to her so that she would know what to expect. On that particular day, she woke up and was told by her mother, "Today you are going to the hospital to have your tonsils removed."

Anita's mother worked a full eight-hour day just as her father had. Often her mother would make promises to her, like to take her swimming, and then her mother did not return home early enough to carry out her promise. It seems she was often breaking her promises to her little girl. Anita remembers at such times how she would cry and scream from being disappointed by her mother. Perhaps this is when she began to devalue herself. At age nine and ten, Anita started to worry about not having enough money. It seems that her parents were always worrying about money. They talked constantly about money in front of her, not knowing how much this was impacting her life. She said, "I feel my whole life has been manipulated by adults." She worried about not being perfect. She worried about not fulfilling her obligations, and she was always trying to please her parents and others. Now, this had carried over into her workplace even today. She was always concerned about her job security.

Anita was never allowed to dance or go to movies. Actually, she was twenty-two years old when she saw her first movie. At age twelve when she went away to boarding school, she felt so "left out" because other MKs could go to see movies. If she went, she felt she would be doing something sinful, and her parents would find out and be so disappointed in her. At boarding school, Anita's classmates went to an English-speaking church, but Anita was told that she must attend the African church. She did, but at the same time, she did not understand the language. This caused her to grow up disliking church altogether. Anita had a deep feeling about all this. She said, "I was never allowed to be a child. In fact, I have had a lost childhood." Anita, a bright young lady and good student, loved ethnic and chamber music, a love that she had acquired at boarding school. She had many good teachers, but for some reason, even resented them as authority figures. Legalism had taken its toll on the mind of this young girl. She said, "I don't want to have to carry so much guilt anymore."

Once when Anita's family was on furlough, and Anita was sixteen, she remembers how her mother bought her a used jacket that was well worn. Actually it was tattered, and her mother put patches on the elbows and other places. As she looked around at others in their new jackets, she felt self-conscious and awkward. She already felt different enough just by being in the States, and now the way her mother was dressing her made her feel even more different.

Some other issues with which we dealt were how crowds of people affected her. Perfectionism, feeling different, and having different values from those of her peers affected her own sense of security. She was also dealing with loneliness, fear of rejection, and depression. She had suffered from some depression since she was a senior in high school, which continued throughout college and now into her daily work. At times, Anita remembers feeling suicidal. However, once she was back in the States in college, she did feel a bit more freedom. She studied hard, and despite her depression she excelled. She had heard so many telling her what she should and ought to do, but now she had the freedom to make her own choices, even if she did have to deal with some guilt.

Since being back in the States, Anita had been experiencing a real identity crisis. Now, at age thirty-two, she still did not really know who she was. At times, Anita, out of frustration, became very assertive to the point of becoming repulsive to some of her coworkers. She described her own mother as being "very brash." Anita was an oversensitive young lady, and sometimes she misinterpreted what her coworkers said and did. Her insecurities were numerous and easily detected by those around her.

One other big problem Anita was facing in therapy was her obsessive-compulsive behavior. One symptom was feeling the necessity to talk, talk, talk, feeling compelled to say aloud whatever she thought or felt. This was a way of trying to be heard and understood. She was so scared that she would miss something. She worried about what she should have said. Then she worried about perhaps not having said enough. She then felt guilty about what she had done or said, right or wrong. It was a vicious cycle. She had brought one false assumption with her to counseling. She did not feel a need to deal with her past in order to find healing. She felt her past, with the passing of time, would heal itself.

As we discussed these matters, Anita was beginning to realize that often it might not be "what" she said but "how" she said things that negatively affected others. Although Anita was a sensitive person when it came to her own feelings, she was often insensitive toward others and their feelings. At first, Anita did not seem to want to change her negative behavior. However she began to see that, in order to live with any amount of peace, she *must* change. This, in itself, made her very angry. She wanted others to change to meet her expectations.

Anita and I, throughout the week of intensive therapy, worked hard. At times she became very angry at me, simply because I was not saying what she wanted to hear. At the end of the week, I encouraged Anita to continue in therapy with her therapist in her home state. She was critical of that therapist to me, and after she returned to that therapist, I knew she would be critical of me. When she told her other therapist that she wanted to write me a letter and express her anger toward me, the lady said to her, "Do you want to write her to try to change Doris or do you want to help yourself?"

Anita did admit that one of the things that I had made her aware of was her obsessive-compulsive behavior. She saw this as being very beneficial to her. Actually she did see me as the "good mother," nonetheless as an authority figure.

Anita was a very emotionally disturbed young MK who was actually a victim of her own background. She carried so much anger toward almost everyone who had been a part of her past and even present. I pray that she has come to terms with her place in life. Hopefully she will keep on acting on her insights and learn a lot about interpersonal relationships. I said to her in parting, "Remember, without good relationships, life can be really sad and lonely." It will take a lot of work, pain, and suffering, but I truly believe she can reach that goal in life.

Unwanted Pregnancy

A phone call came from a particular mission board asking me if I would be able to spend time in counseling with one of their MKs. She would be coming from the West Coast and would arrive in two or three days. I was also asked whether I might be able to find some housing for her while she was in my city.

Marie, a petite, cute college student, had been date raped and was pregnant, and she was in a real quandary about whether she should have the baby or abort. By the time she reached my city, she had definitely decided to have the baby since she had strong religious convictions about abortion under any circumstances. The man who had date raped Marie was not a Caucasian American. Nevertheless, she had decided to have the baby. She was certainly not a person of prejudice since she had grown up in an Asian country. Thus, race really was not an issue or a factor in the equation.

When Marie arrived in my city, I had already secured housing for her. Marie seemed shy but could become a bit feisty. As it became apparent that she would need to be in my city for an extended period of time, she did not want to lose a semester of college credits. I took her to a college campus and talked with some very influential people about accepting her at the last minute as a special student. They thought it would also be wise to give her a fictitious name lest the young man who had raped her might be calling or trying to contact her in any other way. This all seemed to work out providentially, for everything fell in place as I had hoped it would.

Marie and I started our counseling sessions the day after her arrival, and she started her college classes a week later when the college year began. Marie's petite body was revealing her pregnancy more and more. Unfortunately, she was becoming somewhat depressed. One day, I accompanied her to a psychiatrist to discuss the safety of her taking antidepressants. She did not want to do anything that might harm her baby in any way. After talking with her, the psychiatrist offered an antidepressant that would be safe for her to take. However, she refused the medication.

As Marie became more and more depressed, she could not concentrate on her studies. Eventually, she was not able to attend the classes or do the work that was required of her. Sometimes she forced herself to go to classes although it was not productive. I urged her to talk to her professors, feeling that they would be sympathetic, and they would figure out a way to help her. She did just that, and her professors were very understanding, asking no questions that might invade her privacy. As her due date became closer, they told her she could simply take incompletes on her courses, write her papers, and complete her work after the baby was born, which she did.

Perhaps I need to note here that MKs who grow up in another culture usually have not dated until they return to the United States. Many, both male and female, have said, "I really don't know anything about dating. I know nothing about American men/women, and I don't know how to choose a date, and I don't know what to expect or what is expected of me." MK young women are both innocent and naive. Therefore, it is not uncommon for American young men on college campuses or other places, for that matter, to take advantage of the MK's innocence. American men can say, "I love you," and it means nothing. The MKs discover this later, but by then it may be too late. Female MKs are so trusting, having grown up in a safe, secure environment with their parents and other missionaries. Thus, they can often not imagine someone taking advantage of them sexually. Since their parents live in another country, these innocent young people don't often have someone whom they trust well enough to share such abuse. In a case of date rape, most would not know that the first thing they should do is report it to the police. Thus, the abuse goes unreported and they are left alone to figure out what to do. Later, this abuse can easily create problems for them when they marry.

After Marie had this traumatic experience, she believed that "you cannot trust men. I don't want to meet any other men or date. I don't even want to be in contact with two of my good male friends." She was very angry and felt so vulnerable. She was cautious and wanted to be independent. She had described her own father as showing no emotion and her mother as being a quiet lady. At age ten, Marie's mother accused her of not having or showing any emotion, of not being compassionate, of having too much pride. She did see her mother as always "having to be in control."

Before deciding not to have an abortion, Marie returned to the country where her parents were residing as missionaries. She needed to talk with her parents about such a huge decision. Of course, she was fearful, not knowing what their reactions might be. She found that her mother was readily available and listened, asking appropriate questions for Marie to consider. Her mother showed compassion and told Marie that the final decision must be her own whether to have the baby or abort. Marie's father did not want to be a part of any of their discussions. When she and her mother would begin to discuss the matter, her father would leave the room. She was so hurt and felt so misunderstood by her father.

After that visit, Marie returned to the States alone, feeling "numb" and "isolated." Now she had to make decisions that she actually had not been prepared for in any way. She felt the pain of losing the dream of her life. She was experiencing lots of confusion and anger. She said, "Suddenly everything in my life changed." She felt so helpless. Some people did not want to believe her when she told them she had been date raped. Rather they showed an accusing attitude toward her. "She was in the wrong place at the wrong time." They almost convinced her that she had actually invited the abuse. When she came to my city for therapy, she had to leave all the friends she had made at her university. Now she was in a strange place, where she was meeting everyone, even her counselor, for the first time. Who can imagine the fear, the anger, and the confusion that Marie was feeling?

As she continued in therapy with me, she was able to meet some "pretty neat" people who showed her a lot of care and concern. I could tell that she was becoming more and more relaxed with her new friends. Now she felt she had a support group. We all assured her that we were there for her, day or night. Fortunately, she was not too proud to ask for and receive help, even for what Social Services had to offer.

Marie, even though surrounded by new friends, felt lonely for her family, particularly her mother. This was a time when this young lady needed her mother. Her parents were scheduled for furlough a few months later, and her mother perhaps felt some pressure to stay until their scheduled furlough. As Marie's due date drew closer, she had decided to take Lamaze classes. She had asked me to accompany her to those classes. Of course, I agreed to do this. However, much to her surprise, Marie's mother sent a letter and told her that she was coming home early. Fortunately, her mother arrived just in time to go with Marie to her first Lamaze class and was with her when her baby daughter was born.

I, as her therapist, and as her friend, was happy to be there for Marie and to have a part in helping guide her through one of the most difficult periods of her life. Marie is now happily married and has more children.

A Grief Revisited

I first met Nicole face to face in Hawaii at a conference for the children of missionaries of all ages. Nicole was by that time an adult who had grown up in Malaysia. She was married with children. She went to Malaysia with her missionary parents and two siblings. Nicole was the eldest.

Nicole had suffered from depression, off and on, for several years. When she was fifteen, her parents were involved in a devastating traffic accident, a head-on collision that involved a large truck. It was proven later that the men in the truck were "zonked out" on drugs. Nicole's father was killed instantly while her mother was critically injured.

Nicole and I spent about three hours together. She recounted her whole devastating experience for me. At the same time she seemed to be reliving the entire experience. At the time of her parents' accident, she and her two siblings were at an American school. She was in the school cafeteria when the principal came in and asked her to go with him to his office. There he told her that her father and mother had been in a car accident, and for her father it had been fatal. Her mother was in a critical condition, and Nicole was told she may not make it. This fifteen-year-old teenager was living in a country far from her relatives. Therefore, as the eldest, she immediately wondered what she and her two siblings would do without their father and perhaps their mother. Can we even begin to imagine the questions that consumed Nicole's mind and the fear that gripped her soul?

Nicole and the school principal had the dreaded task of calling to the office her two younger siblings, ages thirteen and ten, and telling them the bad news. Of course, not only Nicole and her siblings were in a state of disbelief, but also their classmates who were MKs, and the faculty, of which many were missionaries.

In fact, these missionaries were considered their "aunts and uncles" and the other MKs were their "cousins." Nicole remembers how these missionary families surrounded them with their love, along with the nationals, who also loved her father and mother. Of course, a few days later some of her biological family, an uncle and others, arrived from the States.

Nicole was very much involved in making funeral arrangements for her father while the missionary family took good care of her mother. Nicole, being a very creative person, told me how she had made the white lining for her father's coffin. Nicole's mother survived but was not able to attend the funeral of her husband. Everyone felt that they would surely wake up and discover that this had all been a very bad dream, but no, it was real!

Nicole's mother improved and was once more able to return home to her children. Now the question for her was whether to remain in Malaysia or return to the States. Malaysia had become home for the children. That culture was all they knew, for the time they had spent in the States had been insignificant compared to their time in Malaysia. Soon their mother was offered a stateside job at the mission board's office. She knew it was best for her family that she accept the job and return where they could be close to their relatives. Therefore, Nicole's mother and their children packed up their goods and returned to the States.

The children had lost their country where they had spent most of the developmental years of their lives, and they lost their friends, school, and many other people whom they loved. This just was a no-win situation. They returned to the States to live among people they did not know, to go to a new school, to make new friends, and to face culture shock and sometimes even alienation. They knew they were Americans, they had the American face, but they did not feel American. They felt different from their American peers, and now they were forced to face the future without their father. How could anyone Nicole's age face such a tragic event and not become depressed?

When I met Nicole in Hawaii, and as we talked, I felt so much empathy and compassion for her. I respected and admired her for being able to get through such a difficult experience at such an early age. Nicole was now married and had children, but this did not lessen the pain of her losses. Her children were even about the same age that she was when her father died. All those memories of Malaysia flooded her mind.

Another tragic event had happened less than a year before we met in Hawaii. Her brother, who was only thirteen when he lost his father, had suffered for years with depression. He had actually been diagnosed as manic-depressive. He had shot himself in his bedroom while his wife was at her workplace. He was a sensitive, intelligent, creative young man. It was another living nightmare for this family.

On the day the brother had taken his life he was to go to an appointment with his psychiatrist. He did not keep the appointment but must have felt completely helpless and hopeless. When his wife returned home, she found her husband's lifeless body in their bedroom. Of course, this death devastated the whole family.

I remember clearly receiving a telephone call from Nicole's mother telling me about her son's tragic death. She and her son's stepfather had had dinner with him just a week before and detected nothing about him that would even hint at the fact that he might be contemplating suicide. Nicole's mother did remember how her son had "thanked me for everything I had ever done for him."

How did Nicole and her family survive all this pain and grief? It was by the grace of God, and the support and love of many friends and family. What an inspiration Nicole and her mother were to me. Nicole had bravely faced her father's death again by revisiting her pain and grief with me. Then, she revisited her brother's death by again sharing, in detail, that painful experience. Nicole had courageously handled her own depression with the help of doctors, medication, family, and friends. Today, I believe that Nicole is an inspiration to all who know her.

Suicidal Ideation

Having been a missionary myself for twenty years in Japan, and having watched the children of missionaries grow up there, I could anticipate some of the reentry issues these young people would confront when they returned to the States to enter some college or university. In fact, I had just finished writing my doctoral thesis on the topic, "An Assessment of the Reentry Issues of the Children of Missionaries from a Firsthand Perspective." During the two years I was working on that dissertation, I was also doing further clinical training in North Carolina Baptist Hospital's Pastoral Care Department. I was actually counseling missionary children and their families at that time.

I had just begun a new counseling ministry focusing on children who grow up in a culture other than that of their parents. The need for counseling seemed greatest among the children of missionaries who return to the States and try to become reintegrated into the American culture. However, this ministry was also for the children of business and military families as well. The children of missionaries seem to be the most affected by other cultures since they are either born in that country or have spent most of their developmental years there.

One night when it was almost time for me to go home, another counselor at the center brought a disturbed young man to me, introducing him as an MK. Jim was actually my first client as I began this new practice. The other counselor politely excused herself and left my office.

As I began to hear Jim's story, I could feel his frustration and see his depression. Jim had grown up in Southeast Asia and lived there all the developmental years of his life. He had gone to a very, very conservative college. He said to me, "I know how to talk their language." But as he moved on he became disillusioned and realized that the degree he held from that college had no real value to him. He was so depressed that he had considered taking his life more than once. In his own words, Jim said, "I came to this counselor after being told by another counselor that I could not afford his services." Jim told me right away that he had tried to see two other therapists but when they asked him how he planned to pay, he told them he had no money. They then told him that he needed to see another counselor.

"When I saw Dr. Walters, I knew straight away that she was a person who understood the special needs of MKs. She took me under her wing and allowed my 'pressure cooker' to explode. Before I came to see her, I was hanging on to life by my fingernails. Were it not for her ministry, I do not think I would be alive today." He said, "I found that she would not judge me but was accepting and compassionate."

As we talked I asked Jim the question that led me to believe that he was a depressed young man. I asked him if he would be willing to see a psychiatrist for medication, and he was eager to do this. Many missionaries would never see or even allow their children to see a psychiatrist, believing that if they had enough faith, they could just pray, trust in God, and the job would be done. Jim had no appetite and was losing weight. He had lost all interest in everything and no longer had a desire to live. He felt guilty and worthless as well as hopeless. He was not sleeping. I asked him what he did to get even a small amount of sleep. He hesitantly replied, "I've been drinking beer, even though I do not like the taste." As it turned out, we could not get an appointment with a psychiatrist for two weeks. Jim looked at me with the saddest eyes and asked, "What do I do to get some sleep for the next two weeks?" I replied, "Keep on drinking your beer." Later, he told me he was totally surprised to hear a former missionary tell him to keep on drinking his beer. Within the next two weeks, I saw Jim four times. I supported and encouraged him and gave him hope. Hope was on the way!

I learned that after graduating from college, Jim went to work in the local police department. Jim was a warm, caring, sensitive, intelligent young man. One day at the police station he was called upon to give CPR to a policeman who was suffering from a heart attack. In spite of Jim's efforts, the policeman died. A few days later he was called to a home where a baby was found in his crib, not breathing. He tried to save the baby's life, but the baby died. A third devastating experience came to Jim when he was summoned to an accident scene where an innocent driver was hit by a drunken driver speeding away from a police chase. The young man, a medical student, had been out late studying with some friends. As he was driving home early in the morning, the tragic accident occurred.

Jim got into the car with the dying young man. His head was in the floorboard. Jim did not want this young man to die alone. He took the man's head in his hands. Soon more policemen who arrived looked at Jim, shook their heads, and said, "It's no use." However, Jim stayed in the car, holding the man's head in his hands until an ambulance arrived. He felt so sad and helpless that he could do nothing to save this young medical student.

Jim went home that night exhausted physically, mentally, and emotionally. He said, "Doris, when I looked down at my shoes that night, I saw the young man's blood covering my shoe soles." All of these experiences were enough to make any caring person depressed. The loss of this medical student seemed to be the straw that broke the camel's back. Jim resigned from the police force and then went into even deeper depression.

I asked Jim what he would like to accomplish in counseling. He replied that he wanted to get over his depression and then go back to school, preferably Wake Forest University, and get a degree. He wanted to wipe out the fact that he had ever graduated from the very conservative college. He was not proud of the former degree. When I asked him how he had chosen that conservative school, he replied, "Doris, before I returned to the States, I did not know of but two colleges, both of them just as conservative as the one from which I had just graduated."

After taking medication for his depression and spending time in counseling, Jim began to make a good recovery. He did, indeed, enroll in Wake Forest University where he earned his master's degree. Now this brilliant young man was feeling real good about himself. During the nine months we spent in counseling, Jim dealt with many issues that all missionary kids must deal with upon reentry to the United States.

As time went by, Jim began teaching in a community college. He now wanted to earn his doctorate in literature. Later he did earn that much-desired degree. Today, he continues to teach, and his students respect, love, and admire this genuinely caring and compassionate professor. I, too, personally respect, admire, and love Jim. I am so proud of his perseverance. He worked hard in therapy, believed in himself, and has become very successful. Jim is a winner. Despite his difficulties, his struggles, and past depression, he learned that with support, encouragement, perseverance, and having others believe in him, he could accomplish his dreams. *He did!*

The Trap of Loneliness

So many MKs say to me, "Perhaps loneliness is my worst enemy." This is an indication, I believe, that many MKs live lonely, isolated lives. They may feel empty and unfulfilled. Perhaps they are not in touch with any other MKs from their host country or any other mission country. Thus, they seem to have no one to affirm the feelings they are having that make them feel different. Still, they are probably dealing with feelings of being different and having different values from their American counterparts. This gets in the way, often, of building some good, solid relationships. At the same time, they know that learning to love and to relate to others is what life is all about. It is just as Dr. Randall Lolley said to a group of MKs at a MK retreat at Fort Caswell; "When all is said and done, the meaning of life boils down to three Fs—faith, family, and friends."

When MKs leave their adopted countries, their families, and their friends and return to the States for college, everything in their lives changes. This creates a vacuum for many whose lives were once filled with faith, family, and friends. Some have said, "In my adopted country I was somebody, but here in the States I am suddenly a nobody." With this thought comes a new sense of loneliness, perhaps even feeling lonely when surrounded by lots of people.

When a person is really lonely, they often feel that no one in the whole wide world cares. They may begin to feel worthless. They may fear that they will never form warm, authentic relationships. They may fear involvement, and thus become afraid to take risks. One young man shared this particular sense of isolation he felt when he returned to the States. He said, "I never felt good about anything. I went home from school every day, wondering if there was another person in the whole world like me. Finally, I decided that maybe the problem was within me, and I tried to talk and get to know them, and accept them, even if they didn't believe the way I did. I can truly say that I actually did find that when I reached out to some of my classmates, they reached out to me. Then I realized that there are some pretty neat American young people here." So, you see, MKs don't need to feel helpless and isolated.

The key to building strong, warm relationships is a willingness to be open and vulnerable. It is a willingness to share just how one feels. Each MK is unique, and each has his or her own unique set of feelings. In fact, one's set of feelings is the only thing that makes a person different from anyone else. One's set of feelings is who they are. When two people begin to share their own feelings with one another, they will find themselves getting closer and closer, and have warm feelings for the other. This is the most important ingredient in forming relationships of all kinds.

Why are some MKs, as well as other people, reluctant to share their feelings? Why do some folks feel embarrassed when they cry or show their feelings? Perhaps it is because they haven't allowed themselves to simply *be human.*

Hanoch McCarty, in an article entitled "Permission to Cry," in a "Soup for the Soul" e-mail, shares a heart-warming story about a man whose wife had left him with their two small children. They were divorced, and the man had full custody. He would always try to put on a happy face for the children, filling their lives with activity. One evening, exhausted after a day's work and doing the nightly rituals with his children, he finally was able to close their bedroom doors and tiptoe down the stairs, where he sat at the dining room table, slumped in his chair. Tired from doing all the things that had to be done for the children, the silence was relief, at least for the moment. Then, his fatigue, his great sense of responsibility, the endless details of running the house caused a great sense of loneliness to rush over him. He felt as though he was on rock bottom. He felt a great sense of loneliness. Before he knew it convulsive sobs overtook him. He sat there alone sobbing. About that time he felt a pair of little arms around his waist, and there was the sympathetic little face of his five-year-old son peering up at him. Feeling embarrassed, he began to apologizing to his son for his tears. He said he knew it was hard for many people to apologize when they cry, and he was no exception. He told his son he was sorry. He explained that for some reason he felt a little sad. His little son told him it was okay. It was okay to cry because he, too, was just a person. In the wisdom of the son's innocence, he gave his father permission to cry.

Feelings do free us to be human—to be able to laugh, to cry, to be happy, to be sad, to express pain and pleasure, to love and to be angry, to feel guilt and despair, to experience fear and relief.

Feelings direct us toward survival and living in groups. Feelings warn and caution us. Feelings tell us something is going on that needs to be modified. Feelings free us to be human. The sharing of feelings brings us closer to others.

Wouldn't it be great if we could stop neglecting our feelings and realize their importance in bringing about warm, caring relationships?

Why be lonely? Or should we say, "Why do we allow ourselves to get stuck in that loneliness trap?" Reach out and touch someone. No doubt, you will find others reaching out to you. Be willing to take some risks. Why be trapped in loneliness?

CHAPTER THREE

Schooling

A Social Cripple

Connie, an attractive young MK, upon entering my office introduced herself like this: "My name is Connie, and I am a social cripple." Connie had grown up in an Asian country where her parents were missionaries, assigned to a small country town. Instead of allowing her to go away to a larger city in that country where she could have been educated in an English school, they chose to homeschool her from preschool through high school. She had friends in the community where they lived, but there were no other Americans who lived near her. She grew up playing with her national friends and spoke their language fluently. Connie's parents were ultraconservative missionaries, and they were overprotective of their daughter. They were also fearful of her interaction with other American kids who might influence her in a bad way or ways that would conflict with their theology. As she grew up under the control of her parents, she heard lots of negative words like "should" and "ought." She received little praise from her parents.

Connie did not have good self-esteem, and she was rather shy. After she returned to the States for her college education, she was sent to a conservative college, as one might suspect. Keep in mind that this young lady had never been in a classroom setting but was homeschooled. Now she was placed in a classroom with many peers. She was also facing the usual reentry issues that all MKs must face upon returning to the States: separation and loss; feeling different with different values; culture shock and alienation. She was left at college while her parents returned to their mission field. Her loss was tremendous. America was the foreign country. Her parents had returned to *her* country. She felt so different. Now she was looking at all white and black faces, whereas in her country she had been completely surrounded by brown faces. She said, as so many MKs say, "I know I have the American face, but I don't feel American."

She was living in a dorm at a Christian college, but her values differed greatly from those of her peers. She was astonished at the behavior of some of the students on this Christian campus. She, needless to say, did not feel at home in the States. Her parents told her she was going to America, "home," to get her education. But this was not home. There was lots of confusion about where home was: where did she belong? The feeling of alienation set in, and she spent most of her time in her dorm room. The culture shock was really tough. Even simple things like how to use a pay phone became a big thing. She had no idea who the other students were talking about when they discussed popular musicians or movie stars. She was really feeling isolated, and was right on target when she labeled herself a "social cripple."

After Connie graduated from college, she was still too shy to seek employment. The college gave her a job cleaning the dorms. She needed an advocate to stand with her, to help build her self-esteem, and help develop her self-confidence so that she could live in this scary world called America. On that first day when I met with her, I assured her that I would be her advocate, and she could call me at my office or at my home whenever she needed to talk.

On that first day, I asked Connie what she would like to do if she could choose any career or job. Her response was that she would like to become a nurse. Connie had received a good education from her parents who homeschooled her, but she had not had the social development that gave her self-confidence. She seemed to be unaware of her brilliance. I asked her if she wanted to begin studying nursing, to which she replied that she would. I then requested admission materials from the local technical college. I reiterated that I would be there for her. With a big smile on her pretty face, she asked, "Will you really do that for me?" I assured her that I would.

Connie was now about to start preparing for her career. However, she still had to continue her cleaning job at the college since she was given a dorm room as part of her pay. She began taking nursing classes at night. After a short time she was able to go full-time. At that time, she agreed to come for counseling once each week. It was such a joy to watch how rapidly she was growing. My goals were to help her develop good self-esteem, to help her to believe in herself and trust her own opinions, and to support and encourage her as much as I could.

After a year in nursing training, one night I received a telephone call from Connie. She was in distress. She said, "Tomorrow I have an exam, and I am so tired I just can't concentrate to prepare for it." My response was, "You have my permission to fail the exam. Go to bed, get some rest, and maybe you can, at least, go over your notes before you go to class." She was so shocked, saying, "No one has ever given me permission to fail." I assured her that she could always take the course again if she failed.

Connie did go to bed and slept well. She was able to study a little before she went to sit for her exam. She received a grade of 98. She was so happy and really felt good about herself. All the time she was growing intellectually, socially, emotionally, professionally, and theologically. She began to claim her own values apart from those of her parents. Her theology was quite different from her parents, but she was now coming to know what she believed.

When she graduated, I was there like a proud mother. Connie, with her great compassion for those who suffer, became an excellent nurse, working with hospice patients. If she was in the home of a hospice patient, and she knew that their death was imminent, she would stay with the family to give support.

Connie has truly grown into a wonderful, charming young woman. She is beautiful, inside and outside. She is no longer a social cripple. Now she has no problem meeting people. She exudes a sense of security, and she now believes in herself. Theologically, she knows what she believes, and she verbalizes her beliefs very well. She is not intimidated by those who are different from her. It has been my wonderful privilege to walk the road of growth with Connie and celebrate her achievements.

A Missionary Kids' Reunion

I was invited to present two lectures and be a facilitator on a college campus for a missionary kids' reunion. There were to be about 250 MKs attending. Most were married and brought their wives/husbands and children. It was gratifying to see whole families attending this special retreat. When I arrived at the airport in this distant state, I was met by a retried missionary couple who took me for a visit in their home. The couple poured out their hearts to me about one of their children who had not been able to find her place in the States. She was an adult but lived with them. Of course, they were deeply concerned about their child when they would no longer be around to take care of her, but also about her present problems.

Later in the day the couple took me to the college campus where the retreat would take place. It would begin with the evening meal at six o'clock. I remember getting settled in my room and then going to the lobby where registration was taking place. As I watched the MKs arrive I could see them searching the crowd to spot someone they knew or someone in particular like a brother or a sister. The best way I knew how to describe the scene is that those were the hungriest eyes I have ever seen. Many MK siblings had not seen each other for two, three, or more years since they lived from the East to the West Coast. There were lots of hugs, screams of joy, kisses, and tears.

Then it came time to go to the cafeteria for dinner. Since this was quite a conservative mission, I soon became aware that many of the MKs were a bit suspicious about this therapist having been invited to their retreat. Standing in the dinner line, an adult MK standing behind me said, "Dr. Walters, are you here to fix us missionary kids?" With a smile, I replied, "Not unless some of you want to be fixed." He relaxed, and we had a very warm conversation.

That evening I made my presentation on "Addressing the Reentry Issues of the Children of Missionaries." As I talked about the main reentry issues—separation and loss; difference and values; and alienation and culture shock—MKs were nodding their heads, "yes, yes." There were many tears as well. My speech was followed by a question-and-answer session.

As soon as the meeting was over, I was surrounded by MKs who wanted to schedule some time with me. There were so many that we decided to put up a sign-up sheet for them to claim some time. Some MKs who had not scheduled some time, since the time slots had filled up so quickly, came and pleaded for "just fifteen minutes." In fact, on two nights I did not even go to dinner because they were so anxious to confront some of their problems.

During those two and one-half days, I met with individuals, couples, whole families, spouses of MKs, and even groups of MKs and missionaries from the same countries. One group was made up mostly of men. Without hesitation they began to share some things they had never shared with anyone before. One began by telling us about having been sexually abused by a male missionary from their mission country. There were looks of shock and disbelief on other faces. Several other male MKs said, "And he did that to you too? I thought I was the only one." We spent an entire morning listening and sharing. It was clear that burdens had been lifted from these men who had carried their secret for some fifteen to twenty years.

Then there was the married couple I will call Alex and Fran. Alex told me that the only reason he had come to this retreat was because he heard that a therapist would be there. He also heard that the therapist's focus was on the adjustments and difficulties of MKs. Alex had been unhappy in his marriage to Fran because one day he had awakened and realized she was making all the decisions for him and his children. The fact is, she had to step in and fill the void since Alex had such a hard time making decisions, and he tended to procrastinate. Alex had been in counseling in his home state with a pastoral counselor and was becoming more and more aware of what was happening. Now he was beginning to understand why he had allowed Fran to make all the decisions. When he returned to the States and started dating Fran and fell in love with her, unconsciously he realized he could count on her to make the decisions. Since decision making was difficult and scary, he was relieved to be free.

Alex told me about his life on the mission field. He recounted to me how, at the age of six, he was sent away to boarding school along with other MKs in their little American community. In boarding school, the staff and teachers made all his decisions for him. At home his parents had made decisions for him without consulting him.

The night before they were to leave for boarding school, Alex said he could not eat his supper as he sat around the dinner table with his siblings and his parents for the last time before leaving. He remembered that everyone around the table ate in silence. He said the food somehow stuck in his throat. Then, as he said goodnight to his parents and siblings, he went to sleep in his own bed for the last time, where his tears poured down on his pillow until it was wet. He actually cried himself to sleep.

Early the next morning, all the children gathered around the big truck with their baggage. Everyone but Alex was involved in loading the truck. He stood in silence and watched. His parents gave him his last hug and kiss, appearing stoic even though their hearts were breaking. They drove all day and all night before arriving at the boarding school. Alex told me how he lay on a blanket in one corner of the truck bed, feeling so sick while many of the children were chatting away.

The next day they arrived at the school. Can you see this first-grader, so far away from home and parents, among so many children whom he did not know, trying to act like everything is alright? Furthermore, can you imagine this being your little son whom you would not see again until Christmas holidays? When it came time for him to go to bed, he could not hold back his tears any longer. The bigger children called him a crybaby. This really added to his pain and hurt, and for the first time he learned that it was "not okay" to cry. Nevertheless, he cried himself to sleep that first night in his dormitory room.

Then he got an idea. There was a big tree behind the school building. So, he decided he would go there each day and have a "good cry." He learned that after having his cry he could make it to the next day. At least he could hold it inside him. However, one day, he had started for his tree, but he just could not hold back the tears. As he passed a classroom, a teacher heard him crying and followed Alex to the tree. There she took him on her lap, and she whispered to him it was okay to cry. He will always be grateful for that teacher who consoled and comforted him.

In 1990, Alex, while in therapy here in the States, was asked by his therapist to write his story. He did and found that it was very therapeutic. Alex shared his writing with me, and I share it with you.

MY STORY

I am a child sent away with good intent.

I am a child alone and scared, in need of love and security.

Instead of love and understanding, I received a rationalization. I must do my part to allow my parents to serve the Lord.

Serve the Lord!

I am an angry child. Angry that my needs were not met and that no one hears my cry. When I fight and express my anger, I am told that young Christians don't behave that way. I must love my brother as myself.

Love the Lord
Serve the Lord
Love my brother
Serve my brother

No one heard my desire for limits when I said I wouldn't clean up another child's vomit. No one felt my shame as I cleaned it up after being scolded for not having done it.

I am a young man filled with intent. Intent to do a good job with all my power. People smile as I hold the door. Teachers praise me for a job well done, both in and out of class. I am gentle, kind, compassionate and carry the burdens of all those around. If I do a good job and carry a cheerful smile, maybe they won't see the pain and anger held inside. Pain and anger buried years ago. I am in physical pain as that buried pain and anger eat at me. People ask why should I, so calm and even tempered, have a bleeding ulcer. So well suppressed, I pass it off and pay no heed to the messages being sent.

I am depressed and wonder why. Why is it that I feel so miserable? Why is it that I find no joy? Why is there no light? Why am I in the middle of this desert so huge, so flat, so plain, so devoid? How can there be so much of nothingness?

I am in psychotherapy. Wondering why I'm here and ashamed to admit it. Where did those mountains come from?

The desert is not so huge anymore. I am shown that I don't need to carry all those burdens. Where did those trees come from? I am befriended and shown that someone cares. Where did those flowers come from? Then reality struck.... I'm married, have three sons, very busy producing the "looking good" family and hating every minute of it. Hate being told how I "should" be living, "should" be in church, "should" join service organizations, "should" attend all school functions to show I "love" my sons. The flowers and trees are gone.

I am a codependent. I can see my dysfunctional family. I am a recovering codependent. I see, I empathize, and I can detach. I see, and I want to do and it hurts to hold back. There is a garden now. Plants of my own choosing. A few weeds appear now and then, but I know that if I work at it they can be removed. I work at it and find that some weeds keep returning. I cut off the tops and new ones pop up in their place. I dig the roots and find that I have only delayed their return. My anger is too large for me to remove by myself. I ask for help and suddenly the old root is gone. There's hope for beautiful flowers and a bountiful harvest.

I am a child of the universe, just as the trees and the stars. I have a right to be here! I have a right to be me!

In July 1989 Alex wrote another paper while in therapy. In it he discusses his boarding school experience, his difficulties in discussing his own feelings, a child who craved a sense of family, his codependency, his difficulty in making decisions and how to approach a career lifestyle. After meeting a friend whom he had not seen for twenty-seven years, a friend who had been in boarding school with him, Alex discovered that he was not the only one going through all this anguish. He discovered that there were other classmates who were still "wrestling with their self-identity and with building healthy social relationships." In a positive way, Alex assures others that "Help can be found, and we are not condemned for seeking it. We owe it to ourselves to search for this health."

Another discovery Alex made some years later was the pain his mother had felt in sending her six-year-old son away to boarding school. Counting the cost is the burden that missionary children carry as a result of their parents' commitment to the church? Alex knew that there was a "cost" to his mother and perhaps to his dad, although he had never verbalized it. Since Alex tells about those experiences better than I could ever condense them and maintain the full impact of emotion, with his permission I present you his paper "Counting the Cost." Many MKs who were sent away to boarding school will be able to identify with Alex.

Counting the Cost

The sun was setting, casting vivid hues of gold, orange, and red in the clear sky. The air was dry as would be expected of the dry season which had not yet reached its peak. The day had been hot, but as evening drew nigh the night chill was already being felt. There was an air of excitement as friends of last semester met again and chatted of their vacation experiences. The excitement was subdued by sadness… the sadness of leaving home, parents, pets, and carefree days… the sadness of returning to school, daily chores, and homework. The day had been filled with the usual tasks of packing those special things that I wanted with me during the semester. Of course, Mom packed the "expected" things—clothes, sheets, towels, and other necessities—but it was up to me to be sure the new truck I got for Christmas went along. As the suitcases were filled and time for supper drew near, these tasks took on a melancholy feeling. This was to be the last time to see the family dog for four and a half months. It even seemed as though the dog sensed this and moped around instead of showing the usual vigor. Supper was always sad. The food seemed to go down in hard lumps, and nothing looked as though it was Mom's good cooking—the same that had welcomed me home just six or seven weeks ago.

It seemed to take forever for all the suitcases to be loaded on the lorry [truck]. Now it was the last chance for a hug and kiss from Mom and Dad and time to climb up into the bed of the lorry. All the suitcases had been laid in such a way that a flat platform was made. Everything was then covered with a large tarp, making an acceptable resting place for the long journey ahead. The dry season had started and most of the scenery was dull brown, the hot sun scorching anything not in permanent shade. There were isolated spots where some underground water gave life to those plants with long roots, but these were few and far between. The lorry lumbered out, and the dust swirled up behind it. Some of the kids watched the trail of dust pointing toward home and loved ones, but they soon turned their attention to the scenery ahead. Shortly, the air cooled and it became chilly as the lorry passed over the river, but the sense of heat returned as soon as the lorry climbed up the far bank.

The night grew deeper and the scenery became dim. For most the vignette provided by the headlights was not enough to hold their attention. Some continued to watch, fascinated by the light's reflection in the eyes of a bush baby in a tree or some other night animal prowling close to the road. The air cooled even further, and jackets were donned. As kids lost interest in the road ahead, they found their blankets to help make the bed a little softer. In the darkness, I was able to find solace. I could think about home and how much it hurt to leave. Now, in the darkness, I could even cry a little and not worry about what the other kids would think. Crying didn't make things all right, but the release made me feel better for a while. After a bit, I became more aware of my immediate surroundings. The lorry bounced and joggled noisily. Once in a while, the suitcases would shift and pinch. I felt as though I'd be all black and blue by the time the lorry pulled in at the school. Above the noise of the lorry, some of the kids were able to chatter. Some of the outside noises could be heard—the laugh of the hyena in the distance or the croak of some happy frogs in a meager pond along the road. Looking around in the dim light provided by the headlights, the shapes of my neighbors made me realize how small this space was for all of us to endure the fourteen-hour trek to school. Looking up, the stars of the tropical night beamed down. The air was so clear that I felt as if I could reach up and touch them. Here were some friends. These were the stars that I had watched lying in bed out on the back porch while I waited for sleep to come after an exciting day at home. The memories cheered me up, only to remind me that that was home, and now I was being sent off to school again. In this melancholy mood, I eventually drifted off despite the noise and jostling.

Those memories were written down over a year ago. It was just a small part of the extensive therapy that I have been receiving over the past several years. I was born to missionaries and was sent off to a boarding school for my formal education. When the pain of leaving home to attend boarding school is repeated twice a year through all your formative years, you learn to survive the pain by suppressing the memories. After a while, you begin to forget the good as well as the bad. By the time I achieved adulthood I was very busy forgetting. I even found it difficult to answer the simple question of where I was from. This suppression became a part of every aspect of my life, and I soon succumbed to the stress that resulted. This led to severe depression, which was where the therapy started. Now, though the road ahead still remains uncertain, I can look back on what I have learned about myself and my background and begin to place things into perspective.

My new perspective helps me to see things that many people are not willing to acknowledge. Because of this I find it difficult to discuss these feelings and even more difficult to place them into writing. What was it that led me to live in this manner and to become so involved in trying to forget? To put it briefly, I hated my upbringing, which by its very nature forbade me to express those feelings of hatred. It was the Christian directive that placed my parents on the mission field that resulted in my being brought up there. Therefore, in hating my situation, was I also saying that I hated

Christianity? Because of this conflict I learned very effectively to suppress other emotions besides just the homesickness that I felt every semester.

The Christian teachings were very prevalent at the boarding school, and we were taught not to express our anger. When a dispute arose, we were taught to "love your neighbor as yourself." When we were angry at the "situation," we were taught to "honor your mother and father," and at boarding school this meant any adult figure. It was impossible to form permanent friendships. The close friend of last semester was often home on furlough this semester or reassigned to another mission. A child who craves for a sense of family and belonging cannot see that this disruption is beyond his control. He soon becomes wrapped up in the only person he knows will not leave him: himself. In order to lessen the pain of constant farewells, he loses the ability and desire to make new friends. Because of the cyclical nature of interpersonal relationships, he grows up in a dysfunctional family. The net effect of all this was that each of us kids became codependent.

Now, the term "codependency" is used in many different ways, usually as applied to the children of alcoholics. At first I had trouble coping with having that term applied to me because of the link to alcoholism. It took a long time for me to recognize that I was a codependent because I didn't "love my neighbor as myself," but I love him better than myself. In order to keep peace in the boarding school environment, we each learned to look out for the others' interests to the extent that we lost our own self-identity. I can recognize now that my only identity or self-esteem was in making others feel good. Even if I was doing something I didn't really want to do, I didn't feel good until those around me felt good. As one author put it, the codependent is a chameleon. He unknowingly senses what others expect of him and then places all his efforts into meeting those expectations. In this manner he can get along well with those around him, but he fails to recognize his own true color. He is always asking what it is that others expect or want and fails to ask what it is that he wants. The codependent, in starting the road to recovery, must learn to ask questions to establish just what his identity is and what it is that he wants. To most people this feels like being very selfish, and by nature Christians are not to be selfish. We must put others first... and the old conflict starts once again. You may be able to see why I find this difficult to express. It is a direct criticism of the Christian faith. We were taught that those who blaspheme against the church are doomed to eternal hell and damnation.

Another aspect of my life that has been very hard to cope with is that of making decisions for myself. This is related to the topic above, but it can be extended further. In the boarding school environment all decisions are made for the students. It's not like the family environment where the kids have some input as to whether or not they want to eat at McDonald's tonight. There just weren't opportunities for the individual to have a choice. This leads to a procrastinating approach. If the decision is not immediately required, then it can be postponed. In time either the decision will be obvious, or the opportunity will pass and there will no longer be a need for a decision. I deeply regret now that this was my approach to my career and my lifestyle. How many others from my boarding school find themselves in a similar situation in their adult lives?

Why do I want to write now and finally express myself in this manner? The most obvious reason is the timeliness for my own healing process. If that was the only reason, I would continue writing my bittersweet memories to be shared with my family and the therapist and then to file it and watch it collect dust. However, a couple of weeks ago I had a conversation with a friend with whom I had not had contact for twenty-seven years. Through this conversation I found out that I am not the only one going through this anguish. She related to me her own experiences and those of classmates we both knew. With few exceptions they are all wrestling with gaining a self-identity and with building healthy social relationships. I want to pass the message on to each and every one of them that they are not alone. Yes, each of us must struggle for our own selves, but we are not cast adrift by society and left to live with our burden in quiet isolation. Help can be found, and we are not condemned for seeking it. We owe it to ourselves to search for this health.

The other reason for wanting to voice myself now is that a collection of thoughts that has been forming for some time came together recently. Shortly after I started my therapy, my mom passed on a book that she had found. The book was Letters Never Sent. *The writer grew up in circumstances similar to mine. As an adult she now expresses her childhood anger and frustrations by writing letters to her parents. Those letters would not have been accepted from any child of missionaries. When I discussed the book with Mom, she said that she felt that the writer was too strong in her writings. To counter this, Mom said she'd like to write of the hurt that she had felt as a parent. I could hear in her voice some of the pain she must have felt as she sent each of her children off to boarding school when they were five or six years old. They were her children, but not for her to raise and have for her own. My own thoughts, with those of my mom, have been rumbling around in the back of my mind for the time being and have recently been joined by thoughts from other boarding-school MKs.*

Just recently, I again heard the Brethren phrase about "counting the cost." Suddenly the word "cost" took on a new light. The biblical teaching is that we should go into all the world teaching the ways of Christianity. This is admirable, and I find nothing wrong with it. The Brethren have always emphasized "counting the cost" before a new project is undertaken. That cost has usually been in the monetary sense and in more concrete terms. Where there is a need and a commitment, the Brethren have been able to find the necessary money and resources. For me now, the "cost" is that burden that we children of missionaries are bearing as a result of our parents' commitment to the church. For Mom, it was the emotional cost of sending her kids off to boarding school, even though there were no real alternatives. Although he has never really spoken of it to me, I'm sure there has been a cost for Dad, too. For the mission society, and the church at large, the cost is the social and emotional trauma that has happened to all these children. The trauma can be healed, but not without scars, for the scars remain in not having healthy relationships with those around me and in not having a clear self-identity. The monetary costs of medical and psychiatric expenses that have resulted from the codependent characteristics are one thing that I must cope with. I know that the bills will some day, somehow all be paid. But the scars of not having healthy and intimate relationships with Mom and Dad, brothers and sisters, spouse and children can never be removed.

In the exciting moments when one receives a call to mission, the cost of this pain is not brought to light and is not considered. It is easy to appraise the financial cost of living in a foreign country, but we cannot fathom the emotional cost to ourselves and to our children. However, it is a cost that some of us pay for a lifetime.

Reflections on the MK Reunion

[Note: After returning home from the MK retreat, I received a letter from those who planned it. They asked me to write a paper giving my reflections, as a therapist and as an objective observer as well as a former missionary. I share this paper that I prepared for them.]

It was a really good experience being your guest and therapist at your Reunion. MKs, you gave me some valuable insights into who you are and what you want in your lives. It was a delight to meet and spend time with middle-aged as well as young adult MKs. No, you are not kids in any sense of the word, but you will always be missionary kids, MKs to each other and to those who see you as a special group of people.

I am most appreciative of the trust that you placed in me in such a short time. At least eighty-six of you shared with me your hurts, struggles, and events in your lives. I felt as if I were walking with you on sacred ground.

Before I arrived at the retreat, my guess was that some of you would view me, a counselor, with suspicion. Why was I attending your retreat? But after that first night with you, the Fourth of July, I felt as if we had really connected. You learned that I was not there to read your minds or to fix you, but to give my support if you wanted it. I could feel the walls of suspicion tumbling down as we spent time together. I must say, that felt very good. I felt your warmth and acceptance. You let me into your lives, for which I am grateful.

As I sat in the lobby that first day, I observed you desperately searching for former classmates and family members. It was like an oasis in a dry, parching desert. Your twelve years together may have linked you to each other more closely than you link to your own blood kin. Your genuine greetings and your embracing each other warmed my heart.

I want to tell you that I have never worked harder than I did that weekend with you on that campus, and I have never felt more rewarded. You shared your joys and sorrows, your pain and suffering. Some of you were searching for direction for your lives. You came with questions, and I hope you left with some answers. You must know that when I left that campus on July 7, I took you with me in my heart. How could I ever forget you as you continue to struggle with your issues of separation and loss, feelings of being different and having different values, alienation from both the country in which you grew up and the country of your parents? Who among us does not, on occasion, still deal with some culture shock as we experience the vast differences in our own two cultures?

Here are some quotes from the persons with whom I spent time over the Fourth of July weekend. I want to share them with you.

> "Sometimes the small tasks in life can be most difficult.... Moving from one city in America is not that much of an adjustment, but when it comes to moving to a foreign country, it is difficult."
>
> "Most missionary families feel called to the field by the Holy Spirit and feel led to do the Lord's work.... When a family is given a country overseas to serve in, most of them do it without realizing the psychological effects it may have on them or their children. The children have to go through a very dramatic change and most times are not helped very much, if at all."

"We need some good counselors to go to the mission field where we have our missionaries and counsel the children of foreign missionaries…so they will not go through such a traumatic and rebellious state as most missionary kids do."

"When I came back to the United States for college, it was hard to get a handle on myself. Who was I? I hardly knew myself or my relatives, and I felt cheated and couldn't go to them to talk, because they were people I hardly knew."

"Of all the missionary kids I know personally, all are having or have had adjustment problems. We need help as missionary kids on the field and when we come back to the States for college."

"It took me a while to realize that it was a privilege to live overseas and to feel proud of my parents, what they stood for, who they were. I realize that missionaries give up a lot when they go to a foreign field, but so do their children. In a way, they give up more than they realize. I sometimes wonder whether it was worth it or not, because missionary kids go through some really rough times. I know of so many missionary kids who are hurting so bad, but they don't feel they can express themselves to very many people."

"I am saddened by the fact that quite a few MKs are burned out on religion right now, and I can see why they feel this way. I believe we need to start giving our children room to breathe, to think for themselves, and to make their own decisions."

"We need to have unconditional love. We don't need to have judgment passed on us for our differences."

In closing this writing of my reflections, I would like to introduce you to a book by Jerry Cook, *Some Things I Have Learned Since I Knew It All*. In this book, Jerry tells the story of his own open-heart surgery.

When he had his heart attack, Jerry was the pastor of a large church in Oregon that practiced healing. While he was recovering, a lady from his church asked him, "Were you embarrassed to have a heart attack, especially since you and your church members believe in and practice healing?" Jerry told her that he was not embarrassed. But the lady was. She wasn't able to handle the reality and totality of life experiences, including pain and suffering.

After Jerry had recovered, a man who was facing bypass surgery visited Jerry. With some shyness, the man said, "I want to see your scars." Jerry promptly took off his shirt, and the man traced with his finger the violet scar that ran down Jerry's chest. The man continued, "The doctor says the most painful part of the operation will be the surgery on my legs. They're going to take out veins from my calf to use in the heart bypass. Can I see your legs?" Jerry rolled up his pants, and the man got down on his knees and traced the scars with his fingers. When he arose, there were tears in his eyes. "Thank you," he said. "Now I have hope." Seeing and touching Jerry's scars had given him hope for his own survival.

Most MKs are scarred. You are not proud of the scars, but neither are you ashamed of them. When you are hurt, I pray that God will send someone whose scars you can trace, and I hope you will do the same for someone else. Thank you for letting me trace some of your scars.

"Little Johnny Still Cries" (1990)
DONALD G. PRICE

Little Johnny still sheds tears
The way it used to be
Way back then so many years
When it was time to leave
Weeks of apprehension
Filled his little eyes
When he took the plane to school
And bid his last good-byes
Though there were many others

And brothers and sisters too
It was so hard for Johnny
To leave for the boarding school
All the comforts of house and home
Of loving parents too
Was left behind as he was sent
To a place where all was new
It seemed a great adventure
As they dropped out of the sky
Two volcanoes and a long dirt road
To the end of his good-bye
It wasn't so bad
There were friends to meet
Four to a room
Was kinda neat
Off and on through the night
Little guys woke up in a fright
Struggling to cope with their fears
They shared their beds and their tears
It was always hardest in the night
They were not allowed to turn on a light
There were so many things they couldn't do
To ease the pain their little hearts knew…
And so it went for so many years
Each of them fighting back the tears
All of those little hurts and pains
Seemed to compromise and no spiritual gain
The conflict of those who would not see
Lies in what now is plain to me
A dichotomy there truly does remain
Between spiritual blessing and experienced pain
Time and distance

Played their role
Taxed little hearts
And exacted a toll
The ignorance of the issues back there
Now played out in hearts everywhere
The price to pay is plain to see
When a child is removed from the parent's knee
Self-esteem is running low
A God of love is hard to know
Of all the things they thought they knew
What did they really learn in school
All missionaries go to share the news
But the message was lost in the schools
All the hopes of spiritual gain
Were washed away in the tropical rain
But then night came
And it seemed bad
Some were crying
And all were sad
For many there will still remain
A lifelong struggle for spiritual gain
Still Johnny wonders at the strain
Of a heart filled with such latent pain….
So often on the radio
Something triggers his poor soul
A lyric or a melody
Strikes a flood of memory….
Still within his crumpled soul
An answer he would seek
Though his eyes still fill with tears
They almost never see his cheek
Johnny still cries about yesteryear

But the struggle remains for today
Why he feels so incomplete...
How he will find his way...?

A Feeling of Numbness

Norman, a male MK who grew up in Europe, received most of his formal education through the Calvert System. The Calvert System is a curriculum used in home school; Mks on the mission field. He and other MKs were also taught by young college graduates who were appointed by some mission board to teach overseas for two years. They often would meet in a missionary home or some nearby building, depending on the number being taught. This school had structure just as public schools do. The class may be made up of MKs ranging from first grade to fifth grade. After that, most of them would go away to some American school located in some large city. Because of this special arrangement, Norman never had to leave his home and parents and attend boarding school. After the fifth grade his family lived in a large city, and he could stay at home and attend the American school there. He sees this opportunity to stay home and get all his schooling without ever leaving family as a real asset, and he cherishes those years with his family.

Of course, when Norman and his family returned to the States for furlough, it was a difficult time for him. He ended up going to schools with large classes. During his first couple of furloughs, he thought little about going to a "real" school. He said, "I did whatever was expected of me." It seemed that this idea took precedent over any feelings he might have had.

However, Norman described his tenth grade in high school as a hellish year. He, as an MK, was trying to be what he was expected to be. This actually squelched his whole personality. The most difficult part was dealing with his extended family, people who were like strangers to him. Yet it seems that these people wanted to take care of him, and he found himself resisting. He said, "I always knew that my real family was the missionaries who I considered grandparents, uncles, and aunts, and their children were my brothers and sisters, but not my blood cousins." He never felt really comfortable with his blood relatives, simply because he did not know them.

Each time Norman's family returned to the States, they lived in the same house and went to the same church where they were welcomed back by old friends. He said, "I had instant friends." However, he felt he was expected to act a certain way because he was not only a preacher's son but a missionary's son. He hated going with his father or sometimes his parents when they went to churches as special speakers. They would always take him and put him in a Sunday school class with a bunch of kids he did not know. He was called upon by the teacher to comment on the lesson. He hated this! As a result he never really liked attending a Sunday school class after returning to America to live permanently.

Norman was always eager to leave the States and go "home." He saw his parents saying goodbye to their parents and family members along with many tears of sadness. They would probably not see each other for at least four years. He said sometimes his mother really "lost it" at the airport, meaning she was having a hard time with her emotions. In some ways he was affected by her sadness and pain, but his excitement of going "home" took precedence over other feelings. Sometimes he felt some guilt about not being sad. He just could not identify with them. Norman also remembers that when there was a serious illness or death in the States, how hard it was on his parents. Nevertheless, he did not feel that such losses affected his life.

As a child growing up in Europe, Norman remembers the preaching of his father and other missionaries and the national preachers. He heard a lot of hellfire-and-brimstone preaching, which really frightened him. There were lots of pressures and expectations of how the MK should be living the Christian life, and how he should be completely involved in the church activities. He was often confused and felt angry.

He would think, *Maybe I need to do this or that, but I do not want to do that.* Then he would ask himself, *What is the proper thing to do? I know that I am not full of joy and happiness that others said a Christian is supposed to feel.* One day Norman decided to write a letter to an editor of a youth magazine in the States who addressed problems of young people. In his letter he told the editor how unhappy he was, and how he did not enjoy his Christian life. In the editor's reply to Norman she suggested that he probably was *not* a Christian; she also suggested that he may be emotionally disturbed and needed counseling.

After receiving such a letter from the magazine editor, Norman became really frightened, so afraid that he would surely go to hell if he died. He was so afraid that he could not easily go to sleep at night. He might die in his sleep and go straight to hell. Everybody had said, "If you are truly a Christian, then you should be happy," but Norman was not happy. This experience was traumatic for him, and about that time another traumatic thing happened. There was an earthquake in his country that killed eighty thousand people. He felt so sad, but the worst part was that he thought the world was coming to an end, and maybe he was not ready. This was all just too much. Perhaps it was at that time that Norman completely "numbed out," in order not to have to deal with feelings or emotions at all.

When Norman came back to the States to go to college, his mother made the trip with him. For three months they stayed at his grandmother's place before college classes were to begin. He remembers getting off the plane in a plaid suit and red necktie, and they were out of style. In his country people could wear whatever they wanted to wear, and no one noticed or cared. Norman said, "I knew I was different, and I really wanted to stay that way." He had the idea that he never would be a part of America. Protecting himself from any insecurities he might have, he decided that he would not even try to conform to American ways and expectations. He often felt himself pulling away from groups. He would rather be alone and feel comfortable

His parents bought him a small car. When his mother returned to Europe, he packed his car with everything he owned and set out to find the college. He had never been on the campus. He knew it was in a certain city, but he had no idea what part of the city. Yet he felt no fear, no anxiety. He felt nothing. Now, as he looks back on being left alone to be completely responsible for himself and make all his decisions without anyone with whom to consult, he said, "I feel afraid right now."

The one feeling that Norman often had was anger. He was angry at his relatives who expected him to "be family," and visit them often. They had no understanding about the complexity of his life and feelings. There was no way they could understand Norman, but he did not like these people who felt they needed to take care of him. They had nothing in common. One uncle tried to choose a career for him. Norman only felt rebellion. If he did not comply with the wishes of these blood relatives, they threatened to withhold money and gifts. He also believed that his own standards were higher than those of his relatives. He was now more determined to live by his own standards.

What is clear here is that Norman was trying to find his identity, to individualize. Apart from his family, he asked, "Who am I?" Working through this process was no easy matter. When in Europe he felt freedom from the States, and when he was in the States he felt freedom from Europe. Instead of dealing with his emotions, he was "living through the experience." He did not feel sad or bad that his parents were not here for him. He had already decided, "They are gone, and that is the way it's going to be from now on." To him it was almost like they had died; at least this was his perspective. He was now simply looking for a place to belong. He always had felt displaced and had no idea what was in his future.

When Norman was a junior in college, he went back to Europe to spend Christmas with his family. On his return flight, there was a large group of MKs and children of businesspeople. They all got together in one section of the plane where they "formed a community." He said,

"Later, after my return to the States, I reminisced about that experience on the plane, and I realized that there, for the first time, I had a sense of belonging. We all spoke both English and German. We understood each other's slang and cues. There I experienced community." Before this experience, Norman felt he had one leg in America and one leg in Germany. He said, "I knew I was American, born of American parents, and even if I had been born in Germany, I would still be American." This was truly a freeing experience for Norman.

CHAPTER FOUR

Suffering

Is God Real or Myth?

Jill called my office soon after I started the special counseling ministry for the children of missionaries. She came on a Friday at 11:00 a.m. after driving for more than two hours. As she entered my office she appeared very shy and even a little fearful. She was a petite, cute, and delightful young lady. She had grown up in a missionary home in Australia.

Jill had returned to the States as a high school student, where she lived with relatives while her parents remained in Australia. There she would finish high school and then enter some American university. Jill faced the usual reentry issues but at an earlier age than most missionary kids do who stay in the country where their parents are serving until they return to the States for college. This naïve, trusting young person fell in love fairly early and got married. It is not uncommon for MKs to marry while still in college since MKs are looking for a place to belong. It appeared that her husband loved her dearly. He was well-educated and even working on his Ph.D. Jill, feeling insecure and even inferior to her husband, fearful that he might leave her, decided she must divorce him before he would "probably divorce me." I suspect that this was more of an imagined fear rather than real. She realized that he was crushed when she asked for a divorce. Feeling insecure and unworthy, MKs often seem to read into relationships messages that are really not there.

Later, Jill met a charming young man whom she married. They had three children. Things were not going too well. When he abused Jill she was able to accept his apologies and move on. However, when he started abusing her children, that was not okay. It got so bad that one night, fearing for the safety of her children and herself, she took the children and left. She stayed with friends. Later he would plead for her to return home. He promised he would never behave in such a way again. After leaving several times, Jill realized her husband would never change. She knew she could not continue to expose her children to his abuse. Thus, one night when he was away from home, she packed their clothes and left for good. She knew he had serious problems but did not have a clue that he might be suffering from some kind of mental illness. Later he was diagnosed as schizophrenic.

For some time, Jill raised her children and provided for them by herself. Finally, she met a man who loved her and one who deserved her love. He accepted not only Jill, but her children as well. He loved them as if they were his own. By this time Jill had become pretty disillusioned about life and particularly about religion. She could not understand why bad things happen to good people. She had grown up in a missionary family where there was much love. After she was sent back to the States as a high school student, she felt deprived of that much-needed parental love. We must remember that, to her and to other MKs, the United States is a foreign country. Home is really the country in which they spent all the developmental years of their lives. It really makes no sense to them that their parents can remain in the country that they call "home" and they themselves must return to the States where they know very little about the culture. It is a kind of paradox that the child would rather be in her host country while often the parents would rather be in America, their place of birth.

Jill said to me, "All of this is very confusing." Her religious teaching said that God created the family, and the children were to be the parents' first responsibility, yet she must be separated from her parents since they are doing God's work of taking care of the people of Australia. Despite her disillusionment, she started going to a small church group that met in a home. She said, "I wanted to believe in the God of my parents. I prayed so often that if God was real, he would please show himself to me."

After several sessions, one day Jill came in and told me about some friends who had been in an automobile accident. The mother was in the hospital, and her son was in a coma in the same hospital. She was very sad. This young boy was one of her own son's best friends. To the little church group this accident was a real shock. They all began to pray for this family. They did many other things to try to meet the family's needs.

Later, at another session, Jill entered my office, seeming very happy, energetic, and rejuvenated. I recognized this immediately and commented on it. Then she began to tell me what had happened. She said, "You know I told you that I had prayed to God, if he was real to show himself to me. Well, this week God did show me that he is real and cares." By this time, she had my curiosity in high gear! She told me about the family who had been in the accident. I remembered her telling me about her concern for them. She reminded me that her son's best friend who was in the accident was still in the hospital, but his mother had been able to leave the hospital. She told me how friends from the little church group had taken turns staying with the boy. One day, Jill was taking her turn sitting with this child, who was in a coma, from 8:00 a.m. to 3:00 p.m. Jill told me how hard and fervently she had prayed for the boy all day. She would talk to him and tell him how much she wanted him to get well and come back to her house. She had done this all day long, and still the boy was in the coma. It was getting almost time for her to leave and another friend would take her turn. One final time, she went to his bed, took his hand in hers, expressing her love for him and inviting him to come to her house when he was well. Suddenly, to her great surprise, the boy squeezed her hand, opened his eyes, smiled at her, and said, "Thank you." Jill was so overwhelmed with emotion, not only that the child had come out of his coma, but that "God had shown himself to me." She went to her car after celebrating with the person who had come to relieve her, laid her head on the steering wheel, and wept openly. She said, "I had to take care of my emotions before I could drive home." What a time of joy and peace!

This MK's life was changed forever. She became positive and optimistic. And since that day she knows there is a God of the universe who really does care about what happens to her. Even during struggles and other sad events in her life, Jill is now a happy daughter, wife, mother, and friend. She knows that *God is real*!

Secrets

Mac, a fifteen-year-old male MK who grew up in a South American country, was having lots of problems in that country. Among his problems was failing almost all his courses in school. His parents, when they saw that nothing they were doing was working, decided to return to the States. Mac had three siblings.

The family arrived in Winston-Salem after flying to Florida. They drove the rest of the way, making the trip as pleasant as possible for the entire family. I met them in the parking lot of the building where my office was located. They arrived a few minutes before I did. My first introduction to Mac was watching him do antics on his skateboard in the parking lot. You might call him a skateboard addict, since that is the one thing he never became tired of doing. He had appeared to his parents to be depressed, yet he never seemed to lack energy when it came to skateboarding.

I had arranged for the family to stay in a local church's missionary residence for up to one year. We did not know how long it would take for Mac to work through his problems, and for the family to work out plans for their future. The parents were eager to learn how they could help

Mac. Before returning to the States, Mac, too, had admitted his need for professional help. After meeting them and showing them exactly where my office was in the four-story office building, I drove ahead of them to show them where their home would be for the next few months.

The next day, I saw Mac with all his family members. He did not hesitate to tell us that he was angry and felt displaced. Actually, he would not have chosen to come to Winston-Salem for therapy but had agreed to come after his parents' mission board made the arrangements. There was no doubt that each one of them missed their adopted country and were somewhat homesick. In the States, everything was so different, and he could not discern between what was appropriate and inappropriate behavior. Mac showed signs of passive-aggressive behavior.

Mac's mother described him as inactive, totally unmotivated, uncaring about anybody but himself, disrespectful, without remorse, manipulative, without concern for his future, rebellious, and having no energy. I heard enough that led me to believe that Mac was suffering from some amount of depression. He recognized that he needed discipline and motivation. He knew he had to get into some school in Winston-Salem, but he had a fear of not being able to "stick with school." He knew his parents disliked his use of cigarettes. He admitted that he had occasionally stolen cigarettes. He was underage, and storekeepers would not sell them to him. He liked to stay up very late at night and then sleep almost the whole day. One thing he did continue was his skateboarding. He often wandered away from the parking lot behind their house. His mother wanted him to stay at home more. In a word, Mac was self-destructing.

Mac admitted to his parents that he had often lied to them. He broke things when he was angry, and he was not kind to his siblings. In fact, he acted as though he did not want to be a part of this family. He wanted to be in charge of the remote control regardless of what the other members of the family preferred to watch on television. In almost all other areas of his life, he was out of control.

In spite of all of these problems, Mac's parents loved him very much. They could see all of his good qualities. He usually was a compassionate, kind individual, at least before all the problems had begun to reveal themselves. Before, it had been a pleasure just being in his presence. He had a good sense of humor and could make the family laugh. Before he became "depressed," he was thoughtful; when he committed to do something, he would "see it through." He appreciated good classical music, Bach and Beethoven. He was interested in all kinds of sports, and he loved to read. What in the world happened? They had lost their wonderful son and were now searching to get him back.

Mac said he loved talking to his mother. He saw her as a happy individual, and he said, "She listens to me." He felt her support even in this time when he was being so difficult. She knew that somewhere inside was that compassionate young man whom she had known before. Mac said that his dad was fun to be with, a good person, had a gentle, kind personality, was competitive and motivated. One thing that bothered him about his father was, "Sometimes he seems to try to force God upon me." He needed his father's support, love, and time. This was actually a period of doubting, which bothered both parents.

I saw the whole family together, then Mac, and then each of his siblings individually and together. I saw the parents individually and together, and then I saw Mac with just his parents. As I began to observe them individually and collectively, I began to get a feel for their situation. Early on, when I met with just the parents, I asked, "Do you think Mac has been using any drugs?" They were very confident that he had not and presently was not taking drugs. In session with Mac alone, I also asked him if he had ever used drugs before they returned to the States. He replied emphatically that he had never had anything to do with drugs, yet I had the deep "gut" feeling that he not only did drugs in the past but also had used alcohol as well.

We were working hard to find the root of Mac's problems. I had put him in touch with a psychiatrist who talked to him and wanted to watch his progress in therapy. We would watch the depression as well. He might need to be placed on an antidepressant. It was clear to the psychiatrist and to me that Mac had a hard time dealing with change. He was in the puberty stage of life and had some facial scarring. The hormones were raging. Was this his only problem? I did not think so. A part of the problem was his search for his own identity. He was trying to individuate. In all this, he was not only resisting his family but also their God. He was suffering from low self-esteem. He also suffered from attention deficit disorder. At this point he denied all emotions and stated that he didn't feel anything (numbness is a part of depression). However, he readily expressed his anger. He knew that the best way to hurt his parents would be to distance himself from God. He knew that their greatest wish for him was to be a good Christian young man.

Some rules his parents laid out for him were that he was to eat his meals with the family, keep his room clean, stop excessively teasing his younger siblings, and get up and go to bed at a designated time. All this was a real struggle for Mac. As things were still not going very well for him, we got back in touch with the psychiatrist who felt it would be good for Mac to enter the adolescent unit at a psychiatric hospital for at least two weeks where his medication could be evaluated. He could also continue his schoolwork at the hospital.

Mac had been in the hospital about a week to ten days. On a Monday morning when I went to my office, I had a call from Mac's counselor at the hospital. That was about 10 a.m. She said, "We need for you to come to the adolescent unit. Mac has been placed in isolation." I could not imagine what had happened to require his being placed in the isolation room.

As I talked with the counselor, she told me that Mac had been very agitated. Around ten the previous night when all the other patients were going to bed, Mac could not be found. He had gone to another adolescent's room where they plotted on how they could escape from the hospital. Mac had actually hidden behind the door in his friend's room. He had something in his hand. When the male orderly began his search for Mac and entered the room, Mac stepped out from behind the door quickly and hit the orderly on the head with a heavy object, leaving a rather large lump on his head. Fortunately, the orderly had the kind of training to deal with such a situation. Mac said to me, "He had me on the floor before I knew what was happening."

After telling me what had happened, the counselor took me to the isolation room where Mac was waiting. He was alone with nothing on his bed but a mattress, and they had given him his school textbooks. Then they led Mac and me to an office where we could talk in complete privacy. At this point, Mac acted really remorseful and was teary. He had been brought face-to-face with himself and his real problems.

In the office, that day, I asked, "Mac, were you using drugs in South America?" He lowered his head, broke down, and told me the whole truth. He said, "Behind our house in South America, marijuana grew freely, and yes, I was using it daily. That's the reason I couldn't do anything in class but sleep." He then told me that he kept a bottle of wine in his desk drawer or actually behind the desk drawer. He would take the drawer completely out, put the wine bottle at the back and then put the drawer back in. Of course, the drawer was always partially open, but his mother never seemed to notice. He had plastic bags of marijuana on his desk in his room. He said, "It looked like a kind of tea we used there." Mom and Dad never suspected his use of drugs and alcohol. Since he smoked marijuana or drank some wine each day before class, he was sleeping away the day in classes and was failing every subject.

A few days after this incident at the adolescent unit at the hospital, Mac came with his father to my office. I spent time with Mac first. I told him I wanted him to tell his father the truth. Then in a couple of days we would have him bring his mother, and he would tell her the whole truth. When we called Mac's father into the room, Mac verbalized very well what had happened and expressed his sincere regrets for his deception. His father was shocked! His face turned pale.

We asked his father not to tell Mac's mother, because Mac was to tell her himself.

In a couple of days, Mac came with his mother. Again, Mac explained to her that he had been deceptive, regretted it, and was now ready to change his ways. As with the father, he embraced his mother and asked for her forgiveness. It was clear that Mac was the most relieved one of all. The truth was known, and now he would no longer have to continue living a lie.

Mac started getting better right away. The depression lifted. One thing he said he had learned through this whole ordeal was not to hesitate to ask for help. The more he lied, the harder it was for him to tell the truth to his parents. Mac did continue to have problems with ADD (attention deficit disorder) but continued his studies, this time not in a stupor.

Some three to four years passed since the last time I had seen Mac. Then one day I was at the local post office. This six-foot-tall young man spoke to me, saying, "Do you remember me?" I looked carefully and recognized him. What a nice surprise and thrill it was for me to see Mac. He was working for a real estate company. What a privilege it was for me to be able to be a part of his family's life in a time of crisis. Now we could celebrate!

The Identified Patient

In 1986–87 I sent out questionnaires to MKs representing three different mission boards as research for the writing of my doctoral thesis, "An Assessment of the Reentry Issues of the Children of Missionaries from a Firsthand Perspective." The questionnaire consisted of six areas of the MK life experience: (1) life in another culture, (2) furloughs, (3) education, (4) religion, (5) reentry to the States for college, and (6) a sense of belonging. A seventh question was one of confidentiality, where each MK was encouraged to address any issues that might not have been included in the other six questions. From their answers to these questions

I was able to identify the basic adjustment difficulties of MKs upon their reentry to the United States.

Most of the responses to these questions were enthusiastic, with some MKs sending me as many as fifteen handwritten pages. However, the longest response—thirty-nine pages—came from an MK born in Latin America who lived twenty hours away by car from where I lived. When I received this large packet in the mail, I sat down and read it completely through. I could not stop reading because it was from an MK who was in severe pain, struggling, reaching out, but no one seemed to step forward to help. Although I had told the MKs they did not have to sign their names unless they so preferred, this one had not only signed her name but had also written her telephone number on the last page.

Upon reading this MK's story, I immediately went to the telephone and called her. When I told her who I was, she began to weep. I waited, telling her my time was hers. Finally when she could talk, she said to me, "I have knocked on so many doors, seeking help and understanding, only to have the doors closed in my face and nailed shut. I almost did not send my reply to your questionnaire, thinking it would just be another door to be closed in my face." Stephanie had dropped out of college. She was tired, and she felt hopeless and alone. She was depressed. She was married while in her depression and could not recall very much about her wedding. In trying to talk to others, she said, "Nobody seems to have an inkling of what I am trying to talk about or just how deep the gash is in my soul." She said that since being back in the States for eight years, her life had been a series of disasters. She had no security of knowing where she was from. She asked, "Do you know what it's like to lack that base?" And she answered her own question. "It affects everything." Another question: "Do you know what it means to be born and grow up and fall in love with one country, but be constantly and rudely hit over the head with the refrain, 'Don't get too comfortable; you can't live here when you grow up, kid.' Can you understand bouncing around all one's life, like a ping-pong ball hit between two wildly contrasting tables, which makes a child, an adolescent, or an adult lose any and all clues to who he or she is?" She goes on to say, "I didn't even understand all this stuff until just recently; I had thought all along that I was the defective one, the one who had something wrong with me because I couldn't cope with a few 'slight inconveniences' connected to all the wonderful advantages of the MK experience. Just think how lucky you have been."

It was so good to hear Stephanie pouring out all her pain, which she had kept inside for so long. Now she felt she was really heard and understood, yet not judged. In her anger and disappointment she said, "I was not called to the mission field. My father was. Nobody asked me if I'd enjoy growing up in this bizarre fashion. Don't tell me, 'God calls the whole family.' I have yet to meet an MK who agrees with that little gem." Then Stephanie asked, "Do you see why I am so lost? My past, my home, my life was stolen from me eight years ago, and I had no say in the matter. There wasn't a damn thing I could do about it. I was trapped, and I am trapped, and there is no solution, it seems."

I heard all that Stephanie had to say, and at this point, I told her I would like for her to come to my home in Winston-Salem for a week, and we would talk, talk, talk. We would find some solutions. Stephanie said it would cost too much money to fly, but she would see if she could find eighty dollars for the gasoline. She did, and she had a free place to stay overnight in Nashville, coming and going.

The day came. It was late afternoon when Stephanie arrived at my house. I met her near her car. This was our first time to meet face-to-face. I gave her a big hug and told her how happy I was that she was able to take time off and come for a week. One real plus was that Stephanie had her twenty-seventh birthday that week and we could celebrate it together. She made lasagna.

As it was late, we had dinner and began to talk right away. Stephanie felt so comfortable and comforted by the people of her adopted country, the place of her birth. She had found immediate rapport and understanding with some warm, caring Latin American young people, as well as many adults who readily accepted her. She enjoyed being a part of a musical group. She also had written several songs in Spanish.

Returning to America after high school graduation in the Latin American country was difficult, challenging, and yes, traumatic. Stephanie, though a product of two countries, felt much more at home in the Latin American country. She graphically described how she continued to struggle for a place to belong. Daily she felt pulled back and forth between the country of her birth and the United States where her parents called home. She said, "Recently an image came to me of my life as having taken place for me inside a wall between two rooms. I live inside the wall, and though I am contained in it, both sides of it are quite flexible and transparent so that I can move quite freely and far into each room." She described how she never felt fully in one country or the other.

> I am never really in either room. The wall in which I am contained always confines me until I figure out how to poke holes into the plastic and extend a finger, then a hand to touch someone on the other side. The plastic on the side of my country of birth is always easier to perforate than the stiffer, thicker American side. I always knew which one I WANTED TO BREAK THROUGH, and which one DUTY instead would push me toward. When I have sliced my way through the friendlier side enough to not only stick my hand through but also both arms, then my head and shoulders enough to give someone a genuine hug and let them see my real face, and then all I have left to do is to open the plastic enough to step into the room, I am grabbed by someone or something inside the wall and dragged back into the middle of the wall, turned around, and shoved against the opposite plastic wall, a black curtain immediately drops behind me, shielding the other side from my eyes, making me think that eventually everything behind it has ceased to exist for me.

In Stephanie's imagery, she searched for tools or ways to feel a sense of belonging in either one country or the other.

> Where are my little knives and nail files with which I used to poke those other holes? I dropped them somewhere around here. Oh, yes, here's one! Let's see what it will do for me.... Oh, my, not much. Let me look for another one. I try them all, over and over again with few successful results. I look for new tools but don't find any. I look for materials from which to make new tools; something new and different will pierce this thick plastic wall, but there is nothing.

She described the helplessness that permeated her whole being. She continued to not want to give up the country of her birth and live as an 'alien' in America. The tug-of-war continued to go on. She told me she had received lots of comfort in the words of Charles Wesley's hymn, "Jesus Lover of My Soul." Of course, it had more meaning for her in Spanish than in English. She also read her Bible in Spanish in order to understand the real meaning.

When Stephanie came to my home, she was facing so many reentry issues even though she had been in the States for eight years. She felt separation and loss. She felt different and had different values from those of her peers. She felt so isolated and alienated, and she continued to experience culture shock as well. She was still searching for "home," a place to belong. So many MKs deal with these same issues. When Americans say, "It must be good to be back home," MKs first thoughts are, *This is not my home. Home is where I came from, and the States is the foreign country for me.* On these issues, we worked morning, noon, and night.

I was living in a house that had the old-fashioned shades at the windows. For the first day or two, she left the shades completely closed. It was dark in that room. Whenever she got too tired from the counseling, she would go to the dark room and lie on her bed with her head spinning as she tried to process so much of the information and deal with all kinds of emotions and feelings. All the time Stephanie was beginning to get in touch with her real self. We covered about every topic you could imagine. On the second day, she raised the shade just a little. On the third day, the shade went up about halfway. Then on the last day, the shade was flipped all the way to the top. To me this was an indication of the way Stephanie's depression lifted. By then, we were laughing a lot. Her spirits were lifted. What a delightful human being! She went away with lots of hope and believing in herself. I could and did affirm and validate her feelings and opinions, and yet so gently was able to confront her when it was needed.

I asked Stephanie to write an evaluation of our time together after she returned home. She did and clearly described it better than I could ever hope to do. Therefore, here you can read her evaluation word for word:

MY WEEK IN WINSTON-SALEM

I drove about twenty hours each way to visit Doris Walters. We had a neat arrangement. She would counsel me, and I would be a case study of sorts for her dissertation on missionary kids' adjustment difficulties. I couldn't believe she would let me come stay with her. Even though I had spent two days in March filling up thirty-nine notebook pages of MK reminiscences in response to her survey, I really didn't expect to hear anything back from her. I mailed the envelope with the thought, *Well, I've gotten some things off my chest again, at least; that's the end of that.* I almost hadn't bothered to answer the survey at all, just out of sheer hopelessness. I had tried to talk to people so many times, and what good would it do to try again? Did she really want to hear it?

She did, and she wanted to hear more than thirty-nine pages. Shortly after I mailed her my package, my phone rang and a pleasant voice said, "I am Doris Walters in Winston-Salem. I just read your life story, and I wanted to talk to this MK." She proceeded to ask a few questions, and with several uncanny, accurate phrases summed up what I was feeling. I told her she was hitting the nail right on the head. She told me I was not alone, that I could call her at any hour (something I'd heard a few times before, but this time it seemed to be more than just words, words, words), and that if I could work it out she would like for me to come spend a week with her, just so we could talk.

I worked out the details somehow or other. Friends agreed to keep my child during the time I would be out of town. Money for gas came through after a lot of asking, seeking, and knocking. An ex-missionary family I used to know let me stay overnight with them in Nashville, a good stopping place coming and going. Thank goodness the car was in good running order. (I probably would have hitchhiked if I'd had to, or perhaps hijacked a Greyhound...ha.)

Monday evening, May 16, at 7 p.m., I arrived at Doris's house. We went out for dinner, started talking, and hardly stopped for the next four days. She worked me till I was nearly blue in the face. She wore me out, but it was a good tiredness because it came from looking at issues I knew had to be faced with someone who would know what I was talking about.

We discussed my family of origin intensively the first day, and that was a recurring theme throughout the week. We talked about the way I was raised, about how I was and am different from all my sisters and about how that difference always was considered bad by the rest of the family. We talked about what it was like to grow up as an MK, belonging completely neither here nor there, becoming neither fish nor fowl, bouncing around like a ping-pong ball from field to furlough and back home to the field, over and over until I had no idea who I was or where I would end up.

We delved into my eventual deep identification as a Latin American during my last three years at home (a process that started for me the day I was born in that country). We touched on how it felt to me when I was forced by my parents to give up my Latin American citizenship in order to come to the U.S. for college, neither of which I really wanted to do, but I was never consulted, and I could never make my objections heard by my parents. We talked about how I have always been the focus of much of the family's negative attention. Doris said to me over and over, "You are the identified patient but you are *not* the problem." That is still a bit hard to believe after years of hearing that the problem was my being cranky, stubborn, spoiled, hateful, etc.

We talked about my parents' relationship and how they probably owe me a debt of gratitude for carrying the results of their destructive control over each other, a sick control where no one helped the other get their needs met.

Doris told me after a few days of sessions, "I am really surprised that you have not had any psychotic episodes, that you haven't ever just flipped out and lost contact with reality." I asked her, "How do I know that I haven't?" She said that I wouldn't have gone psycho and then just gotten over it by myself. I then asked her, "How do I know I won't flip out in the future?" She said something like, "If you haven't by now, you probably never will." It was a big relief to be told that I had the right to feel as I did all along. It's bad enough to be told what to think (even though I wasn't even told clearly, I mostly had to guess at what my parents wanted of me), but to be ordered *not to feel* a certain way can really make a kid crazy.

The event that Doris thinks might have sent another person over the edge was when I went into deep depression in late 1981 and had to drop out of college. My parents had selected for me, by family tradition, the worst possible school I could have gone to. That university has become in recent years a very "moneyed" place; you have to look, act, and *spend* a certain way in order to "belong." Needless to say, I did not fulfill the requirements to fit into the socioeconomic campus scene, nor did I want to. I didn't want to be there. I was terribly lonely. I didn't know how to talk to people. I didn't know *who* to be there. I had formed my identity as a Latin American within an American-looking body during my last three years in that place, and then had that stolen from me when I was pushed into the Good-Little-Girl mold. For a while I honestly tried to fit in at that university and become an American, but after a year and a half of crying out for help and being ignored, I finally just couldn't get out of bed one day, and I had to drop out of school. My parents implied at first that I could come home with them and rest at least for a while, and that gave me enough hope and motivation to get through the final exams that semester and get my things packed, but later my mother put her foot down and refused to let me come home, and my father went along with her wishes and didn't stick up for me. They drove off and left me here. Ever since then I've been sort of a semi-person, just functioning and existing, but not what you could call living. Praying to die. Trying to think of painless, nonmessy ways to do the deed. People have flipped out over similar things.

I know one MK who will never be normal again after the breakdowns she has suffered. I knew two other MKs at that university who killed themselves. They'll never get to tell their stories. They probably tried over and over, like I have, but they couldn't get the right person to listen to them. They finally gave up. Who is going to tell their stories? Who at the Mission Board is going to keep these tragedies from repeating themselves? What's the big holdup? Is money the problem? Are children pieces of furniture to be moved around from place to place, shipped off to boarding school, put on display back "home" on furlough with little or no explanations or chances to express their own questions and concerns? Are MKs ornaments to be used to make their parents and the system look pretty? Are we pets to be trained to do tricks for the amazement of the missionaries and nationals?

Are we whipping posts for our parents' frustrations to be poured out upon? Have we no rights? It appears not, we are *just children*.

God told Abraham to tie up his only son and sacrifice him on an altar. Abraham was ready to do it. Did anyone explain things to Isaac? He was old enough to wonder, to panic, to question. "Father, where is the lamb for the sacrifice?" But wait, there is more to this little scenario. When Daddy Abraham had the knife high in the air, a second away from plunging it into his child, God sent an angel with an updated message: "*Don't do it!*" God said, "Don't. Don't sacrifice your child." How many MKs have committed suicide due to the woes they collected during their years in God's service? Apparently at least one MK from one Mission Board has committed suicide each year. Is this not considered outrageous? Is it just a job hazard? Is this little statistic shared with new appointees at orientation? Probably not; after all, it's *only* one per year, and that means hundreds of others are still walking around out there. Whew!

But consider this: How many of those hundreds are walking through life with invisible knives stuck into our chests, dripping invisible blood, sacrificed by our parents for the good of *the work*. OK, so it doesn't happen to *all* of us. Yes, I know there are many who rave about their wonderful lives on the mission field. I've even done my share of spouting pretty platitudes for the benefit of the annual Mission Offering. But what mission board cares what I really think about the system? I am not the only one who feels this way: unheard, discounted, hopeless about any changes being made to help the next crop of poor innocents going to the field, or being born overseas, or sent to the U.S. at age eighteen to sink or swim.

I don't know what's going to become of me. I don't know for sure what I'm going to do with my life. A week with Doris helped me get a lot of issues clearer in my mind, but it also brought others almost to a boiling point. I am back in touch with my anger. Boy, am I ever. I am bitterly angry about so many things. But this time I am expressing it. I am *not* wrong to feel this way. I think after I get cleared of this anger, resentment, and bitterness, I'll be able to work through the events that caused the emotions my anger was shielding me from: fear, insecurity, confusion, powerlessness.... I was sacrificed, but I didn't even have the luxury of dying. I refuse to kill myself now. Life owes me. I'm going to get all the good that I deserve.

In a letter from Stephanie after she returned home, she wrote:

Re-entry has been very difficult. The first week I cried a lot; the first two weeks back I slept a lot in the afternoons, and my sleep habits are still in disarray so I can tell I'm down in the dumps. It's been rough coming back and being around my sisters and their judgmental attitudes; they act alternately interested in what I've done and discovered, and disgusted by my observations. It reminds me of a child coming across a dead frog squashed during a rainstorm on the street: a kid will often approach it to get a good look and may even poke it with his shoe or stick, but immediately draw back with an "Oh, yuck!" They want to see it, but they don't want to see it; you know what I mean, don't you?

Stephanie also sent me a poem she had written after she returned from the week of counseling.

          PETRA LOOKING IN
But mommy I don't understand your eyes afire, jaw set, lips pursed, What did I do this time?
Just go away, I will be Nice.
You're wrong: it will NOT hurt you more than me.
You aren't my mother, you don't love me.

You're just mad, leave me alone.
You make me bad.
I guess I'll have to leave the room.
I'll take a hike again since you won't go.
Why is that lady standing with a hairbrush in the air? She—
DON'T—
The little girl submits, just sits, immobile
Stone faced
Not a flicker of a shudder, not a shadow
On the mask as down it comes
Whack
Smack
Crack
Get up you dummy, run away.
It can't, the statue has to stay but where's the child?
She will be back, where did she go?
How can this be?
It can't be, NO

Disillusioned

Steven is an MK who grew up in Africa. He was born in Chicago to devout evangelical parents. Religion was a very important part of his family's life. Before Steven was one year old, his parents were appointed as home missionaries but later appointed to foreign missions.

I was working as a pastoral counselor at the North Carolina Baptist Hospital where I first met Steven and his father. In November 1986 Steven's mother and sister were murdered in their home by a rapist. The rapist was a man they had thought was a friend of the family. He had done chores around the house for them, and they felt comfortable when he was around. However, at this particular time Steven's father had gone to the boarding school which was hours away to bring Steven home for Thanksgiving.

This rapist/murderer went to their house, did some work, but later that night returned claiming he had missed the last bus to his home, and asked if he might spend the night, which he was allowed to do. Steven's mother was a very trusting person but perhaps a bit naive. Missionaries sometimes think they must accommodate every request by nationals if they are to be seen as "caring for the people."

It was that night that he raped Steven's ten-year-old sister in the middle of the night and then bludgeoned Steven's mother to death with a knife. In order to silence Steven's sister, the only witness, he also cut her throat. The mother and daughter were discovered the next morning when the daughter did not show up at the bus stop to go to school. The father was called and given the sad news. He and Steven returned home immediately by plane. Steven did not see his mother and sister's dead bodies, but he did see the house before it was cleaned, a sight that was imprinted in his mind forever and caused him lots of problems in his future. The man was apprehended within a week and was eventually executed. Steven, his father, and all those who knew his family were in a state of shock. They had gone there as missionaries to help the people, and look what happened. This made no sense to anyone. After a funeral was held there, Steven and his father returned to the States where there was another funeral. Steven's father spent some time giving words of comfort to their extended family members.

As both Steven and his father entered the counseling suite, it was clear that they were in shock. As the father began to tell their sad story, I asked him where he was when he heard the news. He broke down and began to let the tears flow. As he wept uncontrollably, Steven sat with no emotion at all, starring blankly into space. The father said, "Thank you, this is the first time I have been able to weep, since I have been taking care of everyone else." They clearly described what they had been through, and yet it seemed that they were describing a tragedy that had happened to someone else. They would wake up and it would be just that, a bad dream.

The next week when they returned to my office, Steven was carrying a notebook under his arm. In the first session and second session, as Steven's father talked about his feelings, Steven simply listened. Then, when I asked Steven about his feelings, he handed me the notebook, saying, "I can't talk about my feelings because I really don't know how to put them in words, but I have drawn pictures to show you my feelings." He had described so vividly in his drawings his feelings of grief, fear, anger, despair, restlessness, revenge, fatigue, and homesickness for his adopted country. He expressed in his art pressure, and finally, inner peace.

Steven, at that point, was a deeply spiritual fifteen-year-old young man. He shared honestly and openly about his life in Africa, his struggles and doubts, his life with his mother and sister as well as with his father. He loved his mother and sister very much and could not imagine going back to Africa and face the fact that they were no longer there. After several sessions, and a few months later, Steven and his father did return to Africa, which was home for Steven. He was very eager to go back *home*. Of course, when he returned to Africa, he returned immediately to the boarding school to complete his school year.

In Africa, Steven, along with his mother and sister, accompanied their father when he preached in churches or in the open air in nearby villages and towns, gaining converts and helping them organize churches. He said, "The presence of our car attracted almost as much attention as the white skin of the preacher's family." At sundown, his father would rig up an incandescent light bulb, powered by a battery, and thus they would have light for the worship services.

At age ten, Steven said that he decided "to follow Jesus." He had just finished a theological education course by extension, which meant the course was held in a village and not on a college campus. This introductory course explained the why and how of salvation, "emphasizing that all those who died without having received Christ as their Savior were doomed to spend eternity in hell." Steven said, "Being deathly afraid of the prospect of dying and going to hell, I accepted the invitation, thanking God for coming to earth as Jesus and suffering on that cross for my sins, and confessing my sinfulness to him with sincere regret. I asked him to forgive my wrongdoings, to take charge of my life, and to give me the gift of eternal life in Heaven." Steven was then overwhelmed with a feeling of euphoria that defied description. But, a few days later, that feeling of euphoria somehow escaped him. He remembered the sermons at the African churches "sandwiched between rounds of ecstatic singing and the beating of loud drums." He continued to say, "The effect of the native African chanting and drumming on the human mind has to be experienced in order to truly be appreciated. It is thrilling and hypnotic, and it creates an ominous aura of compelling importance for the message being preached."

Steven was baptized at age eleven. He tried very hard to be the best Christian he could be, only to find that his zeal and willpower soon wavered. He said, "After a few weeks, I lost interest in living to please God." At the age of twelve, Steven had read the Bible through cover-to-cover. Later, he even read most of the books of biblical canon several times over. He said, "I can argue the contents of the Bible with the best." He had become an avid "witness," but that too was short-lived.

When the family had come home for furlough, Steven had enrolled in a public junior high school and "was totally unprepared for what I would find there." He found that his classmates were interested only in looking "cool." "I was naïve, socially inept, culturally ignorant, sickeningly polite, goody-goody, had a not-so-cool hair style and was from Africa (which of course meant that I lived in a mud hut, ate bugs, and knew Tarzan personally). Outside of class, my classmates' conversations consisted mainly of profanity. When they asked me why I didn't cuss, I replied that I was a Christian; their response did wonders for my social standing. I made many enemies that year simply by being a naive geek, but friends, I had not one."

After returning to Africa after that furlough early in 1986, his mother and sister were murdered in November. That year, before their deaths, Steven suffered from malaria and typhoid fever, two potentially fatal diseases. Steven said, "It was the worst physical torment and suffering I had ever experienced. My body was jolted with freezing, cyclical chills, and I vomited up every meal I ate, and the intensity of the searing pain in my intestines was so great that I seriously longed for euthanasia."

The following year, after his mother and sister's deaths, Steven suffered severe depression. He and his father moved back to the States where Steven entered a small college. During that year, Steven liked to dress in his African attire, perhaps mostly to get attention and identify himself as being different. He stopped going to church and professed that he was an atheist. One day, I received a telephone call from a ladies missionary study group in the church on campus. Steven had spoken to this ladies group about his experiences in Africa. He had told them that even though his parents had been missionaries, he himself had decided that he was an atheist. He said, "I no longer believe there is God." This was so disturbing to the ladies, all southern, zealous Protestant Christians. They wanted to know what they could do for him. My reply was, "Just love him and show him your care. He will be okay. He is trying to find himself."

To say the least about Steven, he was and is a very brilliant young man. He said, "Mommy and Daddy had taught me that there was a God when I was a child, and I had simply never questioned it, until now." He concluded, "Christianity, I now realized, was, for me, little more than a Jewish version of Hellenistic mystery religion." He continued, "And so it was that I moved in with the atheist for a while, until I found the inner resources to build a house of my own, one which is neither evangelical nor Christian, one whose foundation is self-honesty and a healthy skepticism."

During Steven's third year in college, I visited him on his campus and took him out to dinner. He ate very little but talked nonstop.

He found in me a person who could hear him out, not judge him, but be empathic, and somewhat understand his struggles, especially being an MK caught between cultures. Soon after we sat down in the restaurant, he said, "I just got out of the looney house [psychiatric unit in a hospital] where I spent two weeks." He had been hallucinating, again seeing the outline of his mother and sister's bodies surrounded by blood on the floor back in their house in Africa. He found himself in his room, stepping around or over the blood-stained floor in Africa. His roommates realized something was upsetting Steven and reported it to the appropriate person on campus who got him help.

That night in that restaurant, Steven shared with me so many things he had never shared with any other human being. I felt we were truly on holy ground. He had written a brilliant paper entitled "Apostate Manifesto," an intelligent masterpiece explaining where he was and had been on his spiritual journey. He might have entitled this brilliant, insightful work "Disillusioned." In so many ways I could share his confusion but not his bitterness. I could agree with much he had written about organized religion in general. He saw hypocrisy and was not afraid to write about it. Steven was stressed by both "religion" and "bad irreligion." This writing revealed that he was on a pilgrimage that was neither freeing nor peaceful. It appeared that Steven was dealing with at least two faith systems competing for his allegiance. Finally, bringing head and heart together has been a great accomplishment for Steven.

Steven graduated from college and went on to graduate school, majoring in vertebrate paleontology, a science of fossils. He was completely fascinated with this subject. He had the rare opportunity to work on a dinosaur dig in the state of Utah in 1994.

In spite of all of his losses, reentry issues, struggles, depression, and diagnosis with ADD, Steven is now free from his depression. He is a fine adult who has found focus and meaning for his life.

(See Steven's drawings of his feelings on the following pages. Drawings used by the permission of the artist.)

CHAPTER FOUR

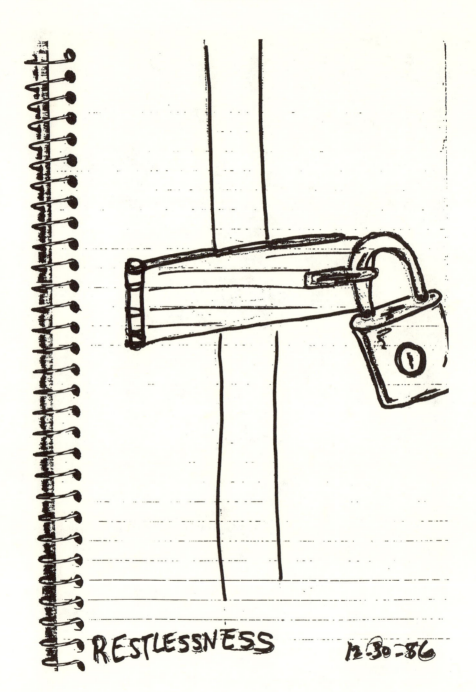

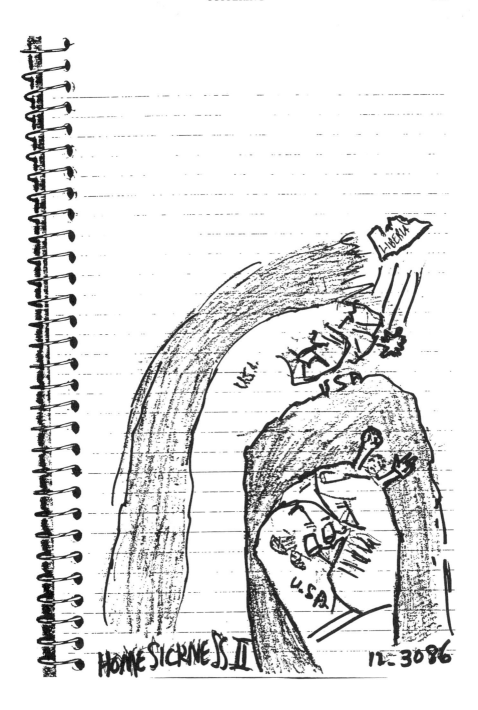

SUFFERING

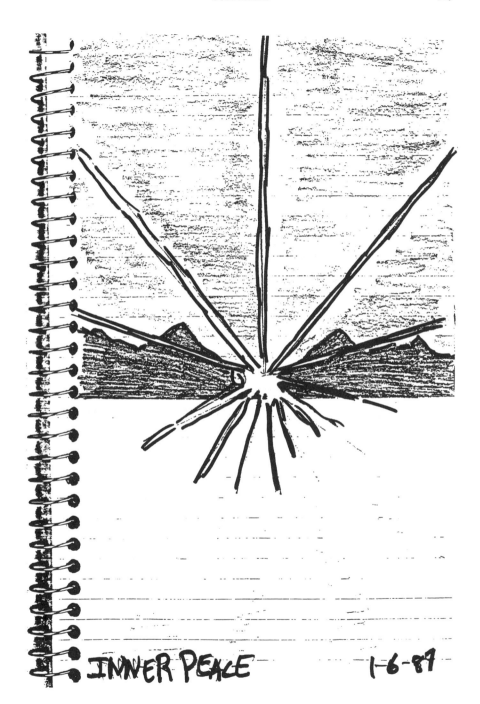

CHAPTER FOUR

I Can't Go Home Again

Richard, a handsome, professional MK entered my office. He had grown up in South America. In all his appearance, he could have been a corporate executive with distinction. I was really impressed. He had come to see me because his wife told him she believed I might be able to help him since I had been a missionary and was clinically trained to look at all kinds of issues. She knew that I dealt with the issues of young people who had grown up overseas and then returned to America to try to become reintegrated into American society. His wife believed him to be depressed.

Richard went to South America with his missionary parents when he was very young, too young to have any memories of America. There they lived in a community of nationals, and his friends were South Americans. It was easy for Richard to grow up speaking both English and Portuguese. He knew there was a certain amount of conflict on a daily basis in his home. He could see that his parents were having relationship problems. Later, he found out that his mother had physical and emotional problems. Now, knowing what he did, he couldn't understand why his father took his mother to the mission field in the first place. One thing he had learned was that if a couple goes to the mission field with unresolved problems, things would only get worse, not better. Living in another culture with all its differences and pressures does not help to improve already troubled relationships. In Richard's parents' case, things did get worse as the years passed.

Richard remembered coming to the States for furlough, but he was always eager to get back to his home, school, and friends in South America. Each time his parents had hoped that their relationship would improve, but somehow it never did. When Richard was fifteen, his father called him into his study for "a talk." His father told him, "We are returning to the States, at least for the time being, but later we may come back to South America." They did soon thereafter return to the States. Richard loved his country in South America, for it was the only real home he knew. He found himself feeling lots of anger toward his father and also toward his mother. "Why couldn't my mother get well enough for us to stay in our home?"

At the age of fifteen, Richard knew that his mother's behavior was rather erratic. What he did not know was that she had little control over her emotions. She was suffering from a manic-depressive disorder. When she was in the manic state, she felt really "on top of the world," but when in the depressive state, she was really "low." She would stay in bed for days with the blinds closed in total darkness. When she got back to the States, she was placed on a medication that gave her more stability, and now she seemed very much in control of her emotions.

Richard, then thirty-two years old, married with two children, had always wanted to return to South America. He said, "All this time, I have tried to figure out a way to get back 'home.' I know I am successful in my chosen profession, but I am not happy. I thought about going back as a missionary, but I don't really feel deep down that I am supposed to be a missionary. I thought if I became a doctor, perhaps I could go back there as a doctor just as nationals come here to practice medicine." In talking with the mission board that sent his parents as missionaries, he found out that there was really no request for doctors there. Doctors who come from other countries to the States come here mostly to learn the latest in medicine. So Richard gave up the idea of becoming a doctor and chose another profession. Yet, there was that gnawing feeling that he needed to go back to South America. The bottom line was that Richard came home expecting to go back fairly soon, but since that did not happen, he had some unfinished business to take care of in South America. He was still grieving his loss.

At one point, Richard began to beat on his knees with his fist, and through many tears, cried out, "I can't go home again! I can't go home again!"

I sat quietly with him as he expressed his grief. Then I said, "Richard, you can't go home again, but you can visit home again."

He said, "You know I have never been back there since I left at age fifteen."

"Richard, I want you to do something," I said.

He asked, "What can I do?"

I told him, "I want you to take two weeks off from your work and go to South America, alone. Do not take your wife and children. I want you to go back to the house that was home during those developmental years of your life. I want you to look in every room and remember all the good times you had there. Look at the places you played." Richard began to smile, and I found that his spirit was already lifting. I said, "I want you to go to the school you attended and see if there are any of the teachers who are still there. I want you to go to the church you worshiped in for all those years. See if you can reconnect with any person in the church who remembers you and your family. I want you to walk around the city, and eat some of the foods you have missed." Richard looked at me and said, "I will do it. This all sounds really exciting to me." That was in November, and Richard made his trip back "home" in February.

A few months later, when I met Richard, he said, "Doris, that was exactly what I needed. I had such a wonderful time reconnecting with people I had known. I even met people whom I thought would no longer be there. They remembered me as a little boy. I asked the people living in our house to show me my bedroom. In fact, I looked in every room of the house. I went to the school and playground where I had played with friends. Of course, there were no MKs there now whom I had known as best friends. I met national friends who were now adults as well." After enthusiastically sharing with me his many experiences of being back there, he said to me, "Doris, I did go home again!"

Yes, things were not the same, but some places had not changed. Richard enthusiastically recommends such a trip back to those MKs who find it hard to settle down here, especially those who have not been back since returning for their college education. He also was very happy to return to his wife and children whom he did miss very much. He said, "Now, I can live in peace in America. I belong here. I can be American. I can settle down and move on with my life and profession."

What a great joy it was for me to see the peace, joy, happiness, and hope that Richard was now experiencing. Yes, Richard, you did go home again, didn't you!

Defining Moments

Where were you on the morning of September 11, 2001? I had just finished breakfast and turned on the television. The first plane had crashed into the World Trade Center. There was a lot of confusion among the news reporters. Was it an accident? Most of them thought it was at that point in time. As I stood staring at the television, the second terrorist plane attack took place right before my eyes. I was in a state of shock!

I had a dental appointment at 10 a.m. for a root canal. Throughout those two hours, the receptionist came back to the room to report the collapse of the first building, the attack on the Pentagon, and then the collapse of the second building. Finally, the news came of the plane crash near Pittsburgh. What had just happened to our world? We were all in denial or disbelief.

This was one of those defining moments for America, for Americans, every last one of us. We can never be the same again. The immense burst of grief like we have never known before descended upon us. Approximately twenty-six hundred lives (at last count) had perished in the World Trade Center, the Pentagon, and the plane that crashed near Pittsburgh.

Americans began to fly their flags. Replicas of our flag appeared on cars throughout our nation. Yes, I put up my flag, too. It was a small gesture to say just how proud I was of our country. What was happening to our country, and when would it end?

Jim Warda sent out an e-mail entitled, "Where were you when the world shattered?" He best expressed our sentiments when he said that we all felt numb from watching the news. There was no way for us to make sense of the attack. From this we experienced at least three things. We put our flags up. Good will eventually crush evil. This was a tragic event that everyone would be talking about for years to come. It was a time in which we were all aware of the fact that liberty and justice are more than just words. We were all scared. We were all shocked, but most of all we were proud to stand together, connected in our grief.

Yes, for all Americans, September 11, 2001, around 9 a.m. was a defining moment.

At a recent retreat at South Mountain Baptist Camp near Hickory, North Carolina, for the children of missionaries, there was discussion on the topic, "Where were you on September 11, 2001?" Then the discussion turned to defining moments in each of their lives.

The children of missionaries are the focus of Missionary Family Counseling Services. We know MKs are strongly affected by the stresses of cultural displacement. Often the country in which their parents serve is the only home they have known. To these children the United States is a foreign land. Their defining moment comes when they leave the country where they have spent all of their developmental years in a culture vastly different from that of America. Without any preparation, these children tackle the transition to college at the same time they must adjust emotionally and socially to this strange society. These children desperately need contact with someone who understands them with their unique needs.

Their defining moment comes when they step on a plane, say goodbye to their parents and their country with all its familiarity, and return to the States to enter college. That experience of separation and loss is often seemingly unbearable.

Their defining moment comes when they arrive on a college campus, "scared to death." On the campus, they suddenly realize just how different they are. "Yes, I know I have the American face, but I don't feel American."

There are all those different values that their peers have, which are very different from their own.

Their defining moment comes when they seek a place to belong, to fit in, to understand this new culture and their peers. In a state of alienation, they feel rootless and lonely. They feel discomfort, dissatisfied, out of place, and restless. At times there appears to be a sense of helplessness.

Then, culture shock begins to set in. Relocation tugs at the roots of the missionary child's identity. They have lost their familiar props. They often feel frustrated and anxious. They may actually feel that America is "bad" because its culture and customs make them feel so "bad." Just to be able to talk to someone who understands them brings some amount of relief.

By the grace of God, these young people deal with their defining moments and are able to move on with their lives and become productive American citizens.

By the grace of God, the people of New York, where terrorism punched a black hole in their skyline on September 11, will be able to move on with their lives. Tim Hobbs, a volunteer who went there to help, said, "It graphically illustrates what evil can do to light, if only for a little while." He went on to say, "Love has counterpunched its way into that void even since September 11, 2001, as New Yorkers and others across the United States have rallied behind the victims."

Defining moments. We all have them. They can completely change our lives. They can make us better people, or they can make us angry and bitter. They can make us more loving, caring, and determined, or they can make us feel hopeless.

> Let us choose love.
> Let us choose hope.
> Let us choose faith.
> Let us choose determination.

CHAPTER FIVE

Family

Who Is My Family?

During the years I've spent counseling MKs, occasionally one would call me for counseling by telephone since they lived far away from my city. One day I received a call from an MK in a distant state. I took her telephone number and then returned her call so that she would not have to pay the phone bill. We talked for approximately one hour.

Margaret wanted to discuss some of the struggles she had dealt with for the past fifteen years since she had been living back stateside. She had thought she should have made a better adjustment after being in America for so long. The truth is that Margaret had faced more than her share of struggles in her short life. She said, "I would like to think that my struggles have been special, not uniquely to me alone, yet certainly hand picked by God in order to grow me into the person I am becoming." I assured her that her struggles were special.

As a single thirty-one-year-old female she was still searching for who she was and who she "was meant to be." She said, "In spite of God's clear directing through my life, I anxiously strain to see further into my future as if I don't trust that God will continue His assured guidance."

Margaret related to me how, at the age of twelve, she was sent away to boarding school in Africa. Even though she was a shy little girl, she said she actually loved her school at the time. She was slightly overweight, but she felt that she was fat, and this caused her to be somewhat withdrawn.

She was clearly aware of the fact that she was now living in two completely different atmospheres, that of the school, and the other at her home where she went for holidays and summer vacations. At boarding school she often felt confused. At home she could depend on her parents. At times she said she felt like two different individuals. She would be at school and be quite comfortable as just one of the other students. She had a sense of belonging at the boarding school. Then her parents would show up on campus, and she said, "Then, I didn't know how to act, or who to be!"

Margaret was also confused about her spiritual life. Upon hearing "spiritual" speeches in chapel at her school, she would try the various methods for "a spiritual walk with God" presented by various speakers. Some of their speech topics were "Three Ways to Keep Your Life in Line with God," "Six Basic Steps to a Meaningful Quiet Time," and "How to Walk with God." She said that by the time she was a junior in high school, she was kind of fed up on how to live the Christian life. She said, "I decided if there were that many different ways to be a good Christian, then maybe it was not for me." She had her doubts, but no one ever told her it was natural and okay to doubt. One day she told her mother that "none of it made any sense." Her mother agreed. This was the last thing Margaret expected to hear from her mother. She said, "As soon as I realized that the Holy Spirit was the Interpreter and actually lived in me, I was relieved to know that I no longer had to understand it all on my own." She then felt angry and wanted to go back and tell all those chapel speakers and Sunday school teachers about her anger and ask them why they had left out such an important ingredient of being a Christian—that is, the Holy Spirit is the One who began to make my relationship with God so very personal." Margaret graduated from her high school and returned to the States for college. In college she was active in various Christian organizations. Margaret said that she never became "American" like she thought most MKs did. She had been told that when she went back to visit in Africa, after being in America a few years, she would realize that Africa was no longer the place she could call "home." That was not true for her, because she had felt so much at home in Africa once she returned there for visit.

Margaret ended up going to another country for two years to teach in an MK school. She realized she had known and understood the culture of Africa, but now this other country where she went to teach was so different from Africa. Teaching for two years in that MK school helped her to realize that there was so much more for her to learn about cultures.

Margaret finished college and went on to divinity school. There she learned a lot about herself as she sought a degree in psychology. She said, "One lesson I learned was that I did not come from the most perfect family or environment. God helped me break through my denial about sexual abuse that I experienced when I was between the ages of four and eight years of age. Another lesson I learned was about homosexuality. I dated a recovering homosexual, and I realized I had some prejudicial views to sort out."

Margaret had taught at a high school where she confronted issues like drug use, abortion, and sexual promiscuity. These issues really challenged her faith. Following divinity school she worked as a counselor in a drug rehabilitation center. There, she was learning a lot about the American culture that she had not yet faced. Later she worked for a state child protective service.

Margaret eventually ended up living with and taking care of her grandparents, where she learned a lot about her heritage and about stroke recovery. Before, her grandparents had been total strangers to her. She had been quite satisfied with her missionary family, the people with whom she could easily relate. She said, "I don't mind meeting my biological relatives and extended family of aunts, uncles, and cousins, but I do not always understand them. This hasn't always been easy." She was reminded of the saying, "We can choose our friends but not our relatives."

I believe that Margaret has put into familiar words her own feelings for which most MKs can identify. Mission family includes aunts, uncles, cousins, and grandparents, though not biological. How can MKs relate to their biological family members the way they do their mission family? Mission family members understand one another's feelings and experiences. Perhaps there will always be the question MKs ask, *Who is my family?*

Who Am I? Sexual Orientation

Jake, a nineteen-year-old male MK, was referred to me by another therapist whose office was out of town. He felt that Jake would be more likely to go to counseling on a regular basis if he could see someone near his home. Jake was born in Bangladesh. He had one brother and two sisters. In 1992, Jake had been diagnosed with mild cerebral palsy, attention deficit disorder, hyperactivity, and acute reaction psychosis. In 1992, he had also spent some time in a mental health facility because of his suicidal thoughts. He said he had been depressed since the eighth grade. Even though Jake was the son of missionaries, he was now feeling that God was distant and said, "God must feel sad that I am so confused about who God is, but I believe he understands me." His parents were third- and fifth-generation missionary children. He stated that his greatest fear was "going to hell when I die." He described his life, in general, as "unhappy." In the last six months before I started seeing him in therapy, he stated that he had been "very unhappy." When Jake was not under stress, or when he was allowed to work at his own pace, he was able to perform at a much higher level. His ability to cope was limited. Psychotic episodes were expected to be repeated.

Needless to say, Jake had low self-esteem and often was self-punitive, and tended to "put himself down," whenever he confronted any degree of difficulty. He spent lots of time ruminating. His underlying neurological involvement expressed by one of his examiners in 1992 was a likely explanation for his mildly awkward motor movements. He even spoke somewhat laboriously with a "thick" speech pattern.

On Jake's first scheduled session with me, he was accompanied by a family friend who drove him to my office. That person, I could readily see, was demanding and expected more from Jake than he was able to produce. Soon after his first visit, we were able to facilitate his moving into an independent, work-related facility where he could be more independent. There he had his own room and eventually was able to receive computer training, although he was extremely slow. This was frustrating. At first, he did minor jobs but whatever he attempted to do he did well. In other words, he was conscientious. As time went by, he was claiming his independence in a healthy way.

When Jake was in the ninth grade in Bangladesh, he was sent away to a boarding school. After graduating from high school at the boarding school, he returned to the States to the West Coast. He was back in the States about three months before enrolling into a small college. He said, "Those were the best three months of my life." He was welcomed as the new MK on campus who had grown up in some foreign country, and was made to feel special. However, during his third semester, he had to leave school because he had a "mental breakdown." His life had been filled with separations, always saying hello and goodbye. The newness and feeling special in America had worn off. He also was remembering the hurtful words of his father who often told him, "You are lazy." Jake had a lot of anger toward his father, who seemed to always favor Jake's brother and never seemed to have time for him. He said, "My dad and I came to just avoid each other." His father was described as imaging a fast-moving train. Jake wanted very much to "get on the train," but all he could see was a blur. It was up to his father to slow the train down and do so in a way that recognized Jake's presence and special needs. Instead, his father was a typical workaholic whose calling to the ministry became an avenue for self-validation, which resulted in his lack of involvement with his family, especially Jake. Thus, Jake felt rejected and angry. He definitely decided that he did not want to become like his father in any way. When I saw Jake, it was clear that he was going through an identity crisis. He was trying to define himself in the American culture, but actually he felt like a foreigner.

Jake told me that he did feel loved by his mother, who listened to him. He felt her nurturing, and felt that she was trying to make up to him for his father's lack of involvement in Jake's life. As I continued to see Jake in my office, it was clear to me that he was not only depressed but also very paranoid. One day, I asked him if he would be willing to meet with a psychiatrist who could evaluate his depression. He agreed and was always cooperative and even seemed eager to see the psychiatrist. This, in itself, seemed to give him hope for something better in his life. The psychiatrist did place him on an antidepressant. Within two weeks he felt better and appeared somewhat better to me. At first, it was like Jake saw himself as a problem to be solved rather than a person to be loved. He was starving for love, attention, and touch. He was willing to take love wherever he could. I facilitated getting him some subsidized housing in town. He was working every day, and was feeling better about himself in his newfound independence. He was taking on more responsibility, which was a good sign.

Jake was open and responsive and willing to be vulnerable from the beginning of our counseling relationship. It did not take him long to trust me. He arrived at his counseling sessions on time or a few minutes early. He often came with a list of things he wanted to discuss in the session. He dealt with his losses from leaving his "home" in Bangladesh to the present. He was still experiencing some culture shock, sometimes feeling alienated. He was very much aware of his being different from others in the States. Jake was trying to discover what his real values were, and was realizing that some were very different from those of his parents. What was clear to Jake was that he was not 100 percent American and not 100 percent Bangladeshi, but a real mixture of the two cultures. He expressed his anger toward his parents, who had left him in the States with no one to turn to except some family friends who "did not understand me." He felt abandoned. One day he would reveal his anger, and the next day he would feel lots of guilt from expressing his anger. Then he would try to make explanations or excuses for his parents' behavior.

As time passed, Jake showed more and more progress. His self-esteem and sense of self improved tremendously. Being a loner, he spent lots of time in his apartment watching television, but then began to venture out to meet and talk to some of his neighbors. He seemed to relate well to blacks in the neighborhood. He had been accustomed to being around dark-skinned people in Bangladesh. He was becoming more and more relaxed and experiencing much less stress. He began to speak less haltingly, yet a little slower than the average. I encouraged Jake and sometimes confronted him to make the best of his abilities.

After gaining more self-confidence, and knowing that I accepted him as he was, and having gained his trust, he openly revealed to me one of his darkest secrets. He said, "I am gay, and I find myself wanting more and more to act out my sexual feelings with young boys." I wondered if the young boys represented his desire to be in relationships that did not demand anything from him. In such relationships, perhaps he felt he could get love and acceptance, that feeling of closeness with other human beings. Thus far, since most of Jake's relationships had been with adult men and women who put demands on him, perhaps he felt younger boys would look up to him. After all, in most of his adult relationships, he had only felt rejection. Perhaps young boys would "give him a place in the sun." He wanted nothing more than to teach or work with children, yet he was also afraid of what might happen if placed in that situation. The fact is that he did quit one job "because of my thoughts I had about attractive children, particularly attractive young boys who came though the lines with their mothers." He finally admitted that he was often confused, but now there was no doubt in his mind that he was homosexual. As we pursued his identity issue, I urged him to accept himself then as a gay male. I do believe he reached that acceptance of himself and felt somewhat comfortable about it. He just did not know what to do with his sexual urges.

I asked Jake if he had ever told anyone about his sexual preferences. He said that he had told his mother, and she "did not preach to me, but I thought she felt that this was something that would pass and I would discover that I was really heterosexual." He told me he had already had some gay experiences since he had been in the States., yet he had never approached young kids, although he had thought about it.

About six months before his parents were to return to the States for furlough, I received a letter from them. They expressed their gratitude to me for working with their son. They wanted my suggestions and input on what they could do to be involved with Jake, other than their "prayers and love." It appeared to me that they wanted Jake to move ahead with his life, "to the place God has for him, leaving his struggles, misunderstandings, hurts, frustrations, losses, and unknowns in God's hands and press forward." They didn't seem to have a clue that their son had some serious problems that would take continuing professional help for the rest of his life. It just wasn't as simple as they thought it was. His father went on to say, "We can't help but wonder if all these struggles are not a strong foundation for his future…. 'The brook would lose its song if you removed all the rocks.' God's power is made perfect in our weaknesses."

Jake, at this point in his life, was no longer depressed. He continued to be a loner, which is not uncommon for MKs. He admittedly said that he was lonely. Another MK once said to me, "Perhaps loneliness is my greatest enemy." Jake was no longer saying, "I do not see any reason to go on living."

While his parents were on a six-month furlough, they saw their son only when passing through our city. They were in the States, but Jake felt they still gave him very little time, time that was convenient only to their schedule. He stated that a part of him would like to be with his parents, but another part did not want that as he would regress and become dependent upon them. If he lived with them for six months, he would again become attached, and it would be hard for him to break away again. He wanted to maintain the independence that he had worked so hard to gain. He stated that he would like to see them often, if either they would come to his place or he go to theirs. Then, he said, "One thing I need is for my parents to come with me to counseling at least once while they are here." He wanted to tell both of them about his homosexual identity and know that they heard him and accepted him, in spite of his sexual orientation. He was also afraid they would not like the person he had grown to be. He was not going to church, which worried both of them because they equated going to church with being a Christian or being a "good" Christian. I told him I would be happy to see his parents if they should like to come with him. They agreed to accompany him.

His parents arrived in the city, and we set up an appointment for the three of them. They came to my office, and we chatted a bit about some things, but without delay, Jake took over the conversation. He told his parents that he had discovered his real identity. "I am gay. I have come to understand who I am and to accept myself. I feel comfortable with myself. Now, I hope you can accept me for who I am." His mother readily said, "Jake, you are my son, and no matter what your sexual preference is, I love and accept you and I always will." The father simply replied, "Well, Jake, if that is who you are, please don't act upon it." Jake looked directly into his father's eyes, letting him know that he was not making a promise he was not sure he could keep.

All Jake wanted was his parents' love and acceptance for who he was. The parents said they noticed how less stressed and anxious Jake was. They noticed that his depression had lifted. Was it because he had discovered his true identity and accepted it? For the father, in particular, it was a "situation" that he could not control. He could not change his son. For a man who had always been in control of his life and family, and even the nationals with whom he ministered, he was now confronted with something in his son's life that he could not accept nor control. He must deal with it! This was *his* son!

As Jake left the counseling session with his parents, he felt relieved that he was able to tell his parents that he was gay. One thing he did learn was that his mother accepted and loved him regardless of his sexual preference. He could only hope that one day his father would accept him as his gay son.

Is It Hard to Say, "I Love You"?

A letter came in the mail from a missionary mother in Switzerland. She told me that her family had been missionaries in Switzerland for fourteen years. They had four children, two boys and two girls. The last two, the girls, were born in Switzerland. The two boys were attending a missionary boarding school six hours away from their home. Trent was a senior, and his brother, Jack, was a sophomore. Up to this point, they had been homeschooled. Now they had gone away to boarding school together. The high school they would attend was well known, and the boys seemed ready and wanted to go away so that they could be with lots of other young people their age.

Trent and Jack were always gentle, obedient boys growing up. The first year at boarding school, however, they began to change, and those changes were not favorable. Those changes were detected more in Trent than in Jack. They, along with their parents, had weighed the pros and cons in going to boarding school. However, there was no way the boys could imagine what it would be like to be in a real school with classmates and dorm mates, yet they voted for it.

Incidentally, Trent and Jack's mother was an MK herself and had attended the same boarding school where her sons were now. Years had passed, and of course many changes had come to that school. It was not like the one their mother had attended, even though it was located in the same spot. When the boys started showing changes, their parents became concerned. They were showing negative attitudes toward authority and rebelling against some of the rules. Their mother credited that to just being adolescents and being with other kids their own age. They were also trying to fit into this new situation.

Eventually, the boys' grades began to drop from A's to B's to C's. The parents were able to explain this away as peer pressure, and now they had many other students with whom to compete. They were showing bad attitudes and a lack of respect for authority and rules, which became even more puzzling to their parents. The mother surmised that it was a spiritual problem and emphasized to them "the importance of their relationship with the Lord."

Then in his second year, Trent, during the first trimester, got in trouble for meeting his girlfriend off campus, kissing and holding hands. For this, Trent was restricted to the campus and placed on probation. The parents were shocked to hear this news. Although he was reprimanded, he began to break other rules. He insisted on keeping the lights on after "lights out time," popping popcorn and cooking French fries at one o'clock in the morning, and then sleeping late and skipping classes. His dorm master sent him to the disciplinary committee, and Trent was suspended from school for two weeks. The dorm master took Trent home to his parents, which was a six-hour trip. The parents were disappointed in their son's behavior and felt very discouraged.

The following day, the mother wrote to me, saying, "Doris, we received your book in the mail from some friends, along with a brochure of your work and other materials about your counseling ministry." She was delighted to know of a counseling ministry that focused on the needs of missionary kids. She thanked me for the book, *Missionary Children Caught between Cultures*. She and her husband saw what seemed like a coincidence as "of the Lord."

Trent was scheduled to return to the States in the fall of that year to enter college. I received his mother's letter in the month of March. She said that her husband was going to accompany Trent to the States and be with him on his first day of college. They would be arriving in the States the latter part of July or early August, and she wanted to know if I could see them in intensive counseling for about a week. I immediately responded, and we set up the first week in August when I could spend two to three hours each day with Trent and his father. I knew it was going to be hard enough for the parents to have their son leave them for college, and it would be a long time before they would see him again. I reminded them that it was not unusual for MKs to start acting out and distancing themselves from their families about six months before they had to leave home. This would perhaps upset their parents who might become somewhat angry with them, and it would then be easier for them to say the word "goodbye" to their MKs. Thus, it would make it easier on the MK as well.

August arrived, and I had decided to devote entire mornings to this father and son. However, their second son, Jack, came too. It would have been too much of a financial burden on the family if all of them had come. I was impressed upon first meeting Mr. Medlin and his sons. They were very polite, open, and cooperative. They were authentic, not trying to impress me at all.

Of course, Trent wanted to talk about the struggles and difficulties he had had at the boarding school. He explained that his dorm master was young and immature himself. He was always watching their every move, trying to catch them breaking rules so he could report them. So, it was hard for Trent, as well as his dorm mates, to respect the dorm master as a person as well as an authority figure. Trent just happened to be the one who "stood up to" him. Trent had built up a lot of resentment and was very angry at the way the dorm master was treating him and his friends. After all, they would all be leaving in the spring that year and would be returning to the States for college, and they felt they deserved a little more respect from their dorm master. When Trent "pushed" him too far, in front of the other students, he recommended that Trent be sent home for a couple of weeks, and he would be on probation for another two weeks upon his return to the dorm.

When Trent went back to the high school boarding campus after his two weeks at home, he was assigned to a different dormitory. He was as "good as gold." When his parents went to visit Trent and Jack, they met and talked with Trent's new dorm master. According to the dorm master, Trent was a perfect gentleman in every way and was a good student. His grades were improving as well. He was happy in his new dorm and respected his dorm master very much. Trent said, "I knew he trusted me, and that made all the difference."

I spent much time with Trent alone, then Jack, then their father, and then with all three together. It was clear to me that Trent was trying to individualize, become his own man. After all, very soon he would be on his own and be responsible for making all his decisions. He was still trying to figure out just who he was. He was in the midst of an identity crisis. He just about knew who he was in Switzerland, but who was he in the United States? Trent was scared about being left alone in the States, and Jack was eager to get back to his home in Switzerland. He would be living in the same dorm where Trent had lived previously.

It was evident that their father truly loved his boys. He verbalized and showed his love for them. He told us that, in growing up, he never heard his own father express his love for him, although he knew his father loved him, yet he wanted his sons to remember hearing the words, "I love you." Until their father was forty years of age, he had not heard his father say those words, and then it was at their father's initiative. He decided he was going to tell his father of his love for him. One day they were driving some place, and the boy's father just plainly said, "Dad, I really love you." Father replied, "luv you too." However, the more he said the words, the easier it was for his own father to repeat the words. At first, he knew his father was uncomfortable, but he saw him become very comfortable. He said, "Doris, soon my father began to tell me he loved me, first. I think he really liked hearing and saying it." One thing was for sure, Trent and Jack knew their father loved them.

Trent's father turned to Trent and said, "I do not want to embarrass you, but when I leave you on that college campus to return to Switzerland, I know I am going to be in tears." Trent said, "Dad, it won't embarrass me. I will also be crying myself." The father embraced his son right there in my office, and they cried together. I was moved to tears as well. What a wonderful experience it was to be a part of this warm father/son exchange of affection.

Born Caregivers

Missionary kids are what we might call "born caregivers." After all, they had two parents, two role models, father and mother, to show them how it is done. Missionaries tend to try to rescue the down-and-out, fix their problems, while all the time the children are watching. Edna, a female MK from Liberia, is one who learned well how to take care of people, even though, at times, it became a detriment to her, yet she did not realize it.

Edna had an eventful, sometimes happy but often chaotic, painful, and unhappy life. She grew up in Liberia and came to the States for the first time for furlough at age five. She has early memories of playing basketball with the national children, and best of all, she remembered playing the part of Mary in the church Christmas pageant. Roy, her first boyfriend, played the part of Joseph. She remembers that he put his arm around her and how good that felt. She felt really special. At age ten, she was sent away to boarding school, remaining there until she was twelve, at which time she and her parents returned to the States for their second furlough. After another tour of duty in Liberia, Edna's family moved back to the States. At that time, at age sixteen and seventeen, Edna related well to the black students in her school. After all, she had lived seeing only black people in Liberia.

Finally, Edna and her family returned to Liberia where she would remain until she graduated from high school. In a church in Liberia she met Antonio at a church service. Antonio raped her, and in her naivete she thought she had to marry him. They were married for five years. Edna hated every minute of that marriage. She described Antonio as a mean, manipulative, arrogant, unfaithful, and abusive husband. He never once apologized to her for his abusive behavior. Edna became depressed, but she never sought psychiatric help. In this marriage she had three children. The marriage ended in divorce.

Edna had a strong need to be needed. Also she wanted to be married. It gave her a sense of belonging to someone and to someplace. Then she met Leon, who had one child by a previous marriage. They were married a couple of years later. She described him as "like a leach." She discovered that he smoked pot on a regular basis. This marriage ended after only one and a half years. She had felt that she had taken good care of his child, but he showed no gratitude at all.

After her second divorce, Edna's parents asked her not to date anyone for at least a year but preferably for five years, and they asked her to spend more time concentrating on her three children. Of course, she resented their request. She had old resentments, especially toward her mother, who, according to Edna, never accepted her black friends in Liberia. She saw this request as just another way her mom was trying to manipulate her.

Edna seemed to be one of those people who responded to life and relationships with an all-or-nothing attitude. She did not know how to draw boundaries for herself or for others in her relationships. Yet she was a talented, loving, generous, empathic, sympathetic, conscientious, thoughtful, innocent, tender young lady. She was a pleaser, with a childlike trust and faith. She could readily see how she drew "needy" men to her as she was a generous person who gave and gave.

Not waiting even a year, Edna met Floyd, who was a loner. She saw him as mysterious. Innocently she believed Floyd, as well as the first two husbands, when he told her he loved her and needed her. She thought she had to marry him and take care of him.

When Edna came to see me for the first counseling session she had just started a relationship with Floyd. She met him at her workplace. After eight months, he asked Edna to marry him. Instead of getting married, Edna allowed Floyd to move in with her and her children. Of course, this was a big disappointment to her parents. The first month in this relationship was "lots of fun." He accepted and seemed to love her children. Even before he moved in with her, he had the habit of breaking his promises. Now that they were living together, he continued to break promises. She could never depend on what he said. Floyd could be very sarcastic and moody, and he had a bad temper. One evening he "lost it," broke a chair, and pushed Edna onto the bed.

On one occasion, Floyd took Edna and the children to Disney World. On the way home, Floyd had a temper tantrum. Edna tried to smooth things over and believed him when he said that would never happen again. After these episodes, I asked Edna to bring Floyd with her to counseling. He did not resist. It did seem that he loved Edna, at least the best way he knew how to love. What became evident was the fact that Floyd was schizophrenic, so his love for her was a strange kind of love. Perhaps to say that he needed her is the best way to put it.

I asked Edna to tell Floyd what she needed from him and see if he would be capable of meeting her requests. She had written out a long list as follows:

> I need for you to allow me to be myself with you.
>
> I need to feel comfortable saying what I feel and think without you getting angry.
>
> I need for you to show some excitement/happiness upon seeing me and hearing my voice at the end of the workday.

I need for you to go to church with me and the children.

I need to have conversation with you without you being sarcastic.

I need for you to trust me. Don't think I'm "out to get you."

I need to be able to go with you to the grocery store and be comfortable without you complaining about what I purchase.

I need for you not to always be asking, "Why?"

I need for you to stop bringing up my past "stuff" in an accusatory way.

I need for you to show that you enjoy being with our children, yours and mine.

I need for you to be able to tell my children what they do that "gets on your nerves." Stop yelling at them and me.

I need to feel comfortable talking on the phone and not feel self-conscious wondering if you are going to find something wrong with my conversation.

I need for you not to hate people.

I need for you not to hurt yourself.

I need for you not to break things when you get angry.

I need for you to listen to me when I try to talk to you, and all you want to do is watch TV. Just tell me you want to watch TV instead of acting annoyed.

I need to feel your love, not just hear the words, "I love you."

I need you to tell me what or who has made you angry instead of sulking.

Floyd promised that he would try to meet these needs as spelled out by Edna.

Edna's parents, upon meeting him for the first time, just couldn't seem to trust Floyd. Edna encouraged Floyd to try to get to know her parents and let them get to know him, without getting defensive. She described Floyd as a person of "few words." When Edna, Floyd, and the children went to her parents' home, he seldom said anything. Of course, that made Edna and her parents feel uncomfortable. Finally, Floyd refused to go to her parents' home anymore.

On the other hand, Edna said that when her father had talked to Floyd it sounded more like a lecture and a quiz show. Her mother finally told Edna, "You are not yourself, the daughter we have known, when Floyd is with you." She knew this was true, and her mother was right. Edna was also afraid that her children would learn deceit from being around Floyd.

Finally Edna stopped talking about Floyd to her parents. Her parents became suspicious that something was wrong with the relationship and wondered if Floyd had moved out of Edna's house. Edna was just angry at her parents for not accepting Floyd. The fact is, Edna had asked Floyd to move out, to leave her home. It seems that she came to the conclusion and realization that this relationship was just not going to work.

Here was an MK, a good person, who put others' needs before her own. She had taken abuse and ridicule, all the time hoping she could "fix" Floyd. She knew that he had a personality disorder, and at times he was completely out of control, and his behavior just was not going to change. In the end, what she had interpreted as her parents' interference was not that at all. They just wanted their daughter not to be abused and hurt over and over again. They had tried to protect her.

Some of the main issues with which Edna was dealing were, first of all, her need for a place to belong. She had not felt that she had belonged in the States or in Liberia, where she had spent the developmental years of her life. She wanted acceptance and love but was often misdiagnosing what real love was. She needed to be able to be herself without feeling rejection. She felt different and had different values from the three men she had taken into her life. She had grown up in a culture completely different from that of the United States of America. She was still trying to figure out her own identity. She knew she had the American face, but she did not feel American. She had loved too much and lost too much, and now she was carrying so much pain from it all. She needed for her parents to be there for her. She realized she had been very naive and had trusted perhaps too much. She did not know who she was. In therapy, we addressed all of these issues. Now, she was beginning to realize who she was. However, it may take a lifetime before she accomplishes this task. Two cultures coming together in one individual can be so confusing. I do believe Edna came to terms with these issues and is a happier person today. She came to believe she was okay not being married. She also came to the conclusion that even though she might always be a caregiver, it was not her responsibility to "fix" people.

Family Depression

Christy, a thirty-year-old female MK from Germany, came for counseling. Her main reason for seeking counseling was to improve her marriage. She was a working wife, and together she and her husband were making good salaries. Therefore, there was not the issue of finances that was interfering with their marriage bliss. The main problem in this marriage was a lack of clear communication.

Mark, who was not an MK, was a good provider, yet he was not as attentive to his wife as much as she needed or perhaps wanted. As their arguments continued, their resentment began to build as well. They were hurting each other with their verbal abuse. The bottom line was that they were actually communicating the best way they knew how. They needed to learn some better ways. Christy really wanted a better understanding of Mark and herself in the relationship. She also needed to come to understand and decide upon the kind of relationship she wanted with her parents, her brother, and her coworkers. She was becoming aware of some of her own destructive behavior, but did not know what to do about it. Christy wanted to learn to be a more responsible person. She also needed to learn how to deal with her anger in a constructive way. She realized that what she had been doing with her anger really wasn't working for her but against her.

Christy, at this time, described her life in general as unhappy, her life as a child as average, her life as a teenager as unhappy, and her present life, at least within the past six months, as happy to average and unhappy. As a college student she had become involved with drugs. She was also having a problem with alcohol. During this time she got married, but the marriage ended in divorce since it seemed that all they had in common was alcohol and drug use. Now, she was in her second marriage. She had changed her way of living. She no longer used alcohol or drugs. She really wanted to make this marriage a good one, and both wanted children.

Mark, Christy's husband, sometimes drank too much, although he did not use drugs. When drinking too much, Christy described him as having a "rotten" attitude. He was cocky and abrasive. She described him as having a personality change when drinking too much. He was temperamental, and at such times, in anger, she called him a "shithead." His addiction to the computer was a real source of contention. She believed he was becoming addicted to pornography. He was also purchasing pornographic magazines which he had tried to hide, but in cleaning she discovered them. This made her very angry. She thought she was not "woman enough" for him, which made her feel insecure in the relationship. She began to realize that she was holding a lot of grudges.

When I met with the two of them together, they were both very honest with each other. They did not hesitate to tell what they disliked about each other as well as what they liked. Since Mark had been unfaithful to Christy at least once since they married, over a period of five years, she had the issue of trust with which she had come to terms. After their first child was born, they both realized they needed to have more patience with each other and even with the child. They became aware of the fact that both needed also to learn better parenting skills.

Christy told Mark that she needed him to help her more around the house, especially while the baby was still an infant. They also discussed how all these other issues had affected their sex life. Once they started working on other problems, their sex life did improve. Christy was a strong extrovert and needed people around her whereas Mark was a strong introvert. He could spend hours on the computer being by himself, and he liked his way of life. As they began to tell each other what they expected from each other, things got better. I discussed with them the fact that when a couple is married, they go into the marriage with spoken expectations, and this does not cause trouble. It is the unspoken expectations that couples take into the marriage that cause them problems. They had been saying, "She ought to know," or "He ought to know." "We've been married five years. She ought to know me by now." I encouraged them to stop playing the game, Guess What I'm Thinking, or Guess What I Want from You. This seemed to help a lot.

As we looked at their families of origin, they became aware that their families were about as different as night and day. After Christy's missionary parents returned to the States, they lived fairly close to Christy and Mark. Christy had lost interest in the Christianity of her parents, which bothered them, especially her mother. She found her mother trying to manipulate her. Her mother wanted to tell her how to raise her son, which Christy resented. Her mother made many phone calls to her each day, which was becoming a problem for Christy. She finally decided to begin letting the answering machine screen the calls. This way her time was not consumed with talking to her mother all day long. Christy felt her mother was lonely and bored and even depressed since returning to the States, while her father was employed and adjusting better than her mother.

Christy realized that her parents were very unhappy in their marriage and had been for a long time. Now that they were in the States, they seemed to have more problems. In the mission country where they had served, they were "important" people whom folks regarded very highly.

Now they were ordinary people. Christy recommended to her parents that they go to counseling, at least try a few sessions with me. The mother came first, and it was clear to me that she was suffering from depression. Later, her father came with her mother. In these sessions they learned how to communicate better, but they still had special issues that did not contribute to a happy marriage. Christy could see that she and Mark were doing some of the same things that she saw her parents doing that caused problems. Her parents were hurting each other in some of the same ways she and Mark were now hurting each other.

Finally, Christy realized she was having some of the same symptoms of depression that she saw in her mother. I referred her to a good psychiatrist, who put her on an antidepressant that helped a lot. Her depression started after their first child was born. It was not postpartum depression, but nevertheless it was bad enough that she needed attention right away, before it got worse. She also was having panic attacks. The month after the birth of her child she began to have nightmares. She complained of increased crying spells and was sleeping around fourteen hours a day. She had also lost ten pounds in fourteen days. She had a decreased appetite and low energy level. Nothing seemed to motivate her. She was not able to concentrate and was having difficulty doing her job, which she finally decided to quit. She felt helpless, hopeless, and guilty for not being able to know what she needed to do. She was becoming more and more withdrawn and isolated. This, of course, did not help their marriage, for Mark had no understanding of depression. It bothered him to come home from work and "find the house in a mess." He could not understand why she couldn't "at least keep the house clean."

Christy admitted to the psychiatrist that ten years before she had an episode with depression that followed her drug and alcohol abuse. She had smoked cigarettes, which she no longer did, but at one point during that time she had made two suicide attempts. Then they learned that both of Christy's parents were taking antidepressants. We discussed that this type of depression could be genetic.

As Christy improved she shared with me her concerns for Peter, her brother, who also had been on drugs for many years. He also misused alcohol. Peter had been married four times. He lived in another state. At that particular time, Peter was "down and out." He now had no relationship with, nor even wanted a relationship with, his parents because "they were always criticizing me." He had no close relationships anymore in the state where he was then residing.

Christy contacted Peter and invited him to come to live with her and Mark "until he could get back on his feet." He did, and she brought him to my office and introduced him to me. He was eager to get into counseling. This was a good, new start for Peter. Peter had a lot of anger toward his parents, and thus he had no contact with them for such a long time. He was very open and willing to be vulnerable in counseling. I could see that he really did want to start a new life. He said, "The old life was not getting me what I wanted. Now I am ready to try something different." I listened to his anger, and we discussed ways for him to deal with it in a healthy way.

As a child, Peter remembered how his dad would provoke him. Sometimes his dad would even hold Peter down on the floor and beat him. He remembered a lot of physical abuse from his father. He described his father as not being affectionate, a strong controller and manipulator. He never encouraged Peter and never taught him basic skills for daily living. He even referred to his father as a hypocrite. His father's ultraconservatism caused him to be a very rigid person. Peter felt he could never please his father, no matter how hard he tried. His father never gave him any affirmation. Christy also talked about her father's rigidity, his abuse, remembering how when left alone with her father, he had spanked her and left welts on her bottom. She was only three years old. It seems that he expected these small children to understand and respond like adults, never realizing that their brains had not developed to that stage.

Peter described his mother as a very insecure person who cried, yelled, and argued a lot. He was afraid of his mother's anger. He said he still hated to hear her voice and described her as a little "crazy." He felt that when she talked to him and Christy about committing suicide, it was coming out of her own self-pity. Finally, he said that he never really had a good role model, someone to teach him how to be a man or a good husband. He definitely did not want to be like his father.

Peter believed that his parents had been missionaries because of the respect and attention they received from the nationals as well as from the people in the churches in the States. In a short time, I can truly say that I saw Peter really take control of his life. Now he was "clean" and only drank beer occasionally. He was able to get a good, promising job and has continued to "move up the ladder." He has also rebuilt a relationship with his parents. His goal for counseling was to regain stable thinking and a productive life, which he has accomplished. He now also has a healthy relationship with himself.

Christy, with the aid of an antidepressant and counseling, was no longer sad all the time. she enjoyed doing things with her husband and son. She no longer had thoughts of suicide. Christy, once again, became a happier person.

An MK Reflects
DAVID SNELL

Sometimes doing the small tasks in life can be most difficult. Moving from one city to another in America is not that much of an adjustment, but when it comes to moving to a foreign country from America, it can be difficult.

Most missionary families feel called to the field by the Holy Spirit and feel led to do the Lord's work. When a family is given a country overseas to serve in, most of them do it without realizing the psychological effects it may have on their children. The children have to go through a very dramatic change, and most times they are not helped or assisted very much, if any.

We need good counselors to go to the field where we have our missionaries and counsel with the children of foreign missionaries so that they will not go through as much trauma and rebellion as missionary kids often do.

When I was growing up, I had to face and deal with this problem. I used to blame my parents for what they were doing. Why should a child have to leave his/her American way of living and sacrifice what a good thing he or she had going? We definitely needed someone there to help us through difficult times.

When I came back to the United States for college, it was that much worse in trying to get a handle on myself. Who was I? I hardly knew myself or my relatives, and I felt cheated and couldn't go to them to talk because they were people I hardly knew.

When one has to leave parents in their work on the field and has to fend for oneself, the person doesn't have an American identity, but a foreign identity. Such people are on their own.

Of all the missionary kids that I know personally, 70 percent are having adjustment problems. We need help as missionary kids on the field and as we come back to the United States for college.

It took me a while to realize that it was a privilege to live overseas and for me to be proud of my parents, what they stood for and who they are. I realize that missionaries give up a lot when they go to a foreign field, but so do their children. In a way they give up more than they realize, and I know of so many missionary kids who are hurting so bad, but yet they don't feel they can express themselves to very many people.

I am saddened about the fact that quite a few MKs are burned out with religion right now, and I can see how and why they feel this way. I believe we need to start giving our children more room to breathe or to think for themselves, as well as to make their own decisions.

We need to have unconditional love. Just because we don't do what someone else is doing, does that mean we should jump right in on them and be judgmental?

I can now say, though, that I am proud to be a missionary kid, and I am proud that my parents are Baptist missionaries. I am proud for what they stand for, but it did take a while for me to see the light.

MK Subgroup?

[Note: This was an article printed in one of our Missionary Family Counseling Services' newsletters, but I did want MKs with this kind of experience to be heard, and we are just as proud of this group of young people who never lived on a mission field, but saw their parents leave them in the States.]

I enjoyed so much the June 1998 MK gathering at Fort Caswell. Since reflecting on that weekend, one verbal exchange keeps coming to my mind. I was asked by another MK, "Where did *you* grow up?" I realized that the Piedmont area of North Carolina was not a desired response when the questioner wanted to know why I was even at the retreat. I explained that my parents left for "the field" when I was twenty-one. I chose to stay here and start out on my own.

In some ways, I felt some kinship to the MKs who were about my age who were coming home to attend college and/or go to work, but I was not in any category, much less any group. The initial pride of my parents going to Austria in 1980 quickly gave way to the realities of "They're gone," and "I'd better grow up quickly!" Taking care of their finances, business interests, and so on was an eye opener as well. My brother, age twenty-six at the time, and I increased contact with our maternal grandmother, the only remaining grandparent. Doing things without my parents close by was a new and sometimes unnerving experience.

The time I did spend with my parents, either in Europe or while they were here on furlough, was always wonderful and full of quality time. I learned that going to the "home place" didn't need to be a certain house or place. It was the relationship with your family or wherever you are.

I felt tremendously for my parents missing out on life here, be it events in their grandchildren's lives, or even something as trivial as a Wake Forest basketball game.

Communication "way back in the '80s" was not as good as it is today. Week-old letters and occasional expensive phone calls were treasured. There were even times when I felt like my parents had passed on.

I am so proud of my parents' dedication to the Lord's work in Austria, Greece, and Denmark. They retired in 1995, well deserved. I love the fact that they are missionaries, but it has been a sacrifice for many. They are returning to Copenhagen this year for a short time to assist the international church there. Please pray for them, the church, and our family here in the States.

I am an MK even though I did not grow up "on the field," and I believe this situation is often overlooked. Thanks to Doris Walters for her gracious empathy and allowing me to vent my feelings.

From the Heart of a Missionary Parent
ANONYMOUS

My dear child,

I am writing this letter as a way of coming to terms with the strong and powerful feelings I experienced when we parted. Something is still very much alive in me of the pain of your leaving home, of your not knowing you could ever come back to the country where you spent your youth. Each time I tried to speak to you I choked inside and the words never came. I wanted somehow to let you know that I really understood how you struggled to say farewell to a world you have known from your beginnings, a world of tenderness and caring, how you struggled to face the feeling that that world may never exist again for you. One day your life was intact. Your family was fully there for you. The next moment this human support was sharply and suddenly gone. I felt the loss too, and wondered what would happen to your basic innocence and trust, to what you've always been able to count on. I wanted to reach you, to let you know that I was there in that shattering awareness of roots left behind, of facing a confusing world alone. I wanted to offer you something that you could take with you into that darkness and uncertainty. But all I could do was to be there with you in that busy airport. There were no words in me to offer you courage and strength. I know that you know I am with you in whatever you do to find a life that will bring you courage and strength. I know that you know I am with you in whatever you do to find a life that will bring you joy and fulfillment. And though I know you must create that world on your own, it is hard to live with this truth, with all the barriers and obstacles that others will put before you.

I wanted to tell you then, and I want to tell you now that you have always been here in my heart and you always will be, that what we have lived and known will be there waiting for you to come home to, a permanent place in you, in me, in others who have held you and helped you grow in your own way.

You did not want to make that final moment final. You took my hand strongly in yours. I felt the love flowing between us as you held onto that last instant, and then you were gone.

None of this really says what's in my heart tonight—YOU—your music, your joking ways, how you enter a room and stand, your quickness, your putting everything you've got into what matters to you, what you've become through steady persistence, what we've shared together all these years. It's all here in me now. It has enriched my life, making sense out of the absurdity, bringing light into darkness, contributing to my life as a human being.

This love goes with you into that unknown world you are now entering. It will be there as a steady presence when you face the problems and issues of living, and it will shine like a beacon to light your way back home.

CHAPTER SIX

Octogenarians and More

At the Retirement Home

Here, I have put together the stories of some older MKs. They were all in their late eighties; the oldest was ninety-four years old. Upon hearing about the four MKs residing at a retirement home in the mountains of western North Carolina, I knew I must meet them and hear their stories, because I believed they had a lot to teach me and MKs of all ages and generations. The first visit was informal, where we sat around in a lounge and got to know one another. However, the second visit was planned, and we would be able to videotape our time together and preserve this valuable part of history.

Octogenarian: Mr. F.
It was a cold, crisp day in early March 1995. I took my friend Frances Lamb and her video camera up that mountain with its winding curves. Waiting on the front porch of the retirement home was Mr. F. This delightful man of eighty-nine years of age was dressed in a dark suit, white shirt, and necktie, with a white handkerchief in his coat pocket. He was the essence of a true gentleman. We were eager to get all four of these MKs on video so that we could preserve their fascinating stories.

The four of them represented 350 years of missionary experience from three countries: Argentina, China, and India.

Mr. F. was born in Argentina in 1905. His parents were among the first missionaries to live and work in Argentina. They had gone to Argentina in 1904. At the age of fifteen, he returned to the States, all alone, by ship. Besides that, he suffered from a hearing impairment, the result of scarlet fever when he was five years old. Can you imagine this fifteen-year-old traveling in silence with people on that ship to a place where he knew no one? It was a very scary experience, to say the least. He had been born a perfectly healthy child until scarlet fever hit him and robbed him of his hearing. This was a handicap that he had to deal with for the rest of his life.

Many years later, in 1992, Mr. F. went to North Carolina Baptist Hospital where a doctor performed a reconstruction on his ear drum, which helped him to be able to hear a little. However, he still relied on lip reading to converse. When he was asked, "What do you think about being able to hear?" He replied, "I can't decide what is most important to listen to, noise or other sounds." Mr. F. expressed his true feelings when he said, "People become human by socializing. The deaf are often shut out from other human beings, mainly because most people do not know how to communicate with hearing-impaired persons."

Mr. F.'s parents felt that he, at age fifteen, needed to be exposed to a good English education. Thus, he was sent back to further his education in a military academy, the Locust Grove Institution, which was a preparatory school. At the instruction of his parents, when he arrived in New York, he was to go to Grand Central Station, send a telegram to his uncle in Tennessee, and ask him to meet his train when he arrived in Memphis. Knowing very little about the country of his parents, he did manage to find his way to the train station. He described a whole mixture of feelings—excitement, isolation, anxiety, fear, sadness, loneliness, and anger. His predominant feeling was anger. There was no one to turn to! He lived in his own silent world in a very strange country and culture. His culture shock was magnified by his inability to hear. He buried himself in his books, all the time feeling unhappy and lonely. Many missionary kids have told me that "Loneliness is my greatest enemy." He said, "What I needed was some counseling, but even in my college years, if they had any counselors available, no one ever told me." Not even college staff or faculty reached out to Mr. F. He said, "I was a very unhappy young man with no one to turn to who could understand where I had come from." He said, "Back in Argentina I know I was spoiled because of my handicap. I was also known as the preacher's boy, and I felt real special. In other words, I was *somebody*." But now, back in the States where he had lived for only one year before going to Argentina with his missionary parents, he went unnoticed and was a nobody. He said there was always someone on his college campus who made fun of him. He explained, "This left me feeling isolated and angry, which was aggravated by my appearance of aloofness due to my impaired hearing."

Mr. F. had vivid memories of how, back in Argentina, the family always talked to him about America, and what a wonderful place it was. Naturally, this young man had great expectations when he arrived in that "wonderful" place. However, he was greatly disappointed when he faced the reality of actually being in America. America just was not what he had been led to believe. He was crushed as the truth came crashing down around him. He was homesick. He was worlds away from his family. He missed his parents and siblings. He said that his anger was perhaps the thing that made him more determined, and in hindsight, he could see that his anger actually helped him endure the suffering and pain he was forced to face.

On his college campus he said, "I was treated badly by some of the other students. They would shout at me. They showed their resentment toward me. I was deeply hurt and tired quickly after being treated like a subhuman being." He was the brunt of their humor, was laughed at, and treated as if he had "no brain." He said that his deafness was his "thorn in the flesh." Nevertheless, he studied hard to succeed and to receive some recognition, a real need he had. His attitude was, "I'm going to show them!" He did show them, for he graduated third in his graduation class. He went on to make exceptionally good grades at Mercer University. He spent some time at Georgia Tech, where someone told him that if he lived off of just water for a month, he could regain his hearing. He tried it, but of course, it failed to give him back his hearing. He became very depressed and went to his uncle's home to recuperate. He said that they were as helpful as they knew how to be, but relatives in Tennessee were just more strangers with whom he had to deal. Later, he spent Thanksgiving and Christmas holidays with them. All the time, he said that he knew his parents had to be worrying about him, and then he said, "But they didn't know what to do." He received letters but they took a month to reach him.

Mr. F. expressed gratitude for the Woman's Missionary Society in Macon, which showed some interest in him but lacked the knowledge to know how to help him. They knew of no specific counselors who could understand him and his MK needs.

After graduation from college, Mr. F. went to work for the Internal Revenue Service. Using his CPA training, he worked in Tennessee and North Carolina. His life's work was with Ford Motor Company where he was in partnership with another man who became his lifelong friend. He met his wife, who already knew sign language. They had no children of their own, but did adopt a daughter who died in middle age. He retired at age sixty-five. Beginning in 1985, he participated in the Senior Olympics, where he won many gold, bronze, and silver medals for his great accomplishments.

Even up until he died in September 2002, Mr. F. talked about the times when he and his younger brother would get together. They would always end up talking about how difficult those years were upon their return to the States. They agreed that it was only by the grace of God and the prayers of their parents that they survived.

Mr. F. was an active member of a church in the mountains of North Carolina for fifty years. He and his late wife were recognized by other parishioners as a remarkable, fantastic couple. Two of my own cousins had been members at the same church, and they referred to him, as so many others did, as "Paw F." He was loved by all who knew him.

When the time came when "Paw F" could no longer compete in the Senior Olympics, he was greatly disappointed. One person said, "Mr. F. was one of those persons who looked on the other side of adversity, the side with fewer bruises." The story is told that, when in his nineties, Mr. F. went on a trip to the Holy Land. As he was going up the escalator to board his flight, carrying a rather heavy flight bag, he missed a step and fell, tumbling down until the security guard stopped the escalator and "pried him from the stairs." He was in great pain, hurting his right hip, but nothing was going to stop him from going on his trip. A retired doctor was on board his plane and took care of him throughout the trip. He visited Athens, Corinth, and Tel Aviv, despite his pain. Then a second disaster happened. As he left his hotel one morning, he discovered someone had taken his flight bag that he had left in the hallway for a hotel attendant to pick up for loading. In the bag was everything he had except his clothes. He lost his everyday needs including his medication. In the bag was a second hearing aid, his batteries, an extra pair of glasses, and his credit cards. Because he lost his hearing aid batteries, he spent several days in total silence. On top of all this he developed a wretched stomach virus. Someone at the local newspaper in Asheville said, "So there he was, stone deaf, stomach cramps, not an ounce of credit or money to his name, having the time of his life. When he returned he was minus a flight bag but full of good stories, and he had had a marvelous time."

On Mr. F's ninetieth birthday, on October 30, I had the opportunity—along with a friend, Frances Lamb, and his pastor—to celebrate his birthday with him. We enjoyed lunch in a restaurant, and Mrs. Lamb took him a specially made portrait cake. The expression on his face was a delight to see. Mr. F. was a great man and a great friend who taught me much about dealing with adversity.

Mr. F. often expressed his appreciation for my counseling ministry focused on the children of missionaries. At one point he said, "Doris, I wish I could have been born fifty years later, or you could have been born fifty years earlier. Then you could have been there to counsel me when I returned to the States alone." He said, "Doris, even this ninety-year-old MK still needs your help." He also said, "I believe that every MK could make a better adjustment in this American society if they had the benefit of a counselor like you who can understand where we come from and could support us on our American journey." He went on to say, "Your counseling ministry is a Godsend in every way to us children of missionaries who have returned to the States. Even though it would have been wonderful to have had someone like you seventy-five years ago, I am already receiving lots of help from my short acquaintance with you and through the pages of your book, *Missionary Children Caught between Cultures*, which I have read and reread. I feel like I am more of a member of the human race now more than ever before. The healing therapy of your counseling works even in a ninety-year-old returnee."

When Mr. F. was asked, "What gift would you give to the children of missionaries who are returning to the States these days, leaving all their friends, families, and all the familiar behind them?" He quickly replied, "Full-time counselors for MKs. Keep track of them as they move through the years, especially college years, and offer them psychiatric help if they need it. Many of my psychological problems have never gone away. I am ninety years old. and I still need help."

Mr. F. shared with me a prayer he had written about his hearing impairment.

> Oh! my soul, do not cry for me
> As the twilight of sound falls on me
> And the night of silences deadens my ears

For more brilliantly shine the stars
as the night darkens and sun fades.
Oh! my soul, bless the Lord for giving me
Increased joy in seeing the beauty
of his creation, a sweet baby's smile;
of feeling the heartwarming touch of a
Beloved's hand, the cooling breeze on a hot day;
of smelling the delicate fragrance of a violet,
the piquant odor of newly mowed hay;
of tasting the full flavors of appetizing food,
and the sweetness of honey.
Oh! my soul, do not cry for me
For in the silence of holiness, my soul
Best communes with God,
With Faith in his eternal heaven bathed in the
intense music of the Angelic choir.
AMEN

Octogenarian: Mrs. L.

Mrs. L., at the time I visited with her, was in her late eighties. She was an MK born in China during the last year of the Chinese Empire. Those were the years that the War Lords were fighting for control and rule of all of China. As a young child, the fighting became somewhat commonplace to her. She said, "I learned early to accept those things I could not change."

Mrs. L. shared with me some of her very tender feelings. One year when her family returned to the States for a year's furlough, she remembers being terrified in her school classroom when one of the teachers slapped the children with only the slightest provocations. This was common. They were slapped if they had not brought their homework. They were slapped if they talked in class. They were slapped if they did not pay attention in class. She was so frightened, never knowing when she, too, would be slapped by that teacher. She remembered crying herself to sleep with her face pressed into her pillow for fear of being heard by her parents. She never shared her fears with her parents.

At age nine, she was left in the States to live in the home of an aunt. She watched her aunt tuck her own children in bed and plant a kiss on their cheeks. At first, she wondered if her aunt would do the same for her. She just craved being tucked in, the touch, and the kiss. Then her aunt did treat her like her other children, and Mrs. L. said, "It felt so wonderful when my aunt kissed me goodnight."

Mrs. L. remembers how she was "shown off" at school. Her teacher would take her from classroom to classroom and have her tell the children about China. Rather than being happy about all that attention, she said that it was so painful, and oh, how she dreaded it. Not knowing the ways of American schools and their practices, she remembers writing on the blackboard when asked by the teacher, and when she finished, she started erasing the blackboard with her little hands, just like they did in their school in China. The teacher scolded her for doing this, but never told her to ask for an eraser. After all, what was an eraser?

When Mrs. L. went back to China for high school, she and her sister were sent away to boarding school. They were at the train station about ready to leave home. She said, "As my family stood there together, I looked intently at the faces of my mother, my father and my younger brothers and sisters and was thinking, 'I always want to have their faces in my mind in case something happens to them or to me and I would never see them again.'" She continued to say, "Even to this day, I can see each of their faces the same as I did that day I left for boarding school." She said that her mother put on a brave front. But then, as the train pulled away from the station, she saw her mother collapse in grief. At the same time she was fighting back her own tears. Her dad watched closely with a sad face.

Once she arrived at the American school in Peking she said she did have lots of fun and good times with friends who were also far away from their homes and families. They shared things, and she was quite happy with her newfound family.

As a young child, she had vivid memories of being bitten by a dog. Since they lived near the small hospital in that village, she started running toward the hospital, her little friends running behind her, and their gardener following behind them. She said it was like a procession. She was crying every step of the way. Her mother's dear friend who worked at the hospital saw Mrs. L. and took care of the dog bite wound. On the way home they passed a vendor who had watched the procession on their way to the hospital. He had mimicked her crying, "Waw, waw, waw." She talked about how embarrassing that was for her as a young child.

Now the time had come for her to return to the States for her college education. She remembered the terrible culture shock she experienced. She studied hard to try to achieve and in order to not have too much time to reflect on what was happening to her. She was an excellent student. One culture shock she received was watching her classmates cheating, which she said was very common. A boy who sat next to her was trying to copy her answers to a test. However, she wrote very small so that he could not read her answers. He said aloud, "I always like to see people write with large letters." This amused her.

Another shock she received was the many American students who lied to their parents. She felt so discouraged with all the cheating and lying she saw, and she just wanted to go back to China. Besides all this, she never felt that she was dressed anything like her classmates. Although her mother had gathered fashion magazines from the States and tried to have clothes made for her that she thought were stylish in the States, hoping she would fit in with the crowd, she felt she never did. She said, "My clothes seemed so wrong. This also was embarrassing to me." She was particularly self-conscious and ashamed of her clothes when dating. She knew her clothes were out-of-style.

Mrs. L. smiled when she remembered the peanut vendor imitating her crying all the way to the hospital and the procession that followed her. But then a sadness came over her face and she said, "That day, I decided I would never let anyone see me cry again." She still cries inside, but no one has seen her tears. At boarding school, she would cry into her pillow, but none of her dorm mates seemed to notice. Why did they not recognize she was crying? My hunch was they were all crying into their pillows as well. One night Mrs. L. left her dorm room and went out to the ball field, and there she cried out to God for help because she was so desperately homesick. She had not heard from her parents in three months. No one ever explained the delay of the mail. She felt abandoned and forgotten. Later, she said she realized that the mail took a long time to arrive, and some of it never arrived due to the situation at a given period of time.

At this point in Mrs. L.'s boarding school days, she decided that she would do all she could to make it easier for the younger MK students coming into her boarding school. She remembered a joke she pulled on three younger students when she told them that all students must use the same toothbrush. The kids became like brothers and sisters, but they never had to use each other's toothbrush.

After two years at boarding school, the war reached Peking. At that time her parents decided it was time to bring her and her sister back home for at least a year, believing it was safer for them where they were living in a smaller town.

On returning by ship to the States for college, it was the first time for her to see young people dancing. She wanted to try it "so bad," but she did not want to do anything that would disappoint or hurt her parents, who had always taught her that dancing was sinful. She was afraid that if she danced, they would never trust her again.

When I asked Mrs. L. what gift she would like to give to MKs coming back to the States for college, she replied, "the opportunity to get with other MKs, gathering to share their hurts, to bond and find healing."

Octogenarian: Mrs. E.

Mrs. E. was a ninety-four-year-old MK who also resided at the retirement home in the mountains of North Carolina. As we sat around talking, sharing, and asking questions, I asked Mrs. E. to tell us about her life. She related that she was a third-generation MK.

Mrs. E's grandparents were missionaries to Nigeria. Her father and mother served as missionaries in the Shantung Province of China. Mrs. E. went to China with her parents when she was only two years old. She told us about knowing Lottie Moon, a Baptist missionary icon who served along with her parents in China. Lottie Moon lived her life in China, and while returning to the States her ship docked in Yokohama, Japan. By this time she had become very ill. Unfortunately, she died on the ship before it left the port of Yokohama.

Mrs. E. remembers that when they first went to China, they lived in the city of Tungchow. Her earliest memories were the strange practices in the Chinese churches. At the age of six her family moved to the Shantung Province. Her parents homeschooled her. An exception was when some American young person would come to China to teach missionary children for a year or two. These young people became her tutors.

Later, however, Mrs. E. was sent to boarding school many hundreds of miles away from her parents. She often wondered why she could not stay in her own home and have her parents teach her like they had taught her older siblings. Much later she learned that she was sent away because her father had had a nervous breakdown. As a young child, she was terribly homesick. She thought their family was a very close one where there was lots of love, but she could never understand why she was sent away to boarding school at such a very young age. She vividly remembers having whooping cough, and oh, how she wished her parents had been there for her. Her pain and loneliness were so great. She said, "At times, I felt like I was going to die." Then she hastily said, as if feeling a need to protect her parents, "But I think my parents also nearly died."

In high school when she was attending boarding school, she said she had become somewhat used to being away from her parents. She seemed to have happy memories of her high school days. In those days, they traveled by horseback. When horses were not available, she said they walked.

Mrs. E. left China and returned to the States after high school graduation in China in 1937. Her parents and siblings all returned to the States together. After a year in the States her parents returned to China to continue their mission work. This time, her parents taught at an American school for several years. This seemed to better suit her father's aspirations and his health. Mrs. E. did return to China one time and actually had her wedding ceremony there.

The emotions that seemed to be the most difficult for her to live with were sadness and loneliness. Holidays away from family in boarding school and stateside without family were her most difficult times. Although people in the States opened their homes to MKs, it still did not feel good being with what you might call "strangers." After all, these strangers had their own children in their homes and were very happy. At times, on holidays she was with MKs from various countries, and she said it felt good to be around these young people who understood her.

Mrs. E. was a delightful ninety-four-year-old lady who looked and seemed much younger. In fact, she informed us that she had gone out and secured herself an apartment in town, since she did not feel she was ready for the retirement home. And, she did indeed move out after our meeting.

Octogenarian: Mrs. H.

Mrs. H. was an MK who grew up in the southern part of India. She lived with her parents in a rather isolated province. There were no American schools anywhere near. She began by defending what her parents had done regardless of the cost to her. She said, "First and foremost I believe my parents did what God told them to do." Mrs. H. was sent away to boarding school in the first grade. Here again, in defense of her parents, she said she did not blame her parents, although she said, "I cried and cried and cried." It was a terrible time, and she felt disoriented. The boarding school she attended was way up in the mountains, a great distance from where her parents lived and worked. There she lived in a large house with other MKs. She said that she did not know how to make friends, and as an eighty-nine-year-old lady, she said that she never learned. She indicated that she had had problems making friends all of her life. She said, "It seems like I always say the wrong thing."

The first time she and her parents returned to the States was when Mrs. H. was nine years old. Then her parents returned to India, leaving her in the States, where she lived from age nine to age eleven. She lived in a home with other MKs. She said that there were five boys from one missionary family, ages three, five, seven, nine and eleven. These boys were also left by their parents. She said that school was very hard for her in India, and she never had time to play. She indicated that it was "all work and no play" for her. She also said that, in the States, high school and college courses were much easier than grade school in India. It seems the teachers at the American school in India did not take a special interest in them and did not offer to give personal help even to the very young children. The only play time she remembered was roller skating, and that was not too often. When Mrs. H. was a senior in high school, her parents returned to the States with her.

Mrs. H. had left India in 1934. On her way back to the States she had a trip though the Holy Land. She talked about her trip to the Holy Land "all the time" until others got tired of hearing about it. That had been the biggest event of her life, up to that point. All the time she was in the States she just wanted to go back to India, the land she loved so much.

It took Mrs. H. seven years to complete her college work and graduate due to "a nervous breakdown." She had to drop out of school at one point and live with her grandmother in order to recuperate. Finally she went to live with an uncle in Tennessee who offered to help her financially and also help her with her studies. This was her first experience living in the South, since she had attended Wooster College in Rochester, New York. She had also attended Crossnore Academy. Each time she changed colleges she lost a lot of credits that would not transfer. She said that she was always restless until she met her husband at Crossnore Academy in North Carolina. Up to this point, she had not known what she would do with her life. Her husband-to-be was just entering the seminary to become a pastor, which meant that she would become a pastor's wife, a lifelong dream of hers. Now she felt happy.

She indicated that her parents had expected much success from her and her sister. She especially felt sorry for her sister who, at first, was very compliant. Her sister, once, in a letter told her father, "Father, I want to be what you want me to be." Her sister was a student at Wellesley College and was always eager to please her father. But there, she majored in philosophy where Mrs. H. said, "My sister lost her faith, and for many years she had nothing to do with the church, but finally found her way back through a Quaker church." She continued, "My parents' expectation of my sister was too great and unfair." She let it be known that she, herself, would always be angry at her parents for this. She said, "It just was not fair." My hunch was that Mrs. H. had plenty of anger toward her parents for their lack of care and understanding, and she was projecting this onto her sister. She could deal with it better if she could make statements and make it appear that they were her sister's feelings

When asked what gift she would give MKs returning to the States today, she said, "Access to psychologists, psychiatrists, and counselors." This octogenarian, in the twilight years of her life, admitted that she had never worked through the difficult issues she had confronted from early childhood throughout her adulthood. She realizes she lived through some very abnormal conditions that continued to affect her life and would until her death.

Conclusion

What an inspiration it was for me to hear the stories of these four dear older MKs, ages eighty-nine to ninety-four, who had struggled and suffered more than anyone could ever dream. Perhaps their stories will help MKs who live in this century have a greater appreciation for all the modern conveniences that have made their lives so much richer even in the midst of their own struggles. Their struggles were perhaps simply different in kind and the period of history in which they lived. Now all four have finally found their "true home" with their God. Their struggles have now ended. Thanks be to God!

Octogenarian: Mary "Skip" Boyles—What a Lady!

Mary Boyles is better known to her friends as "Skip" Boyles. She is an MK who was born in Rio De Janeiro, Brazil, on Sunday morning, April 2, 1916. She reports that her father, after a sleepless night, stood in the church pulpit of a small storefront Baptist church in Rio and announced to the congregation, "An interruption to our normal routine took place early this morning. That interruption came in the form of a baby girl with a loud mouth." Her parents named that baby girl Mary Emma. Her father thereafter often referred to her as the "loud noise maker."

Skip's parents were Dr. and Mrs. A. B. Langston. Dr. Langston was the dean of the Baptist Seminary in Rio. Her mother taught music in the Baptist Training School for young women.

At the age of three, Skip was taken to the United States for her very first time. She said that during that year, many "firsts" in her life took place—her first time to see snow, her first Christmas tree, and her first experience with death. It was in the summer in the month of July, and they were spending that time with Skip's grandparents in Kentucky.

On a particular day, at the age of six, Skip sensed a strange atmosphere in the house since everyone was so quiet, and she said, "No one seemed to have time for me except my granny, who kept saying to me, 'Be quiet, child.'" She remembers how her "papae" (Portuguese for daddy) came to her, took her by the hand, and led her to the parlor. He pulled up a chair to a pretty white baby bed where a baby boy was lying quietly. He held Skip close, and in a soft voice said, "Sister, he is your baby brother, but God decided to take him to heaven." Skip remembers touching his tiny white hand with her finger, and then she squirmed to get down, and left the room. Skip said, "Since I was too much of a noise maker, my aunt in South Carolina took me to her home where I spent the rest of that summer." Uppermost in her memory is her father's reassurance and acceptance of her, which continued throughout the years.

After they returned to Brazil, Skip said that school seemed to occupy most of her time. She remembers at age nine Dr. John Sampey visiting in her home in Brazil. It was during his visit that Skip "accepted Christ as my Lord and Master." Her father was supposed to baptize her, but that Sunday morning he woke up with the flu. Another missionary, Mr. Baker, took her father's place and baptized her. She remembers the baptistery as a homemade concrete tank filled with water, and it was rather deep for a petite nine-year-old girl. It was made to accommodate adults. However, Mr. Baker told Skip to tread water as she came to meet him in the baptistery. She did, but when she got right in front of him, she went under the water. Mr. Baker pulled her up, said a blessing and sent her on her way.

Skip's elementary education included attending Brazilian schools. She was also homeschooled and was taught in a county school by "Aunt Ta." She remembers that the year of her fourteenth birthday turned out to be different but a lot of fun. As a teenager, Skip played the piano and a portable pump organ for various groups in Rio. On one occasion she was invited by a missionary couple to go with them on a mission trip to the interior of Brazil and play the portable pump organ. One evening, the couple's daughter played the violin and Skip accompanied her on the pump organ. An amazing thing happened. While playing the organ, a very large lizard made its debut from under the organ.

What did Skip do? She stood up, stopped pumping, but continued to play the notes, making no sound but never missing a note.

After participating in those services, and returning to Rio, she and the missionaries had to go by sailboat out into the water and then boarded a salt barge which was also carrying a herd of pigs that had the run of the barge deck.

The time came when MKs are expected to be sent back to the States, their parents' homeland, to complete their education in some college. Upon graduation from high school in Rio, Skip attended Greenville South Carolina Women's College, which later merged into Furman University. She loved Furman. It was there that a classmate began calling her "Skip." The name has stuck with her throughout her life. After Furman she transferred to the Stuart Circle School of Nursing in Richmond, Virginia, on the campus of William and Mary. This was a time of difficult transition. There were many adjustments to be made. She did not feel understood. She felt that even her grandmother did not trust her, but neither did she trust any other teenagers. She said, "This really bugged me since up to this time everyone trusted me." She said that the American way of life was so different from the Brazilian way of life. She said, "Brazilian teenagers and American teenagers are two different breeds of 'cats,' with one exception, and that was all teenagers want to be accepted."

Skip's only brother was four years older than she. Even though he was already in the States, he lived many miles away from where she lived. Therefore, he could not give her much support. She said, "I was homesick for Brazil. I missed my friends, and I was lonely. During my first semester in college I did my best to fit in but found that most American girls were immature and silly." At midterm her parents agreed that she should go to Furman University. There her school work was challenging. She found lots of satisfaction in speaking in various churches about Brazil. Most gratifying was her participation in the college chapel choir. She said, "At graduation time, while I was only a junior at Furman, I was selected to be a page or usher to my father who was receiving his doctor of divinity degree from Furman."

During her college years Skip had a particular interest in entering the medical field. Even though she would like to have gone to medical school, she realized that, financially speaking, it was not one of her options. She said that because of the Depression, missionary salary, and already having her brother in medical school, she gave up the dream of medical school. She then began investigating nursing schools where she could put to use her academic learning with her nurses training. Therefore, she enrolled in the Stuart Circle School of Nursing at the College of William and Mary Richmond Extension in Richmond, Virginia.

After receiving her RN (registered nurses) degree, she realized her mother really needed this "noise maker" to care for her. Her mother was missing Brazil and her Brazilian lady friends. At the same time, there was a need for a nurse at the county hospital in Laurens, South Carolina. She could work and still be at home with her mother. She said, "The combination was a good choice, and I was able to pay off my college debt."

One day a letter came to Skip from the American Red Cross Emergency Service requesting her to get a release from her job in the local hospital and make herself available to the Army Nurse Corps. It was during World War II, and there was a great demand for more nurses.

On January 15, 1941, Skip reported for duty at Fort Bragg in Fayetteville, North Carolina, and became Second Lieutenant Mary E. Langston, N-T26-097. Their nursing quarters at Fort Bragg were some of the original barracks, with large rooms and iron cots. Later they moved into the Contonment building that had thirty beds to a ward. Then Skip was sent overseas. On April 29, 1943, her unit sailed from New York with the Fifty-fifth Station Hospital. Ten days later they landed in Oran, North Africa, where they set up camp in a staging area known as Goat Hill near Algeria. That was her first experience in living in tents with eight nurses to each tent with water rationed (one quart daily). That one quart of water was to be used for drinking, bathing, and washing clothes. All this was to be done using their helmets.

It was at Goat Hill where she got her first taste of war in the form of an Air Raid. After eight days, orders came to pack up, load up the trucks, and roll out. They ended up at a train station. She said, "This was our introduction to the French 40-8 trains, forty horses and eight men. The only thing left on the train were fleas and plenty of them." She went on to say, "This train had one outstanding feature. Its brakes were not worth a hoot. We discovered this when the train gained speed going down an incline, completely out-of-control."

They arrived in the Arab holy city of Kairowan. By now, war was becoming more real. Their "Fifty-fifth Station Hospital" was set up in a badly bombed-out building, and they also used tents. She said, "Soldiers came to us proud of their jumping boots and clinging to their helmets." There, Skip's noise making came in the form of singing for the chapel services. One day, as she was singing, they heard planes overhead, the sounds they knew all too well. Those planes were carrying many men jumping into combat. Yet Skip continued to sing and pray.

Later that day, they were notified that they must prepare for a large number of casualties since a serious mistake had occurred, and the navy had opened fire on its own planes. Immediately they started setting up thirty beds to each tent to accommodate the wounded. They heard the roar of vehicles in the distance, jeeps and trucks driving very fast toward them and stopping at the receiving deck. She said, "All personnel moved quickly, lifted stretchers with bleeding soldiers and assisting those who were able to walk to the hospital. That night 114 wounded men were brought on stretchers and placed end to end on the floor to be moved into surgery as soon as the surgical staff could take them." She remembers how nurses on their knees went from patient to patient, giving aid and medication for over thirty-six hours straight. When they could take a break, the nurses would take turns going to clean up and change their uniforms, eat on the run, and then return to continue taking care of the wounded. She said, "Sleep could come another day or time. The hospital capacity had been 125 patients and already it was almost full, and now with this sudden large increase of patients we set up double-decker bunks wherever we could."

Kairowan was home for Skip until November 10, 1943, until the monsoon rains and storms hit suddenly and with tremendous force. The place became flooded quickly. Off came their shoes, and they waded barefoot around packing equipment, discharging or sending patients to a drier place for a hospital. This sudden move took them to the staging area in Brizertia, Tunisia, where they stayed eleven days in the rain and mud, with dripping tents and boredom…. Just waiting! Finally, orders came for them to leave North Africa and head for Toranto, Italy, via the Bay of Bari.

At Toranto, Skip and her unit of nurses boarded a beautiful white hospital ship with the Geneva Convention Red Cross. They were reassured that they were now in safe territory but warned not to become too smug, since the Germans had their own plans. When enemy planes were spotted coming their way, they grabbed their helmets and backpacks, and over the side of the ship they went, climbing down a wiggly rope ladder and crawling onto open barges that were floating nearby. The excitement of the Italian fishermen grew more intense. About two feet from shore they were ordered to get off the barge and run to some trucks that were parked in an alley. They climbed into the trucks quickly, tied the side flaps down, and stopped talking. Two frightened young soldiers were driving the trucks when they heard a tremendous blast and flash of light. She said, "Our beautiful white ship was no more. Then softly, the hushed voices of the nurses were heard singing, 'Nearer My God to Thee.'" That was in December 1943.

The nurses were stationed in Sagezia, Italy, until August, 1944, and then moved to Leghorn, Italy, and then to Florence, Italy. She said that "While in Leghorn, as night supervisor, I had a religious experience. Rounds had been made, and I had double checked all the prisoner patients' tents. When I came out in the night, I heard the roar of an enemy plane hovering above. Bad Check Charlie, a frequent German visitor, was hovering over our area. It was soon obvious that this was not a random visit because a flare was dropped, lighting up the entire field with very white lights. I stood completely visible to the pilot of the plane, and my whole self was standing in the presence of my God and Maker. This was strange, but fear did not take over. Instead I had a sense of peace and affirmation that God was always near, caring for and protecting me."

Florence, Italy, was the city everyone came to love. R&R (rest and relaxation) came, and Skip spent time in Sorrento. She said, "Officers from the Ninety-first Division Headquarters were also assigned to Sorrento for R&R. Among them was a Lieutenant Colonel S. Julian Boyles." Skip and Julian became friends and kept in touch until the end of the war.

Skip spent a short tour of duty in Pisa, which she describes as "distasteful" because the patients were the army's "bad boys"—rapists, looters, and so on. The day soon came when Skip was to fly home. She left behind her brother and Julian Boyles. She described this as "a bitter-sweet farewell." Finally the war years were behind her. Her service in North Africa and in Italy included twenty-seven months of active duty in combat zones. She served a total of five years in the Army Nursing Corps.

Skip married that army officer, Julian Boyles, whom she had met in Italy. They had seven children, three daughters and four sons, including two sets of twins. However, one daughter, a twin, died as an infant. Julian died in 1985 after a battle with cancer. Her grown children have gifted her with seven grandchildren. One of her granddaughters said, "If I want to see my grandmother, I have to make an appointment because she is always so busy helping others." Skip's children and grandchildren are careful not to interfere with Skip's busy schedule. Nevertheless, she is always there when they need her.

Skip noted, "My children are all grown and now on their own. Julian's days on earth are over, and I am now eighty-nine years old, and

I am still being a 'noise maker' by singing with our Senior Singers at the First Baptist Church in Winston-Salem, North Carolina."

Skip Boyles has served in almost every position in her church at First Baptist, and with almost every age group. She has served on the Worship Advisory Committee. She has served as a deacon and the director of Women's Missionary Organization, a natural for a child born of missionary parents. She served as a volunteer visitor to the elderly, as a volunteer on the Food Services Council, and as a volunteer coordinator for the annual Blood Drive for the Red Cross.

In her community Skip has volunteered many hours for Habitat for Humanity, where she prepared and then served food on site. Not least in her volunteer work has been her efforts at Wake Forest Baptist Hospital Medical Center for the past twenty years, helping cancer patients in the Cancer Patient Support Program. She has already received recognition for five thousand hours of volunteerism. By now, she has probably accumulated close to six thousand hours. When one of her cancer patients dies, most of the time she attends their funeral, and has been heard to speak of them as if they were her own family members. *She cares!*

Skip has kept fit even in more recent years by doing aquatic exercises two to three mornings a week at the YMCA. She has also driven some of her older friends to participate as well. Skip is a volunteer with the Retired Army Officers Association, the Military Order of World Wars, and the Baptist Nurses Fellowship, which means that she is a liaison for missionary nurses who serve all over the world. Skip is an active member of the Alumni Association of her alma mater, Furman University and the Stuart Circle School of Nursing. Most recently she has become a member of the Red-Hat Ladies Society.

She has been an encouragement to the children of missionaries when they return to the States for their college education. Upon their reentry, these children of missionaries feel like foreigners in their parents' homeland. Skip knows how this feels and how much they need to talk to people who understand them. After all, seventy-three years ago she returned to the States and knew the frustrations of not being understood and accepted.

In 1997, a group of Skip's friends, fellow church members, colleagues and neighbors nominated her for the Jefferson Award that is presented each year by News Channel 12 in Winston-Salem, North Carolina. I now share with you some of the things they have said about Skip.

> Skip is an unassuming eighty-nine-year-old lady who has always adapted to the times and situations in which she has found herself. She has equally adapted those to her own needs; and more importantly, she has graciously helped to do so for many with whom she has come into contact. PAUL L. MCCRAW

> Her specific acts of services are many, but in my mind, what distinguishes Skip Boyles is her unwavering sense of optimism and contagious positive spirit which she not only demonstrates herself, but which she elicits from those around her.... When Skip accepts a task, she applies an energy and perseverance far beyond what one might expect from a woman of her age and small physical stature. JOANI R. HUGHES

> Skip is consistently loving, caring, understanding, giving, and hard working. She has excellent judgment and outstanding organizational skills. ANN RYDER

> One evening I was very sick and needed help. I called Skip, and she was at my home in a few minutes. She spent the night with me and part of the next day. She's my friend. WAVA HOWARD

> Recently, when I was afflicted with an unusual malady which necessitated many visits to doctors, labs, early morning tests, X-rays, etc., I was able to meet all those appointments, thanks to

Skip and her unfailing care and devoted attention. She drove me to my appointments and even stayed with me in order to drive me home. DOREEN GODDARD

Skip has a great motto: "Where there is a need, I try to meet it." TEDDIE MARTIN

Skip is strong in her belief that all people are special, important, and deserve an opportunity. THE LATE CLARA NORWOOD

I have been in awe of Skip's energy and stamina in relation to her service to others. Everything she does is connected with helping others. MARGARET POWERS

Skip is recognized for her endless energy, efficiency, and delightful sense of humor while carrying out her volunteer work. GROVER C. BURCHETTE

Skip Boyles is an extraordinarily loving, compassionate, and energetic volunteer. She brings her experience as a professional nurse and caregiver of a cancer patient (her husband, Julian, died of cancer in 1995). She has a gift for healing that was born out of her own distress and suffering that accompanied the death of her husband. However, she has reached out to others in our program for many years. She has demonstrated the capacity to grow from and give to others out of her own adversity. RICHARD P. MCQUELLAN, PH.D. | DIRECTOR OF PSYCHOSOCIAL ONCOLOGY & CANCER PATIENT SUPPORT PROGRAM, WAKE FOREST MEDICAL CENTER

The Cancer Patient Support Program offers psychosocial support to patients and their families and friends during diagnosis and treatment of cancer. For twenty years, Skip has acted as hostess in our Support Room. She offers each person a warm smile, a caring attitude, and a listening ear. For many of our patients, a trip to our Clinic would be incomplete without time spent with Skip.... Skip is a genuinely caring person who has gone though the cancer experience with her late husband. Her life experiences give her invaluable insights in the needs of patients and families. PAT DECHATELET, ASSOCIATE DIRECTOR | CANCER PATIENT SUPPORT PROGRAM, WAKE FOREST MEDICAL CENTER

Perhaps the greatest gifts she shares are her smiles and loving hugs. Somehow she always seems to know just the right time to give encouragement and share a hug.... Sometimes it is easy to forget that Skip is a senior citizen. GREG POWERS

Missionary Kids have made and are making a great contribution to their communities and to society in general. However, there are not a great number who have lived as long as Skip Boyles and who continue to make such enormous contributions to her church and to her community. To say the least, Skip has been a person who joyfully takes on numerous responsibilities and one who seems to enjoy all that she does. Her ministry to cancer patients for twenty years is remarkable in itself.

CHAPTER SEVEN

Challenges

Incompatibility

Edith is an adult MK from Nigeria. She had been married for twenty-five years. She met her husband, Bailey, in college. They have three children. The more recent years of their marriage had been filled with all kinds of difficulties and disharmony, with her husband going into a rage at the least provocation. Whereas they used to go to church as a family, he no longer attended church, while Edith continued to be faithful and sang in her church choir.

It seems that Bailey had been suffering from depression, but he kept denying it. One day when Edith returned home from work at 5:30, she found her husband still in bed. Edith felt she could not do anything "right" or please her husband regardless of how hard she tried. His agitation was affecting every member of the family. Often when he would be out of control and go into a rage, he would fake a heart attack. Edith would call 911 for an ambulance, and he would be taken to the hospital only to find out there was no problem with his heart. At such times, he was unreasonable and uncooperative.

In his unhappy state, he would try to do and say things that would humiliate his wife. Since he was not working, when he was not in bed, he would be on the computer. Edith was actually becoming fearful of her husband, but never feared that he would hurt their children. However, the children were becoming afraid of his bizarre behavior. Bailey's behavior seemed rather schizophrenic. It was believed that his mother was also schizophrenic. This kind of life was leaving everyone in the household confused as well as concerned.

When Edith came to see me for counseling she said, "Doris, I don't feel that I can go on living this kind of life. On the other hand, I do not want to be alone." I assured her that divorce would be better for her and the children if he was not willing or if he was not capable of change. She told me of a unique dream in which she was strapped in a chair with three straps across her body holding her down. How revealing of the actual situation in which she found herself. It became clear to Edith that her husband perhaps was not only suffering from depression but had a much deeper psychological problem. Of course, she had no idea how to help him even if he would agree to seek help, which was unlikely. She knew he would never go for help on his own since he denied that the problem existed. It was all Edith's fault, no matter what happened. Sometimes he would go out and come home in the wee hours of the morning with no explanation of where he had been.

Since Bailey had been sent away to boarding school in high school, Edith knew that he had felt abandoned by his parents. This was perhaps one among many consequences of living with a mother who was sick. At one point, Edith was thinking seriously of having Bailey institutionalized. At such times, he packed his things in his car and left, and would be gone for days.

Bailey decided that they did need to split up, and he felt it would be in the best interest of the children if they stayed with their mother. He would pay child support, although at this point he had no job. Both Edith and Bailey came to the conclusion that they would never be able to resolve their differences and problems. They were just too overwhelming for both of them. He admitted that his verbal abuse of Edith was never justified. All trust of each other had diminished. Contempt seemed to be the only mutual feeling they had for each other.

Bailey felt that Edith had undermined his authority as a parent, whereas Edith saw Bailey as being unreasonable in his demands of the children. He felt somewhat sorry for himself and neglected. His faking heart attacks no longer concerned Edith. He accused her of not having any compassion for him.

Then Bailey got the idea of changing his name, using his middle name instead of the given name by which he had been known for forty-plus years. His father and brother had switched their names in like manner in their later years. Bailey's constant talking about changing his name became a dissenting point that Edith never understood, and he could give no specific reason for wanting to do so.

Edith, who worked a full-time job, would come home from work and then take the children to their ballgames and practices as well as prepare supper for the family. When Bailey would go to the games he always arrived late, and he was upset because Edith would not leave the friends with whom she was sitting and join him, no matter where he chose to sit. At times, Bailey would then leave the game in disgust, saying that she was not sitting with the right kind of people.

Since Bailey was apparently making no effort to find a job, Edith's patience was wearing very thin. She was feeling more and more resentment and contempt for him. She admitted that he was right when he said that she was kinder to the family dog than she was toward him. Then they stopped talking, realizing that neither was listening. At one point, Edith told Bailey just how angry she was toward him. He accused her of a lack of basic human kindness toward him, and he let her know that he felt her contempt. The best resolution had occurred to both of them. The kindest thing they could do for each other was to separate. Then he would pursue the divorce.

Later, Edith discovered that not only was Bailey sent away from home to boarding school, but also that he had been sexually abused at an early age by two different older women. Therefore, Bailey had seemed terribly confused about his own sexuality. This, in itself, seemed to be chronic and associated with his abuse. This abuse also may explain why he had such difficulty with his own sexual partner, his wife. Other factors included his restricted upbringing, some disturbing family relationships, inadequate sex education, and his own unreasonable expectations. His anticipation of failure, his guilt and discord, the loss of attraction for his spouse, and his impaired self-image portrayed someone suffering from a personality disorder.

Nevertheless, both suffered from the dissolution of this marriage relationship. The children felt that the house seemed quieter and more peaceful after their father left. By living in this kind of situation for so long, Edith was now clearly suffering from depression. She was having anxiety attacks, and at one point she was afraid of losing control or "losing my mind." At times she felt completely helpless. She was also a perfectionist, especially when it came to her work in the office. She expected her colleagues to be as perfect as she was. This caused her a lot of stress and anxiety on the job. She described her co-workers as a dysfunctional family.

Edith was diagnosed as having major depression, single episode, and anxiety disorder. She readily agreed to take an antidepressant. Otherwise she was afraid she would become dysfunctional and perhaps lose her job, which she could not afford to let happen. She began to improve within two weeks. Her husband had left the state, which relieved her of a lot of anxiety. Edith was a beautiful person who had her plate full. However, she managed to continue her work and care for the children as well. They appeared to be very close to their mother, and somehow knew they could trust and depend on her.

So many unusual marriage problems often seem to raise their ugly heads when a MK marries a non-MK. Their total family and environmental backgrounds are so different. They have a really hard time understanding why each does things the way they do, never stopping to realize that a lot of it results from cultural differences. In trying to bring the two cultures together, often there are misunderstandings that just can't seem to be resolved. On the other hand, I have noted that when an MK marries another MK, regardless of the country in which they have spent the developmental years of their lives, there still seems to be a camaraderie and mutual understanding. I have observed that when MKs get together for retreats and other gatherings, they feel like they are with family, with brothers and sisters. This is a very unique kind of relationship. It is hard enough to create good marriages, and these young people bring some unique second cultural thinking to the relationship.

On one occasion when I was counseling with an MK wife married to a non-MK, her husband described what it was like when they went on automobile trips. His MK wife would get a map, study it, and write down "every turn in the road." I asked him if he would start out on a trip in her country not knowing anything about the geography, without studying a map? Suddenly, he realized that he didn't have to study a map when he went to her country because she knew her way so well that she was his guide. MKs are a group of wonderful people who have so much to offer people in America if they would care to listen.

What Went Wrong?

Virginia, an MK from Nigeria, came for counseling after reading my book, *Missionary Children Caught between Cultures*. At that time, she was a freshman in college, and she was dealing with depression. She felt a lot of confusion over her parents' separation and divorce. She described her parents as good, well-meaning people who became completely absorbed in the culture of the country where she spent the developmental years of her life. Her mother dressed conservatively in order to blend in with the women of that country. It was her way of trying to identify with them, but most missionaries know that, no matter how hard one may try, they will never be completely accepted as "one of them." They will always be seen as Americans.

At one point in Virginia's life, since returning to the States, she suffered from bulimia/anorexia nervosa. She remembered that she had taken on at a very early age more responsibility than she could handle. This had made her life complicated. So often, she felt helpless and out of control. Swahili happened to be her first language and English her second language. Being a young child she often could not distinguish one from the other. In Nigeria, the family moved often, from one rented house to another.

Being a college freshman in the States was not easy for her. So much of the time she felt she was living in a fantasy world. Some issues with which Virginia wanted me to help her were her unrealistic expectations of others, her lack of trust, her anger, and her seemingly growing lack of respect for authority. She was feeling a lot of disillusionment. She felt misunderstood and disappointed with life in general. Here, she and her siblings were trying to figure out what went wrong in their parents' marriage. It appeared to me that most of her issues came out of the break-up of her parents and losing her family as she had known it.

Virginia had a lot of difficulties with relationships herself. Being very pretty, she had no trouble attracting young men who wanted to date her. However, most of the young men Virginia dated felt that she had unrealistic expectations of them. They could never measure up. When each of these relationships dissolved right in front of her, she was asking the question, "What went wrong?"

Since she was dissatisfied with living in the girls' dorm, disliked her peers, and was unhappy with the relationships she had with the staff who were authority figures to her, she decided to move into a co-ed dorm on campus. Even though there were twenty-nine guys in that particular dorm, she never had a steady boyfriend. This was a big disappointment to her. She had had good conversations with several of them, and they had watched movies together, but her male friends never asked her out for a date, and there had never been any physical contact or affection shown toward her. She had a thirst for being alive and free. She could see beauty all around her, but could not understand why she only had worries and fears.

Seldom do missionary couples separate and get divorces. When that does happen their children become quite disillusioned. They think, "I know this happens to couples, but how could this be happening with my parents who served several years as missionaries, trying to share God's love with a people in a different country? This just can't be happening to me!" After all, she and her siblings had been taught great values, had lived around Christian missionaries and national Christian pastors. If this could happen to her parents, what could she really trust to be permanent in her life? Her parents' marriage problems had been kept a secret from her. She didn't know about it until they returned to the States. One night her parents called the children into the room and told them they didn't love each other any longer, so they were getting a divorce. The children had thought their parents had been such good missionaries. They had studied the language and culture with such enthusiasm, and they had known and followed the customs. They had appeared to be committed to the work they were doing and to each other. What went wrong?

Too often, missionary parents eagerly give all they have to witnessing and caring for the people to whom they have been sent, and then they have no energy left to give to their spouse and children. Perhaps some, especially the men, suffer from burnout. Then they begin to question their own religious beliefs, and some think, "Why should I be working so hard, when I am seeing few or no results?" Real disillusionment sets in. They become dissatisfied with themselves, their spouses, and even the responsibility of taking care of their children. Then it becomes easy for them to become attracted to someone of the opposite sex, and the first thing they know, they have become more deeply involved in what may have started out to be an innocent relationship. Then, of course, they start dealing with a lot of guilt. They find themselves in a real predicament.

Virginia's parents had been married for twenty-five years, and now they had teenagers, one in college and three other younger children. The parents were living apart. Her mother was now trying to find employment and seek a new career in order to support herself. Each member of the family was feeling out of place, and particularly the children felt displaced. Fears of the children were, "Who will pay for my college education?" "What will happen to me?" "Where do I belong?" "Did I cause my parents to divorce?" "Where will I live, with my mom or dad?" Everyone was suffering from deep emotional pain. Virginia felt sad, negative, and full of anger. She could not think straight and was becoming more and more depressed. Just being back in America had triggered all kinds of issues, such as separation and loss, feeling different and having different values, culture shock, and feelings of alienation. Now her pain and suffering included the issue of her parents' divorce. Needless to say, she did feel some embarrassment when people asked her about her parents. How would she answer all the questions? Virginia was trying to adjust to her many losses, to this strange and different culture, to living in America, and to coming from a broken home.

Perhaps Virginia's extreme conservatism, the same as her parents, was partly what caused her not to be able to connect with the youth in America. The men liked her as a friend but not as a potential wife. It created problems in almost all of her relationships. Virginia, nevertheless, was doing the best she knew how. She was forced to reevaluate her own faith and beliefs, all that she had been taught by her parents. It was going to take time to confront her own preconceived biases and prejudices, but Virginia was now questioning the reality of it all.

Virginia had been fluent in the language in Nigeria, and now she was trying to get used to hearing and speaking only English. This, in itself, was a real struggle, and it made her feel even more different from her peers. In her culture shock it was hard for her to distinguish between what was real and what was fantasy.

Needless to say, Virginia had good reason to feel depressed. I made her an appointment with a good psychiatrist for evaluation. She went to see him right away, and he put her on an antidepressant. At first, she did not want to take the antidepressant, feeling she could "beat this" on her own. If she had enough faith, then she should be able to pray and get through all this by her own effort.

Virginia and I spent many sessions in therapy, and through many tears she was able to express her anger and other feelings. Within a couple of weeks of taking the medication, she was able to concentrate, and we were able to accomplish much more in each therapy session. She was able to continue her studies at the college. Life will not be easy for Virginia for a long time. She will never be completely American. My prayers have been that she will begin to feel more comfortable with her living situation as she continues to make many adjustments.

What went wrong? Perhaps she will never know the answer to that question. The question now is, "Where do I go from here?"

Discovering Interdependence

Eloise, a female MK, made an appointment and came to my office for her first therapy session. I immediately liked her, perhaps for one reason: she was so open and willing to be vulnerable. She wanted help and was willing to work as hard as it took. She had been left in the States to live with an uncle and his family as a senior in high school. To be left in the States with people she barely knew was really scary for Eloise. Even among blood kin, she felt different and was very lonely. Therefore, when a certain young man expressed interest in her, she began dating him on a regular basis. At first, he seemed to be the perfect gentleman. She thought she was in love and, at the same time, was looking for a place to belong. They dated for a little over a year, and then Eloise dropped out of college during her second year to marry this young man.

To her chagrin, soon after they married, he became verbally, emotionally, and physically abusive. At times she was terrified of him. She never knew what kind of mood he would be in, not only from day to day, but from hour to hour. She began to feel that he might really harm her. She also found out that he was on drugs, which partially explained his "weird" behavior. While Eloise was in high school she had smoked cigarettes, and she did try speed once. When she was in college she had also smoked marijuana once. She had been exposed to crack cocaine, hashish, and acid, but she never would partake of them since she was smart enough to know that they could really be harmful and habit forming.

The main issues with which she was dealing were low self-esteem, anger, rejection, fear, guilt, shame, rebellion, insecurity, lust, and terror. She had no idea what to do with her sexual feelings. The big issue was her marriage. She had a deep need to be loved, and at the same time, she was fearful of becoming dependent. After several sessions, I asked her to invite her husband to come to see me. I experienced him to be completely controlling, and he expected Eloise to do everything he told her to do. Eloise, this independent young MK, just could not comply with his wishes and his commands. The marriage ended in divorce.

Eloise remembered, as early as the second grade, that some of her emotional needs had been neglected. Also, because she wore eyeglasses, other kids made fun of her. At that early age, she got the idea that she could not be loved for who she was. She also had needed her father's attention, but as a missionary, he was always, it seemed to her, away from home "doing God's work." Now, she felt that her husband's grandmother was blaming her for his use of drugs. She had always refused to get caught up in controversy. She just wanted to fix things when they were broken. Now she was learning that she could not fix everything. She felt a lot of confusion about what was the right or proper thing to do. Like most MKs, she felt very responsible.

When it came to religion, she felt a lot of confusion, mostly with Christianity versus the Muslim religion. She wanted peace in her heart, but just couldn't seem to find it. In seeking this peace, she pushed herself—doing, doing, and doing things for other people until she became exhausted. She said, "I would push until I dropped." Perhaps this was her way of seeking approval and acceptance by others. She agreed. She was so stressed and irritable, and she felt as if she were going around and around in a vicious cycle. She began to realize that a lot of resentment was building up inside of her. She felt she could not do some things simply because she was an MK. She thought she had to be a perfect Christian example.

In high school, Eloise had tried out for the basketball team, but soon she realized or was told that she had not been in that high school long enough. This caused her to feel unworthy. She said, "At times I felt plain weird." "Weird" is a word that lots of MKs have used to explain their feelings at certain times since they had been back in the American culture. They felt different, and at that time, they thought they could never be accepted in this culture.

Eloise was suffering from depression. Here she was: a high school senior, left by her parents who returned to the mission field. She was living with relatives she hardly knew. She had dropped out of college to marry a man whom she thought she loved, and it had ended in separation and a divorce. With all these things occupying her mind, she was often distracted when driving her car. She had four car accidents, totaling three of the cars, but fortunately she only received scratches. She even said that she had had premonitions about the accidents before they actually took place.

She recalled that at the age of six, she had a recurring nightmare where she was being ambushed by soldiers, who were killing and cutting up bodies of people. This fear was created very early and continued to follow her even into adulthood. Eloise had always yearned for the day when she would have someone to protect her, but now, instead, she had a husband who was abusing her. It seemed that most of her struggles showed up in her dreams. Her husband had told her what hours she could work, and what hours she could not work, wanting her to be at home whenever he was at home, which was unrealistic for the kind of work she was doing. He was sarcastic, and "he put me down." This kind of treatment had just about destroyed her already-harmed self-esteem. She said, "All I needed from my husband was his acceptance." Although he had told her he no longer "smoked pot," she discovered that he was only lying. He lied about many other things as well. She knew she could no longer trust him. One of Eloise's greatest values was honesty.

Eloise's resentment continued to build until she told her parents about how her husband was treating her. She told them how he would "jam her against the wall, jerk her around, and his general lack of self-control." Her parents did not believe in divorce, but when they saw how badly she was hurting, they suggested that she leave him, which she did. The first time Eloise came to see me, she was miserable and desperate. It was time to get a divorce and move on with her life. Once she made that decision, she felt some amount of freedom. However, she did move out while he was at work. She felt she had no one to turn to who could really understand her. She was just plain tired of being abused. It was time for her to take control of her life. I assured her that I would be her advocate. When she asked me what she should do, I hesitated, because it was not really my style as a therapist to tell individuals what they should do. Rather, I asked her what she thought she should do. She said, "Leave him." I replied, "Then do it!" When it came to her personal safety, it was time to leave him. Even though he tried to get her to come back to him, she told him, "Enough is enough."

Eloise was now free. She could pursue the career she had wanted. Eventually she dated other young men, but she had become somewhat skeptical and was now cautious. After a couple of years she met a very fine young man who was gainfully employed and who even owned his own home. As time went by they fell in love. Since Eloise had such a bad marriage, she wanted to bring this new man in her life to talk with me. This new man in her life had never been married, and he was quite independent. I told Eloise if she did not work through the problems she had in her first marriage, she would only take them into a second marriage. I reminded her that in a second marriage, her husband may do or say things that would remind her of her first husband's behavior that she strongly disliked. Thus, she would be responding to him like she had with her first husband. She must remind herself that this man was not her first husband, but he was a different person. I warned her to not project on him the behavior from her first husband. I therefore began seeing each of them separately in counseling and then together.

One fear that I often heard MKs verbalize throughout my years of counseling was their fear of being left alone, no matter how good their marriage seemed to be. "Being left alone" is a real MK issue. The separation and loss they feel from leaving their home, family, and all that was familiar to them when they returned to the States is so powerful that it would continue to affect some of them for the rest of their lives unless they entered therapy and worked through that fear. When their parents leave them in the States and return to their mission field, MKs often feel abandoned. When an MK lives in dread of a spouse leaving, that old feeling of abandonment and fear causes great unrest.

Some of the issues that Eloise and her new love had to discuss were communication skills, how to listen, and how to be open and honest with each other. Each wanted to know that they would always come first in each other's life. We worked for months on these issues. One thing that her new love had to change was the way he had always consulted his parents first about problems that arose in his life. Eloise let him know that she wanted him to continue to seek his parents' advice, but to please discuss things with her first. She saw this as being real partners in marriage.

At first, it really bothered Eloise when her new love, whom we will call Harry, did not always include her when he wanted to meet with some of his guy friends. At first, she took this as "not caring about me." Sometimes he would go out with his friends and not tell her what time he would be back, which bothered her. Harry was in a band, and he never could be sure when he would return home. In this way, he was continuing to live his bachelor life. At times she felt he was simply ignoring her, but as time went by we dealt with these issues, and they both were able to sort out things and communicate their own needs with each other. Some negotiation had to take place.

Eloise and Harry would need to tell what they expected from each other if they indeed planned to get married. The unspoken expectations would cause them the most trouble. When they each would forget their promises to let each other know about their plans and expectations, they would get defensive, feel hurt, and then become angry. I stated to them that when they did feel anger, they should stop and think about what they felt before they felt anger. Anger is never a first feeling, but it comes second to feelings like rejection, being ignored, or even "put down." For Eloise, that first feeling was fear. Both worked very hard, and when they left my office they were exhausted. Because they really did love each other, they persevered. Harry never refused to come to counseling with Eloise.

Eloise had grown up going to church every Sunday, but for some time, Eloise had not gone to church. She had gotten out of the habit. But now she was feeling guilty. She wanted Harry to go to church with her, and he did, but events would come up for each of them that again distracted them from church attendance. They did learn to schedule time for themselves together and separately. Even with all this work, Eloise was feeling a lot of pressure and anxiety about when they should marry. She found she was not able to focus as she had before. She was not sleeping well, and her appetite wasn't as good as it had been. I noticed she was developing symptoms of depression. We caught this very early, and she started taking an antidepressant. She began to pull out of her depression in a couple of weeks.

When I asked Eloise what was most important in her life, she replied, "My faith, my husband to be, relationships, solitude, having fun, trust, being organized, and learning to be more interdependent rather that having to be independent or dependent." When I asked the same question to Harry he replied, "Life itself, my wife to be, our relationship, enjoyment, family, and honesty." So it appeared that they had worked through most of their issues and were now ready to make wedding plans. Fortunately, Eloise's parents were in the States on furlough. Therefore, they asked her father to officiate at their wedding ceremony. They realized that after the wedding they must still work on their relationship on a daily basis for a lifetime if they wanted to be really happy. They recognized that their family backgrounds were so different, with Eloise growing up in Egypt and Harry in the rural United States. They learned it would be to their best interest not to assume things but to check things out with each other. Basically, they had to remember that in marriage interdependence must take precedence over being too independent or being too dependent.

The Missionary Kid Syndrome

One day I received a desperate telephone call from a male MK. He was then thirty years old, married, and with one child. A second child was on the way. He owned his own home, and both he and his wife were professionals. They really seemed like the ideal couple and were living the American Dream. However, Mitch had grown restless, and he really could not describe the feeling nor why he felt this way. He said to me, "I have just left my wife and child, and my wife is expecting our second child in a few months." Mitch knew something was going on, but he could not identify or put his finger on it. He was carrying so much guilt, and he was so confused. Needless to say, his wife was in shock and asking the question, "What did I do or not do?" "Does Mitch not love me anymore?" "Could there be another woman in his life?" He declared to me that he didn't know if he still loved his wife or not. He thought he probably loved her but maybe was not "in love" with her. No, there was not another woman. The only one thing that he seemed most sure about was the fact that he just felt restless and unhappy. I asked him if he thought it was his wife's responsibility to make him happy. He didn't seem to be clear on that. He just knew he was not happy.

Mitch and I talked about the meaning of happiness. He began to realize that happiness must come from within him, and he should not expect his wife to hand over that happiness to him. He queried, "But she can add to my happiness?" I agreed, and he could admit that he did have feelings of love for his wife. Then, I said, "Mitch, I think you are suffering from what I have come to call 'the MK Syndrome.'" He quizzically replied, "What in the world is the MK Syndrome? I know we MKs have some pretty unique issues, but I have never heard of the MK Syndrome." I told him I had never heard of it either, but it was a conclusion and a term that I had personally created after watching several MKs, particularly males, describe to me what he had just described. Then I explained what I meant.

I started by telling him I saw the syndrome less in females than I had in males. I asked if he had noticed that about every four years he found himself getting restless. He thought a moment, and said, "Yes, that's about the time span." I then shared with him the story of one MK who said to me, "About every four years I really get restless, and I want to go somewhere, *anywhere*. It does not matter how I might travel, by plane, by train, by car, or by bus. I just know I don't understand why I have to experience this restlessness."

Then I helped him see how, being a MK, he was really set up to experience such restlessness. Every three to four years, as he was growing up, he and his family moved back to the States for a year of furlough, and then after a year they went back to their adopted country.

There was lots of excitement in their travels. Mitch's eyes lit up, and he said, "So now it is time for me to go back to the mission field or travel somewhere. It's time to move again. The furlough is up, it's time for me to do something exciting again." Also, many MKs with their families moved around a lot on the mission field. They moved from one place and one house to another. In some cases there is very little stability when it comes to where they live. Incidentally, Mitch and his family had lived in three different cultures other than the American one. I said to Mitch, "So, I believe you are suffering from the MK Syndrome. Four years have passed, and it is now time for you to move again. But you are now an adult with a family. You are thirty years old. You can't go back to your mission field, but you are anxious to go somewhere." As I spoke Mitch shook his head, "Yes, yes." Now he was beginning to understand the reason for his restlessness.

I told Mitch, "I want you to take a vacation by yourself for two weeks, all alone. I want you to go anywhere you choose, and I want you to think about your total life, past, present, and future. Take a look back at every four-year interval of your life. Remember all the good times as well as the unpleasant times. After two weeks, come back to see me, and let's talk about your experience." He agreed to do this. He said, "I believe we are on to something here."

A short time after Mitch returned from his two-week vacation, I had a telephone call from him. I could tell by the sound of his voice that he had lots he wanted to tell me. His spirits seemed lifted. He came in, and right away, Mitch said, "Doris, I took the two weeks off and drove out West, took my time, and did a lot of thinking. I am back now, and I know that I do want to be with my wife and child, and now I feel excited about the coming of our second child." He went on to say, "Yep, you were right, I was suffering from the MK Syndrome." We both laughed, talked, and celebrated his new understanding. He fully realized now that he had almost lost the most important people in his life. Mitch continues to enjoy his life, his work, and his family. I do suspect that he will plan a trip about every four years in the future, but the best part is that he will understand if he grows restless.

Some time later, Mitch and I had the opportunity to spend time discussing his past history as an MK. Mitch was the youngest of four siblings. He had lived in three different countries and cultures. Each place was very different culturally, socially, and geographically, and with regard to the language spoken. Mitch remembers being the little squirt to his older siblings. He remembers his mother rocking him to sleep in a large rocking chair. Whenever his dad "had enough of me and my siblings, and our noisy, disruptive behavior," he remembers his father "pulling off his belt." This sent everyone scampering, but they most often had to bear some of the stripes of the belt anyway.

In the second country, Mitch remembers being very lonely since all his older siblings had left home for boarding school or for college in the States. The boarding school happened to be five hundred miles from their home, so his siblings did not come home very often. He did have good memories of talking and sharing a lot with his mother. He did acknowledge that in the second country where they lived, his father seemed to be under a lot of pressure, and often he would "blow up" at home, and he often yelled at Mitch's mother. Mitch was perplexed at his father's show of anger. He went on to say, "Americans think pastors and especially missionaries are next to angels, that there is some kind of hierarchy when it comes to people being closer to God, and they should never make mistakes." I agreed that his summation was true, and we need to see that all are imperfect humans, whether it be Mother Teresa, Billy Graham, or Pope John Paul.

There were times when his dad was so frustrated and angry and his yelling became so bad, Mitch could hardly wait to leave home. He wanted to leave as soon as possible. But then they moved, the three of them, to the third country where his parents served as missionaries. In that third country, Mitch had grown up enough to want to "do my own thing." He wanted his parents to let him grow up without each night asking him if he had brushed his teeth or washed behind his ears. In the first two countries, there had been lots of Americans, but in this last one, it was completely different. He said, "We lived in the boondocks." He remembers lots of isolation when it came to being near a lot of other people. However, Mitch has good memories about Mission Meeting, when all the missionaries in that country came together for a week of business and fellowship once each year. He remembers the great times he had being with other MKs.

As mentioned before, for that particular country, furloughs came once every four years, when they would return to the States for one year of rest, replenishing, and sharing with churches about their work on the mission field. Mitch always loved coming to the States and seeing his siblings, but he was always eager to return to his mission country.

Then Mitch shared with me some of his thoughts on religion. He could readily say that his own religious beliefs are much more liberal that those of his parents. Yes, he had had his mental battles, running from Christian liberalism to agnosticism. At that time, he said, "Still, I am not very steady as far as sticking with something for any length of time." He said that even in college his thoughts about religion were different from those of his peers. He continued, saying, "I've always had a bit of rebel in me, and unfortunately I sometimes switch to different positions just because everyone else seems to be against it."

When it came to having roots in a definite place, Mitch said he felt as much at home now in America as he had in the other three countries where he had lived. He said, "I don't think I'll ever have a complete sense of belonging in America, or for that matter, overseas, because I have been split in two or three culturally." One thing was sure, Mitch did not feel like a "full-blooded American." In all, Mitch lived outside the United States for fourteen years.

Most MKs, like Mitch, confess that their parents never talked to them about sex. Once back in the States, Mitch found himself volunteering to do some work for Planned Parenthood, which had a program geared to helping parents talk to their children about sex. He felt some empathy for his parents because he presumed that their parents never offered them any sex education. He did discover that many other MK friends were also ignorant when it came to knowing much about sex. However, he was able to glean some facts from some of his MK friends whose parents had taught them about sex from an early age.

After discussing many issues with Mitch, I asked him to state one thing he had learned during our sessions together. He said, "Now, I know the meaning of the MK Syndrome. I will share this new bit of information with my MK friends, and others who will listen."

CHAPTER EIGHT

Good Enough

I Did My Best

Josh, a fifteen-year-old male MK, had returned to the States because he was having more than usual struggles with his course work in school. He grew up in Nigeria with his missionary parents who served there. Now they were taking an emergency leave from their work to get help for their son. Josh was very suicidal, due partly to sheer discouragement from not being able to keep up with his classmates at school. I really admired Josh's parents, who clearly let it be known that Josh was their first priority. Their missionary work would remain second to Josh's needs. Josh had a history of learning disabilities, but more recently, he showed symptoms of depression, and he had lots of anger.

Earlier I had received a phone call from his family in Nigeria and also a phone call from their mission board, telling me of Josh's urgent need for therapy and possibly the need for antidepressants. Within a couple of days they arrived at my office. First, I noticed that Josh just did not feel good. Perhaps he was suffering from jet lag. Not sure of that, I told him that it appeared to me that he was not feeling well. He told me that he had a sore throat. As his parents and I looked in his throat, I said, "That looks like strep throat to me." When we finished our session, I walked with him across the street to the hospital. We saw an ear, nose, and throat specialist. The doctor confirmed our belief that he did have strep throat. He was given medication and told to get lots of rest and drink plenty of liquids.

The next week, he and his parents returned to my office for their second appointment. I first saw the three of them together and then spent more time with Josh alone. He began to tell me about his depression. When asked if he had thoughts of hurting himself, he replied, "Yes." I detected that he had a lot of anger and mentioned it to him. Then he began telling me about how, in one class, he was to write an essay. He had stayed up most of the night working on it. Later, his parents found copy after copy of his essay wadded up and thrown into his wastebasket. He just couldn't seem to get it right. In the wee hours of the morning he finally finished his essay, felt good about it, and went to bed.

The next morning when he handed his essay to his teacher, the teacher looked at it, crumpled it up, and tossed it in the trash basket. This action devastated Josh, who had stayed up practically all night, did his best, and this is what his teacher thought of his best. He went home from school that day and went to his room where he sat in utter darkness. He felt he had reached the end of his row. He saw no hope in improving his work at school. He kept saying to himself, *I did my best.* Josh just wanted to die. He was attending the Christian school associated with their mission where he had attended since kindergarten. Is this the way Christians should act? If this was the way he was treated in a Christian school, how would it be to attend a non-Christian school? He decided a non-Christian school might treat him better.

I experienced Josh as a very warm, healthy, affectionate fifteen-year-old boy. He was five–feet-seven and attractive. He had smiled a lot, but not lately. He had many friends back in Nigeria. His parents described him as fun, creative, observant, and with a real sense of humor and a great personality. However, since all his disappointments at school, they had watched their son become quiet, not laughing anymore, and withdrawn. He wanted to spend all his time in his dark room. They wanted their son back with his great personality.

On a more recent furlough Josh had been tested, and the test revealed that he had several learning disabilities. The teachers at the school in Nigeria had made efforts to adapt Josh's education to recommendations derived from his assessment. It seems that the school really didn't have a special class or teachers who knew how to meet Josh's needs. Thus, his spring semester was very frustrating for him. Although his grades had been acceptable, he had become more and more frustrated and overwhelmed. Over the next semester, his parents saw no improvement, and now he was suicidal. His parents knew it was now time for them to bring Josh back to the States and "find some answers" to their son's problems and needs, especially in regard to his depression and his education. They had watched long enough, seeing their son become angrier and angrier, more withdrawn, and demoralized as a result of his stress and pressures.

Josh had expressed his feeling that his teachers, with the exception of one, had been "hard on me," and that made it hard for him to feel good toward his other teachers. Therefore he stopped trying to get along with them. He felt they were not flexible and were more demanding of him than he was capable of accomplishing. At the same time, he perceived his classmates as having little trouble with their class work. He was struggling so hard to do B and C work, but he was giving up. It seemed hopeless. He struggled with reading comprehension. When he failed the test in that course, his teachers often accused him of "goofing off."

Although Josh had a high IQ (intelligent quotient), he began to think he was not smart. He said, "I have the worst memory." He would forget his assignments and get scolded for not having his homework ready to hand to the teachers. Because he had long hair, he believed that he had been stereotyped by his teachers as being a rebel who was not interested in his schoolwork.

The test results showed that his most significant weakness was his short-term auditory memory. In his achievement test, he scored in the 85th percentile. In his performance IQ test, he was measured in the 95th percentile. Thus, he was performing below what would be expected of him by his teachers. Josh was above the average in abstract and social reasoning abilities as well as visual motor skills. You can imagine how frustrated and angry Josh was when he was told all these great test results, yet he could not seem to perform even to his own expectations. He had become more morose and apathetic. His school had given lip service to the idea of an individualized educational plan, but they had not put it into action. When his performance had not lived up to his own expectation, Josh's motivation and character were questioned. He was like a person standing on the edge of a cliff; it would take only one more disappointment to push him over, and he would fall through space that seemed bottomless. He felt his best efforts were wasted, and he began to identify with fellow students whose mental abilities and motivation were less than his own. His self-esteem was significantly damaged.

In working with Josh, I tried to help him acquire an understanding of his strengths and his weaknesses. I knew, and we all knew, that Josh had the capacity to be a happy, successful young man, and I encouraged him to work to that end. In order to help Josh get the most out of his education, I enlisted the psychologist who had administered his latest test. This psychologist was more than willing to go to Josh's new school nearby and talk with his teachers. This school happened to be well equipped with teachers who knew how to help him. The psychologist laid out a plan for his teachers, which they were happy to follow. He needed help in short-term auditory memory work. He needed help with written instructions, in order to complete his work. He did well with people one-on-one. He had excellent talent in drawing, copying, and reading, yet he was forgetful and had a hard time keeping his mind on his work. In other words, he was easily distracted. He would become bored easily. He did things unintentionally and impulsively, but was performing inconsistently. He demonstrated an awkward pencil grasp, which reduced his speed and efficiency for handwriting, resulting in having trouble finishing his work.

The psychologist gave the teachers at his new school in the States a list of modifications that he believed would be necessary to ensure adequate classroom performance and success for Josh.

- Be allowed to do makeup work with his resource teacher.
- Give him a study guide for test preparation.
- Do not penalize him for spelling errors.
- Give him extended time for major assignments.
- Don't scrutinize him too much.
- Give him reduced assignments.
- Let him give oral instead of written answers to questions.

He added, "Josh should be allowed to take tests and quizzes, allowing extended time, in a small group setting and with the use of textbooks, notes, study sheets as deemed appropriate by his classroom resource teachers. He could also benefit from computer-assisted instruction."

The teachers in Josh's new school were very sympathetic, and they put into practice the plan made by the psychologist. Guess what? It worked! Josh went on to enjoy his high school years. He made new friends easily with his big smile, and graduated without losing a year. Today, he is successfully employed and happily married. All this could happen, and Josh's life was changed because someone stepped forward to intervene for him. When Josh became productive and happy, his parents too were relieved and happy. Now, Josh and his parents had great hope for him and his future. His father later sent me a letter saying, "Doris, thank you for all you have done for us. The Lord placed you in our path for a very special purpose and you have been an instrument of His blessings. Thank you for being there and for the advice and guidance and counsel that you gave us during the time of great crisis in our family."

What a joy it was for me to watch this intelligent young man go from depression to being a happy individual. Since then he has brought joy to the lives of many people, those his own age and older ones as well. This happened because people cared and were willing to go the second mile for him. All that was done was bathed in prayers, while acknowledging the frailties that were found in one life. "Rejoice and be exceedingly glad."

Adopted but Not Adapted

Teresa, a seventeen-year-old female MK from France, came to see me with her missionary parents. They had suddenly returned to the States since Teresa was having some unique problems and struggles. Her presenting problems were that she had an uncontrollable drive to steal things and then to lie in order to cover it up. Teresa said that she had begun to isolate herself but did not know why. As she described this behavior, "I put myself in a box."

Teresa had begun to steal from her parents as well as from others. She said she did not feel guilty about it nor did she regret it when she stole from people, parents, or stores. When she felt she had gone undetected, she did feel some excitement and it gave her a high. In taking these risks she said, "I do sometimes scare myself." She lived under a premonition that something bad was going to happen to her. She expected only failure from herself. She lacked motivation in her schoolwork and in her personal life. She described herself as "living on the edge."

Even though Teresa was well liked by her friends, who found her to be funny, she did not feel popular. Her friends thought she was brilliant, personable, and admirable. Nevertheless, Teresa felt worthless and stupid, and had lots of anger toward her father. Then she felt guilty about having anger toward her father.

Teresa had spent most of her seventeen years outside the States in a country where her adopted parents served as missionaries. She was adopted when she was only a few days old. Teresa's biological mother already had one child when Teresa was born. Having her own problems with drugs and perhaps alcohol as well, Teresa's mother realized she could not take care of Teresa. Thus, she gave her up for adoption.

During her seventeen years, Teresa had lived with her parents in eight different places, including two countries and six states. She had attended nine or ten different schools. She always felt like the odd one out. She never seemed to stay in one place or one school long enough to feel that she belonged. In other words, the permanency that she needed in her life was absent.

At age seventeen she was in the stage of individuation. She was trying to individualize and discover who she was apart from her parents. Now she was back in the States. She had just about formed her identity in this other country and culture, but it just did not fit in the States. Now she was experiencing a lot of confusion as she tried to re-form her identity. One thing she did know was that she wanted to become her own best self. She wanted to become an interior decorator or an occupational therapist. She would also like once again to visit France, where she had spent some happy years of her life. She would love to graduate with her former classmates in France, with students who had known her best. However, she knew, due to circumstances, that was not going to happen.

The truth of the matter is that the entire family was going through a grief process because they had loved their adopted country, and presently the likelihood of their returning was nil. It appeared that the parents were angry at Teresa, and she was very angry at her controlling father who did not seem to understand or even try to understand his daughter and her problems. Teresa wanted her parents to trust her and realize that she wanted to work on reclaiming their trust. Her father clearly stated what he wanted from Teresa. He wanted her to stop stealing and lying. She was hurt and discouraged when he made the harsh statement that he was afraid Teresa would end up pregnant or in prison. This was very devastating to Teresa. Her father was stressed out because he could not "fix" his daughter.

Teresa seemed to have a good relationship with her mother. She knew her mother really loved and cared for her, and Teresa saw her as a good teacher. She was kind and fun to be with. She liked her backrubs, her smile, her laughter, and her originality. Her mother described Teresa as affectionate, liking her hugs, her goofy moods, her compassion, her freckles, her eyes, her smile, and her "cute little sneeze."

It bothered Teresa's mother since it seemed so hard for Teresa to share any affection toward her father. Sometimes she was persistent, annoying, selfish, and made a fuss about what her mother called "petty things." Teresa did not like her mother's overprotection. When something happened, her mother seemed to always blame Teresa. When Teresa saw her mother's tears, she felt so sad and helpless.

Teresa's father simply said that his greatest fear for Teresa was that she would end up as a prostitute on the streets. She would have a bad reputation and maybe even end up in prison. Can anyone imagine a father even thinking, much less saying these kinds of things to his daughter, adopted or not? It seemed he could only think about how people would view him rather than being deeply concerned for his daughter and her problems. The bottom line was that he wanted his daughter to change and meet his expectations without understanding the ramifications of her own pain and suffering. He wanted to look good, and he simply felt helpless. Thus, all he could do was strike out at her and blame her for all the family's problems.

As a toddler, Teresa had suffered a concussion with a brief loss of consciousness. As a small child she had correctional knee surgery. She had an impulsive control disorder, specifically kleptomania. She had also been diagnosed with attention deficit disorder with symptoms relating to inattention and impulsivity. She was easily distracted and had difficulty concentrating.

Teresa had problems with stealing and lying since she was age four, which had become progressively worse. Her lying and stealing technically would not be diagnosed as antisocial personality disorder. She simply had a temptation to steal that was too difficult to resist. All the items she stole were for her own personal use.

In counseling, Teresa made a contract with me to keep a log of every time and every place she was tempted to steal or lie. For three weeks she declared she had not had the urge or temptation at all. In class one day, a student left her handbag in an empty classroom. Teresa took it to a teacher, not even looking into the bag. She felt really proud of herself, and I commended her for such good behavior. This had been a perfect opportunity for her to take something, but she said she was not even tempted to do so. She said that one of her teachers had said something that had inspired her. "Every time you steal something from a shop or mall, the cost of things rise and everybody is required to pay more."

I fully believe Teresa had the will to not lie or steal, but basically she was out of control, sometimes more than others. My hunch is that the biological mother's participation in the use of drugs while carrying Teresa had left some irreparable damage.

I want to share here some things I have learned about the feelings and needs of adopted children. Usually they say, "When I was born I was given away." Often they feel rejected, not wanted, and not good enough. They often have a great need to have friends, to impress, to accomplish, to be loved, to receive praise, to be complimented, to know where they come from, to be trusted, and to feel comfortable with their adopted parents. Usually the time comes when they feel a need to find their biological parents, particularly their mother, in order to come to terms with their adoption. This is seen as unfinished business. They have a need to know their mother's face, to feel her touch, to hear the sound of her voice, and to let her know her child.

One adopted young man described what it was like to find his adopted mother, "It is like growing up with many of the threads of your being disconnected." Another said, "You have no idea where the parts nor where the whole of your being comes from." Finally, "Knowing you were rejected at birth leaves a dull ache that you can no longer mask." Some experience acute loneliness, helplessness, and even abandonment. On the other hand, there are some adopted children and adults who do not even want the subject of their adoption discussed or mentioned in any way.

Some questions adopted children ask are: "Who am I?" "How much of who I am results from my upbringing (adopted parents) and how much from the genetic code paired in my mother's womb?" "How did my mother come to give me up?" "What tragic circumstances surrounded my conception and birth?" Some are afraid of finding their birth mother because they are afraid of discovering something bad and would just rather not know. Others say that there are always two forces inside them pushing them forward in the search, and the other holding them back.

To my knowledge, Teresa never found her mother. However, when Teresa was given up for adoption, her mother wrote a letter to Teresa, left it with a friend of the adopted parents, and told them to give it to her when they thought she was ready to receive it. She discussed this with me and said that she felt she was ready. The person who had the letter had held on to it for seventeen years, and he sent it to her adopted parents, who in turn gave it to Teresa. One thing that greatly surprised Teresa was her mother's handwriting. She said, "You know, my mother and I write just alike." She was not sure if she wanted to go further in the search at that time.

I emphasized to Teresa how important it was to continue in therapy after they moved from my city. We discussed how her behavior could deprive her of some very good, pleasurable relationships. I encouraged her to take responsibility and stop blaming others for her problems. She understood that her persistence could work for her or against her. The road for Teresa may be rough and rocky, but hopefully her persistence will help her to realize some of her dreams.

Understood and Empathic

When I met Vivian for the first time, she was a senior in college. Vivian was a beautiful young lady—vivacious and with contagious laughter. She had gone with her missionary parents to an African country when she was only two years old. Therefore, she had no memories of living in America. Her first memories were of Africa, which she always considered home. She heard her parents talk about America and what a wonderful place it was, yet she could not even imagine what they were talking about.

When she and her family returned to the States four years later, she was six years old. Can you imagine what her perception of America was really like? She saw mostly white people whereas in Africa she saw mostly black people. She actually felt more comfortable with blacks than she did with whites. Everything in the States was so different. They spoke a different language. They dressed differently. Their church services were really different. She thought church services in America were really boring, because in Africa, there was lots of singing, beating of drums, dancing to music, and raising of hands toward the heavens. However, she really enjoyed the difference for a year. She enjoyed all the gifts and attention from her grandparents, all the fast-food restaurants and ice cream parlors, but after one year, she was ready to go home. Her very first year of school in America went well.

When they returned to Africa, Vivian was sent away to boarding school. She was so homesick! She had grown up in a home filled with love and had a real sense of security. Now her sense of security was really shaken. She was so miserable. Her parents went to see her since she was having so much difficulty adjusting to her new environment. They said to her, "If you want to leave boarding school it will be all right. You come first in our lives, and our work comes second. If we need to return to America, we will do that. We will do whatever you want us to do." What a big decision for a little girl to make. After all, Africa was home for her, and to return to the States would be like going to a foreign country. She loved her parents, and she loved Africa, and she wanted to stay in Africa. However, what was most important to Vivian was to hear her parents tell her that she was more important to them than being missionaries. She agreed to try real hard to adjust being away from her parents.

Vivian had missed the structure in her family life at home. When she and her siblings went home for holidays and summer vacations, they had to be out of bed and at the breakfast table at seven in the morning in order for the whole family to be together at the beginning of the day. Her father read a portion of Scripture and prayed before they ate. Vivian really did not like getting up so early. After all, this was her vacation and she wanted to sleep late for a change. Her dad would go off to work, and other family members did whatever they chose to do. Although she was glad to be at home with her parents and siblings, she did admit she really missed her classmates at school because they had become her family as well. One of her memories about going home was on the first day back, her mother always prepared spaghetti, her favorite food, for dinner.

Vivian's social life was mostly relating, playing, talking, and studying with other MKs at boarding school. She remembered that for about two years, she was the only girl in her class. Even today, she says she feels more relaxed talking to guys than she does to girls. Time did pass very quickly, and before she knew it, it was time for them to come to America where she completed her senior year in high school. Her parents were in the States with her that year, which was very comforting, and it gave her some time to become a little more adjusted to Americans and their "funny ways."

After she graduated from high school, her parents went back to Africa. Then she felt so alone and lonely, even more than she had when she went away to boarding school. However, her first semester in college was really good. Everything was new and different in college. It would be exciting as she could meet new people and start her new curriculum of studies. She said, "This was the first time for me to be completely on my own." She had heard someone say that it takes two years to get used to a new place.

In her sophomore year, Vivian began missing her country and her parents more and more. She had relatives in America, but they lived in a distant state, not close enough to go to see often, or for them to visit her often. By this time she was suffering from culture shock. She found herself finding fault and criticizing Americans in general. She was critical of their materialism, and even their ideas about Christianity. She was asking herself the question, *Where do I really belong?* At one point, she said, "I felt like I was on the edge." I asked what she meant by the term "on the edge." She knew she was not coping very well and didn't know how long she could go on feeling this way without having a nervous breakdown.

Vivian did have an older sister in a college far away. Then her sister got married. They began to talk by telephone, and her sister tried to encourage Vivian. She had one good girlfriend, but she did not want to burden her with her constant talking and complaining. How could this good friend understand where she had come from anyway? In her lowest moments, she felt anger toward her parents for abandoning her in the States and returning to *her* home country. It just did not make sense. She did not think that even her parents could understand her predicament. After all, they had chosen to leave America and go to Africa, but Vivian didn't think she had a choice. From the time she was little, her parents were always saying, "Now, when you go back to the States for college…" Of course, when Vivian was in the midst of culture shock, she did not recognize it. When we talked about what was happening, she said she had heard people talk about culture shock but did not really know what it was or how it felt.

Vivian also had a hard time finding a church where she felt comfortable.

One thing she did know, she did not like Sunday school. Everyone in the classes seemed immature and not serious about their faith. In other words, they did not seem to take their Christianity seriously. At the same time, Vivian was having a struggle with her own personal faith, and she also had many doubts. She wanted to be treated just like anyone else. She had not expected to be recognized as special just because her parents were missionaries. On the other hand, in watching and listening to her parents, she believed that they did expect people in the States to treat them as special and provide for them. This was a little confusing for her.

She said that even as a child she knew about the "Missionary Barrel Syndrome." Americans who had outgrown or gotten tired of their old clothing would give it to a church, and when the missionaries came home for furlough, they were given some of these hand-me-downs. She said that this really was an insult, at least to missionaries and their children. One MK told me about watching someone giving her mother some hand-me-downs. She said her mother was very gracious and said, "Thank you," but never wore them. She said she couldn't help admiring her mother for her gracious spirit. Today, I think the missionary barrel has become obsolete. This MK said, "Thank God, we don't have to deal with that anymore."

Vivian expressed some sympathy for her older sister, who had taken a lot of responsibility for her and her younger siblings when they came back to the States for college. She said that even on the mission field when her parents went to meetings, her older sister was left in charge of the younger children. They were told to obey their sister. She loved her sister but said, "She is too responsible and bossy." Later, she saw her sister showing some resentment for all the responsibility that had been placed on her, especially when she had wanted to go to graduate school to get a master's degree. Her parents told her they couldn't really help her financially. This hurt her so badly that later when her parents sent her money from the mission field, she would put it in an envelope and mail it back to them.

Vivian had gone through many struggles and had learned a lot about herself and others. She met a young man and fell in love. The best part was that he was a son of missionaries. They would be married right after her graduation from college, which was only weeks away. He attended a state university. She said that he had gone through his rebellious period and for a while had nothing to do with the church. He was trying to individuate and find himself.

Vivian had found a good church, and it had become a vital part of her life. It was at that church where she had met her fiancé. Both Vivian and her fiancé kept asking themselves the question, "How in the world did our parents end up as missionaries?" However, neither had ever confronted their parents with that question.

Vivian remembers an occasion when she felt truly understood and found someone with whom she could really empathize. That was her grandmother. One day at college she received a telephone call, telling her that her grandfather had died. The next day, she flew to her grandmother's and found that her mother and sisters were already there. She remembers so well the sadness and grief of her mother and her grandmother. She did not know her grandfather very well, yet she felt a lot of sadness. Other family members had arrived. There was a house full of people. When the members started talking about where they would sleep, Vivian chose to sleep with her grandmother. She remembers how they comforted each other and cherishes that close feeling they shared. Vivian and her grandmother were identifying with their separation and loss. It seemed that her grandmother could empathize with her granddaughter in the loss of her country as well. After three days and nights, Vivian returned to her college campus and to her fiancé.

When Vivian and I spent time together, I sensed that this was the happiest time of her life as she was making her wedding plans. For her to find another MK to be her husband was really special, because they could identify in so many ways. They had each found their soul mate. They could understand and appreciate each other's life experience.

Creative but Not Creating

When I first met Karl, a male MK from Mexico, he seemed overwhelmed with the various issues that he was suddenly confronting. He was so tired from trying to "figure it all out" by himself. He was thirty years old and did not have a clue as to what he wanted to do with his life. He had gone from one job to another and from one relationship to another. In the meantime he was taking some college courses but was not enjoying his studies. He said to me, "For too many years I have felt lost in the labyrinth of America. But this year, I heard about Doris Walters, who was devoting her time in counseling the children of missionaries. I was impressed that she would make such a commitment to MKs. I called for an appointment. In no way could I have afforded to pay the high cost of counseling."

Karl was such a delight to counsel. He was very intelligent and handsome. He had a winning personality. He began to name some of his issues. He was aware that he was a "pleaser." This came from his fear of rejection. He was not financially independent, which troubled him a great deal. His perfectionism caused him to procrastinate. He could understand and admit that he procrastinated because he was afraid of failure. Karl was passive-aggressive and dependent at the same time.

Karl recognized that his father was handsome, eloquent in speech, and an intellectual man, yet he saw him as undisciplined and insensitive. He saw his father as needing more structure to his life. He had learned from his father that "it was bad to have too much money," but Karl never seemed to have enough to pay his bills. Somehow, Karl had gotten the message that he needed to be perfect in order to receive love and acceptance.

Karl's mother was dependent on Karl to the point that he was feeling like his mother's surrogate husband. Since his father was away from home a lot, one can readily see how his mother would come to depend on her son more and more. Due to Karl's lack of self-confidence, he felt out of control much of the time, which caused him to sometimes become immobilized. Yet when he was in charge, he found he could function well and felt more accepted.

Karl talked about the double messages he received from both of his parents. For example, they would say, "Karl, you are great just as you are." In the next breath they would often say, "You are not good enough." He heard them speaking out of their own theology. One message was that he must accept people as they are. However, the other message that came through to him was "but you need to be a Christian to really be good." They talked a lot about "us," meaning us missionaries, and "them" in referring to the nationals.

Karl felt that his mother derived her sense of well-being from her children and her husband. They gave her a sense of worth and self-esteem. She did seem to enjoy being recognized as the wife of a missionary. Karl often saw his mother unhappy and angry. She often made verbal threats and was judgmental. He picked up the double message that "men are good for nothing" versus "men are terribly needed." His mother felt her husband should provide more than he did for the family. Karl often experienced his mother as seeing the tasks of a missionary wife and mother as being distasteful, yet she felt compelled to do those tasks. This made Karl feel angry toward the mission board and the church.

As Karl lived with his family on the mission field, he said he sometimes felt embarrassed to have his national friends visit in his home. He was embarrassed and felt some guilt at his friends having so much less. He remembered feeling angry and unhappy a lot. Sometimes he felt as if he had no life. He also felt anger at not having a home, a place to belong. He had to please "in order to survive." In his anger he said to me, "Doris, I don't know who I am, and I have a hard time dealing with that." He also said, "I truly want to make a contribution to the world, but I also want to receive remuneration, feel financially secure, and I want to be respected." Since he was financially out of control, Karl felt weak, impotent, insecure, anxious, and afraid about his whole future. He recognized all these feelings but said that he had not learned how to integrate his knowledge and feelings into his life with his daily struggles.

Karl had some great values. He had learned to distinguish his own personal values from those of his parents, even though they also had some great values. He was sensitive, genuinely pleasant and kind, tolerant, honest, accountable, and fair, and he was well educated. He believed in justice and freedom for everyone. He understood "integrity," and he knew he must be true to himself. He did recognize that his set of values were at the core of his being. At one point, Karl wanted to be a physician, but being realistic, he recognized that he did not have the energy, commitment, time, or money.

As I listened to Karl expound about so many things, I recognized what I believed to be depression and perhaps attention deficit disorder. On several occasions during counseling, I said to Karl, "I believe you have two problems: depression and attention deficit disorder." However, he would just pass over my comments and move on to another topic.

Karl mentioned that he had also been "pushing against the spiritual." He knew what he ought to do but found it hard. Being an MK and growing up in a different country and culture, he felt he had missed out on so much, and he resented this. In all this, I urged him to be aware of his own humanity and that he would never be perfect.

At the age of thirty-two, Karl read *Further Along the Road Less Traveled* by Scott Peck. Karl had let his moral values slip and found out in so doing that he was sabotaging his own life. He was taking the most demanding courses in college, and yet he felt a lot of resistance and resentment. He lived constantly with the fear of failure. He was disorganized and undisciplined, and he even felt hopeless much of the time.

Now it was time for me to confront Karl as he continued to talk about his symptoms. He had a low energy level. He fantasized and did a lot of daydreaming. He was often unaware of the passage of time. He could not concentrate and found that it was getting tougher to follow through on his assignments and studies. He was also holding inside a lot of anger. He felt lethargic. He was just feeling awful. His relationships were short-lived, particularly with women. He had a fear of being entrapped in a male/female relationship. He wanted intimacy, yet he was fearful of it. In relationships with women he felt intense and uptight. This handsome, gentle, warm, intelligent man was depressed. I told Karl I felt it was time for him to see a psychiatrist in whom I had lots of confidence. Without hesitation, he agreed to make an appointment. He knew he had to do something or he would never finish his college work and get his degree.

Karl did see a good psychiatrist. After being on an antidepressant for a short time he began to feel much better, more energetic, and more able to complete tasks, and he found that he was more consistent. He was able to concentrate and began to enjoy things that he had not enjoyed for a long, long time. His relationships, in general, began to improve. Yet he was continuing to deal with his attention deficit disorder.

One day, Karl suddenly appeared in my office. Fortunately I was available for that hour. Enthusiastically, Karl said, "I just came from my psychiatrist's office, and guess what! Dr. G. says I have attention deficit disorder, and he has given me a medication that he thinks will help me." I smiled and waited. Then he said, "You have been trying to tell me this for so long, and I wouldn't listen, but when Dr. G. told me today, I heard him. Why did it take so long?" I responded, "I guess you were just not ready to hear it." This was a powerful awakening for Karl.

Week by week things got better and better for Karl. He was now working on his master's degree. He was able to do his class work but was still finding it hard to write his thesis. This was a young man who in the fifth grade tested close to being a genius. Finally his college professor allowed Karl to do a project with a company related to his thesis topic, which lasted for three months. He would keep a daily log of what he did and what he had learned from what he did. This he could and did do. He subsequently received his master's degree.

Karl and I worked on many of his issues, and Karl grew by leaps and bounds. He was still concerned mainly about finding a good woman, getting married, and having a family. At his age, it was time to be thinking seriously about this issue. He said, "Why do I need to love and be loved so much?" My reply was, "Because you are a human being." He learned that he had been "blocking," as he put it, "my heart from my head." He had paid more attention to his instinct that said "danger" when he was getting close in a relationship. He also learned that to love he must also take some risks. In a relationship he also learned that he had a deep fear of "losing himself" if he fell in love with a woman. In reading Thomas Moore's book, *Care of the Soul*, he said, "It was so great to realize I didn't have to continue feeling the way I did about being in a relationship."

Karl was now getting a sense of direction for his life. He was gradually tossing aside the excess baggage that had been holding him down. He realized that he, indeed, was creative, but he had not been creating. Now he was sleeping better, had more energy, was not agitated anymore, was less passive, was more focused, and could retain what he read. He came to another conclusion. He said, "You know, I believe my dad has always been depressed, but he just didn't know it, just the way I was." He was able to discuss this point with his father.

Finally, we began to pursue what he wanted in a woman who could become his wife. He wanted an intelligent woman, one who would be strong enough to be her own person, and one who would stand up for herself as well as "even call my hand on things of which I may not be aware." He wanted to respect and be respected. He wanted love and acceptance. He wanted to be able to see in her eyes, in her smile, and in her touch the love he so desperately wanted and needed. Fortunately, Karl found just such a person. He has now what he had longed for for so many years: a wife and a family. He continues to be creative. At this writing, he and his wife have a beautiful baby girl. I am convinced he is a good daddy.

Acceptance and Appreciation Needed

Pete is a male MK who had been back in the States for several years. He was still having a hard time trying to figure out his identity. The one thing he did know was that he was a mixture of two cultures. Now that he was living in the States, he still carried within his soul much of the culture of the country in which he spent all the developmental years of his life. That was home for him. In America, he often felt like a stranger. He had had some good years, working as a professional, but it seemed that all of his jobs were short-lived. At the time I saw Pete, he was employed, but he was actually overqualified for the job, which did not do much for his already suffering self-esteem. He even felt a lot of shame and humiliation as well as a lot of pain. He had married and had one child whom he loved dearly. He had strongly believed in living up to his wedding vows, but somehow had gotten off track and was suffering lots of guilt from cheating on his wife. He had good values but had violated them. He felt he had disappointed a lot of people, including his own family of origin. At this point, he had practically broken off all relationship with his parents. Besides all this, he was facing financial pressures and was in debt. His wife worked every day and was carrying the load of supporting the family. He had practically stopped believing in himself, feeling a complete failure.

Pete had made a commitment to his wife, but a big part of him wanted to be free from that commitment. He talked about being bored. He was looking for some excitement and was ashamed to admit that he had a desire to be with other women. His sex life with his wife was nonexistent. He was intimidated by her religious commitment and dedication to the church and to Christian living. He described her religious beliefs as "pure child-like beliefs." He did not like her walking around the house singing hymns. A part of him wanted to be free, but a larger part wanted to remain in the marriage. He was very ambivalent. He said that his wife's expression of love for him was "smothering."

Pete carried a lot of resentments. His wife's expectations of him were reasonable. She expected him to get a job and support the family. This caused him to pull away from her emotionally. Then he felt rejected and alone. He also felt her resentment toward him. Not bringing in any money to help pay the bills became a big item of discussion almost every day. She resented him for not being there for her emotionally. Not least of all, she resented Pete's "betrayal" in breaking his wedding vows "to be faithful to me unto death." Yet she did not give up on Pete, always hoping that he would change. On the other hand, Pete resented his wife's not trusting him. He knew he had made a mistake, but he could not understand why she couldn't put the past in the past. Pete's secretiveness kept her from being able to trust him.

One observation I made in working with Pete in therapy was that he was an all-or-nothing kind of guy. Things were either/or, black or white, never both/and. From a psychological viewpoint, this type of perspective results from not having a strong bonding with the mother or a caretaker. Pete had some unresolved issues with his mother. He described her as always talking but not listening. Thus, he felt she never really heard him and his feelings. He felt she treated him as insignificant. Whether it was actually true or not, Pete believed that his mother saw him as weak, not assertive or aggressive enough to get to where he was really capable of being. Yet she would tell him he was "a good boy." Often he saw her as out of control to the point of being hysterical. He knew his mother had a lot of anger, and she got defensive easily, especially if one touched on her insecurities. At the same time, he felt she was focused on the "super spiritual." It was like a "one-up mom, and one-down for me." She referred to him and his brothers as "the boys" instead of speaking their names. In his mother's presence he felt like a little boy all over again. He said that when she was speaking of him or his brothers, she often got them mixed up and called them by the wrong name. Because his mother was such an "authoritarian," Pete realized that he also had problems with authority figures in his life and in his work. His confusion mounted as his mother "put me down" and in the next breath told him how good and sensitive he was compared to his siblings.

Pete's father described Pete as very intelligent, sensitive, honest, compassionate, and handsome, with good athletic skills and a good sense of humor. Pete believed his father really did care about the family. The father, too, was handsome. However, Pete did have some childhood memories of abuse that continued to haunt him and make him feel helpless. His father had beaten him as well as his brothers, making them pull down their pants, and lean over the foot of a bed. He said, "Dad would beat us until we cried." However, Pete refused to cry, which meant that he had to endure what seemed endless pain. His brothers learned to cry immediately. He said, "My mother condoned the beatings and did not seek to intervene for us." Pete said that he felt helpless, powerless, and vulnerable, and saw no way out. In fact, Pete remembers his mother asking his father to beat the boys for what seemed to him the smallest offenses. He felt that his father complied with his mother to keep down arguments between the two of them.

Pete's father's expressed desire was "to see Pete come back to his spiritual roots." At times, he felt that his parents were more concerned about his spiritual condition rather than accepting him for who he was. Pete had also become a codependent. However, I experienced Pete as being thoughtful and kind, yet having low self-esteem. It was as if his spirit had been broken.

The first thing that I did was to get an appointment for Pete with a good psychiatrist. I knew, without a doubt, that he was suffering from depression. He was willing to go for an evaluation. Pete admitted to the psychiatrist that he indeed did feel depressed, was anxious all the time, and had obsessive ruminations for at least the last two months. He also admitted that he had been having either anxiety or panic attacks. He suffered too from mild agoraphobia. He had increased crying spells, insomnia, and a decreased appetite. He had low energy and was not motivated due to a lack of energy. In general, Pete felt helpless and hopeless as well as guilty. His concentration level had diminished. He noticed that he kept checking things like whether the doors were locked, and he washed his hands a lot. He shared with the doctor that at the age of twenty he had been hospitalized for attempted suicide.

Pete was suffering from major depression. The psychiatrist discussed with him his different options for medication, and he decided to try one particular antidepressant that brought about good results in a short time. Pete revealed a lot about himself on an internalized shame test. He responded by saying, "I almost always felt that something was missing in my life, because I have felt empty and unfulfilled, and lonely." He also said, "I have this painful gap within me that I have not been able to close." He saw himself as striving for perfection only to continually fall short of his goal. He also said, "I have an overpowering dread that my faults will be revealed in front of others. And, I replay painful events over and over in my mind until I am completely overwhelmed. I would just like to shrink away when I make mistakes." He also talked about how he felt intensely inadequate and full of self-doubt. He said, "I am always scolding myself and putting myself down."

It was clear to me that Pete had the desire to be different, successful, predictable, and true to himself and to others. However, his depression had full reign over him and had beaten him down to the point that he felt worthless. After being on the antidepressant for a short time he improved a great deal, and he became relieved of some of his aggravating symptoms. It does seem that his depression is genetic, and perhaps he will have to continue on medication the rest of his life. He did not like the idea of being on medication, but I encouraged him to think in terms of having a problem with high blood pressure, and thus having to take medication for that problem the rest of life or at least indefinitely.

Why is it that we human beings do not see mental problems just like we do other physical ailments? We are one whole human body, and what affects one part is going to affect the other parts. With time, effort, therapy, and medication, I believe Pete will be able to live a more satisfying life in the future and feel some real peace of mind.

Down but Not Out

Brenda and her second husband, Ronald, came to my office seeking counseling. Immediately, I was told that Brenda was an MK. Brenda and Roger, her first husband, had five children, and Brenda and Ronald, her second husband, had two children together.

Brenda and Ronald had come to discuss with me their two daughters who were students in North Carolina universities. They had grown up in a South American country, and now they had plans to spend their college years in the States. One of the girls was a sophomore and the other a freshman. Since Brenda went to South America when she was a young child, she had spent most of the forty-two years of her life there. Brenda and Ronald at that time lived in South America and had come to visit their two college daughters. The younger daughter wanted to go back to South America with her parents. Heather had found it difficult to leave her home in South America to come to the States for college. After all, that was the only home she had ever known. However, since her older sister, Monica, had already been here for a year, she decided it would be a good experience. Her grandparents and other relatives were in North Carolina. Monica was more of an extrovert, whereas Heather was more of an introvert. Heather was quite shy, and she wanted to spend most of her time with Monica and her friends. She actually found it difficult to reach out and make new friends of her own.

The parents' purpose for this visit with me was to ask if it might be a good idea for them to take their younger daughter back to South America with them. After some discussion I discovered that Heather planned to stay in the States after she graduated from college. I told them that I believed that if Heather did go back with them, it would be a big mistake and she would regret such a decision later. The parents seemed to be relieved and admitted that they had felt the same way but needed to get a professional's opinion. I assured the parents that I would visit their daughters on their college campus, and would be available to help them in any way I could. The parents went on their way, but did say that perhaps they would be moving back to the States in a few years.

A few months later I went to the girls' college campus. We went out to a nice restaurant and had a delightful time getting to know each other. Monica had a boyfriend back in South America and would return there after college graduation and marry him. She was excited but fully intended to graduate from college before getting married. As it turned out, Heather decided to transfer to a different college so that she would not depend on her sister so much. This, she knew, would force her to make her own friends. She wanted to become more independent as well. I stayed in touch with them, and occasionally talked to them by telephone. They both settled down in their two different colleges. Monica, after graduation, did return to her country and was married. Heather met her husband-to-be at her new college where she had transferred.

By then, their parents had moved back to the States from South America, with their three younger children. Brenda shared with me her joys and her heartaches. As an MK she had grown up in a missionary home where there was lots of love and nurturing, and she felt pretty secure. She said, "As a child, there must have been some struggles, but I can't remember any right now. I remember often hearing my parents speak lovingly of the people they knew whose lives were changed due to my parents' ministry to them. They loved the South American people, and they taught us to love them as well."

When Brenda was only fifteen she fell in love with a young native boy. She said, "I was having a very exciting and romantic life at that time." After one year of college, Brenda and Roger decided to get married and live in the jungles. Now she began to live her own life. She came to realize that life and people were more complicated than she had thought. She was almost nineteen years old when she married, and four years later, she had three children. Her life was filled with all the details of taking care of her children. Her husband's father was a cattle and agricultural farmer. She, along with her husband and children, lived in isolation in a house similar to what one would see in the television show, *Little House on the Prairie*. Upon moving there, Roger was working with his father but could not foresee the problems of land invasion by squatters who eventually did destroy their farms. Then her husband began a sawmill to clear the land. He would also continue helping his father build fences to try to keep out the invaders.

In their house, they had no electricity and no running water. They had a thatched-roof house, simple board walls, and canvass for windows. Brenda washed their clothes in a stream of water, and her husband milked the cows. They were both so busy, she said, "We neglected our personal relationship with Jesus Christ, and it was reflected in our family life." It had become hard for her to respect and appreciate her husband. They moved nine to ten times in eight years, even though Brenda protested. Realizing that she was not the kind of wife she wanted to be, she began to read the Bible again. She and her husband began to work on their problems and dramatically found peace again. She said, "Our relationship became much happier, not because of us but because of our relationship to our Lord Jesus."

When Brenda and Roger were expecting their fifth child, they were still living on a farm, struggling to make a living. Then her husband's father asked him to spend three to four months helping him deal with land invaders who were cutting their fences and stealing their cattle in the jungles. Brenda did not want to go there, but she eventually felt it was the right thing to do. She did not realize that she was headed for the worst tragedy of her life, but by now they were used to living with danger. There had been threats with guns, and one of their camps had been burned. Roger had a brother who was studying for a degree in the

States, and he came home for one month to help his father and brother. The tragedy was that the three of them walked right into a trap, were ambushed by forty-five men who lay in waiting to kill whoever was related to the land owners. Brenda was in their camp with her four children. Her mother-in-law was in the States visiting Roger's brother's wife along with her own six grandchildren. All three men were shot—Roger, his brother, and his father.

A sawmill worker's wife "came trembling into our house... I looked at her trembling hands, wondering what had happened." She told Brenda that Roger, his brother, and his father had been shot, only her father-in-law was not killed, but was severely wounded. Brenda said, "I refused to believe it. It couldn't be true.... I knelt down and prayed with my children for it not to be true." Although she knew her husband Roger would not be coming home again, a Scripture verse kept coming to her mind: "Let not your hearts be troubled or afraid," and she continued to say, "And do you know God did not allow my heart to be troubled or afraid? Sad, yes, very sad. Everything I had loved, planned for, cared for had been taken away from me, but I found that God was there, like a rock, stronger and more real than any of those things I had thought so important to me. He gave me the strength and trust I needed. People spoke about how strong I was, but I had been a very dependent, simple wife." Her strength was from God. She said, "I felt how fragile and short life is and how real heaven and eternity are."

Brenda, at age twenty-six, was a widow with four children and one yet to be born. Since her missionary parents were in the States at the time, she decided to return to the States to have her fifth baby. With two suitcases she returned with her children to the States. She said, "I began to appreciate how hard it is to be the head of the house, make decisions, answer all the children's questions and give emotional support to five children who did not have a daddy." Family, relatives, friends, and church people were all so very helpful. She said they received more than they needed.

After living in America for two years she began praying for a good husband and daddy for her children. At first, nothing happened. Then after three and one-half years, she had finally decided she could be happy and handle the children alone. She was now in Texas and was trying to move to the East Coast to be near her parents and other relatives.

Finally, one day she received a telephone call from the son of a doctor from her adopted country in South America. The family had known Ronald and his family for a long time on their mission field. This young man had visited her and Roger on their farm. He was one of Roger's friends as well. Ronald had called to tell her he was in the States and had gotten a job, and he wanted to visit her and her children. They were living about one hour apart in Texas. After three visits from him, and watching him play with her children, she began to think that he was awfully nice. This went on for several months. Brenda realized she was falling in love with Ronald, but she waited patiently. Then, one day, surprisingly he drove up to her house. He spent two days with Brenda's aunt who lived nearby, yet he never said a word about the two of them. When he left, he mentioned coming back and taking her and the children on a picnic. However, he left saying, "See you sometime." Brenda was confused and rather angry. She decided, then and there, that she would tell him just how she felt about him. Thus, she wrote him a short letter. Later, he told her that after hearing that she had special feelings for him, he realized that he had been loving her without recognizing it as love. They got together. Ronald told Brenda that he had first visited her out of respect for her dead husband Roger and because Roger had been his best friend. He truly wanted to be able to help her children, but he never thought about the two of them falling in love with each other.

Ronald responded to Brenda's letter telling her he had shared his feelings about her with his parents. Fortunately, his parents were both very pleased about having Brenda as their new daughter-in-law. Brenda said, "We decided to get married before we had even kissed." Then he asked her children for permission to marry their mother. The children already loved him, and they were pleased to have him as their new daddy. Five months later, Brenda and Ronald were married. Brenda said, "Ronald was a gift from God to me." Brenda and Ronald had two children from their union. Now they had seven children to parent. She said that she knew Ronald was not perfect, but she dearly loves and appreciates him.

Brenda, a delightful human being and MK, came though a lot of struggles, disappointments, pain, and grief, but her eyes shone with delight when she spoke of her husband, her seven children, and her deep faith in God who had brought her through it all and had provided so well for her and her family. She concluded by saying, "God has helped me change so much that now even moving is easier for me."

CHAPTER NINE

Secrets of the Heart

Learning to Trust Again

I received a telephone call from a Mission Board telling me that they had a young lady, a daughter of missionaries, who needed some intensive counseling and asked me if I would be able to spend some time each day for about two weeks with her in counseling sessions. Since she was coming to Winston-Salem from out of state, I told the Board that I would not only counsel with her but would also arrange some housing for her. In our city, several local churches own what they call "missionary residencies," where missionaries and their families could move right into a completely furnished house and live there for the duration of their furloughs. They would pay only for the cost of their personal phone calls.

I first met Meagan, an MK from Kenya, at the airport and drove her to the missionary residence where she would stay for two weeks. It was a beautiful spring day, the most beautiful time of the year for Winston-Salem, since the dogwoods and the azaleas line the streets in all their glory. When I met Meagan, I knew immediately that I was going to like working with her. She was an attractive, warm, and friendly young lady.

When we arrived at the missionary house, the chairman of the house committee was there to greet us. Meagan was warmly received and was shown throughout the rather large, beautifully decorated house. It would be within walking distance of my office. Then Meagan met some of the church staff. We went to the supermarket to purchase foods of her choice.

The following day, Meagan came to my office, and we began our first counseling session. Meagan began telling me her story about how as an MK teacher she had gone to teach MK children in a country other than the one where she had spent her MK years. She had been sent home from that country before finishing her contract. She felt that although she had made a serious mistake, she did not deserve being sent home. She was so sad and deeply hurt to leave "my kids" before the school year ended. I detected that she was not only hurt but that she had some anger as well. I assured her that I believed that the people to whom she had been responsible had made the best decision they knew how, although I did see how it could have been handled in a more caring way. Meagan seemed relieved and glad to hear me affirm what she had been thinking.

Saying goodbye is always a big issue for the children of missionaries. It was difficult for Meagan, who felt she was always saying goodbye or hello. MKs spend three to four years in their adopted country where they live with their missionary parents and then return to the States for one-year furloughs. Then they are off again to their adopted countries for another three to four years.

MKs learn very quickly not to invest themselves too deeply in friendships in the States since it is just too painful to have to leave them at the end of the year of furlough. In spite of this, Meagan had invested a large part of herself in the MKs she had been teaching. Actually, saying goodbyes for Meagan had always been difficult. She indicated that, as a child, when going back and forth she could never remember saying goodbye to people, whether it be friends or relatives. Perhaps she had blocked out such experiences since they were always painful.

At the age of thirteen, Meagan did remember saying goodbye to her rabbit when she was leaving her country and returning to the States. She said, "That was hard." Then, at the high school graduation, she did say goodbye to her classmates, not knowing if she would ever see them again. To MKs these experiences are a bit like death. At age seventeen, Meagan remembered getting on a plane to return to the States. Saying goodbye meant separation and many losses. This time she would not be returning to her country. Now she would be a college student. This was so painful. As one male MK said, "When I left my country to return to the States, I felt like I was experiencing a thousand deaths at once, including my own. And, I believe I was."

As we began to look at Meagan's childhood and family history, she became quite energized. She became animated as she told me about growing up in a country where she had spent all the developmental years of her life. She loved her country, and during all those years, she said, "My mother was my best friend."

Meagan's earliest memory was an underwater ride she took at Disney wearing a Mickey Mouse sweatshirt. She was in the third grade at the time. One of her most vivid memories was her intense feeling of dislike for America. She did not like going with her parents from church to church when they spoke to congregations about their missionary experiences. Even on her second furlough, when she was in the seventh grade, she felt angry because she did not understand all that was going on around her. The school she attended that year had between seven hundred and eight hundred students. She felt a lot of confusion.

When the day came for her to return with her family to her country, Meagan was so thrilled at the prospects of "going home" to their own house, where she had lived most of her life. She looked forward to sleeping in her own bed in her own room once again. The one thing she did not like in her adopted country was the long church services and activities that continued into the late afternoon every Sunday. She said, "It was just plain tiring." I could empathize with her and told her that I certainly did not enjoy spending all day in worship services and then meetings that lasted all day long on Sunday when I lived and worked in Japan.

Meagan graduated from high school and returned to the States for college. After college she went abroad to teach MKs in a junior high school. There she had some unfortunate and sad experiences. She had little support since the missionaries there seemed consumed with their own problems. From her perspective, Meagan did not think they were communicating effectively. After dealing with their own problems, it seemed they had nothing left to share or to give to Meagan. Being an extrovert, she needed people. Actually she related better to the nationals than she did to the missionaries. In this situation she made some unwise decisions. At this point, Meagan had become so discouraged, she thought, *What the heck? I might as well do whatever I want to do.* She had already heard that she would probably be sent home. She felt she was in a real predicament. To go home before she was due to go would be to lose face. What would she tell her friends and relatives? How could she cope with leaving "my children, my students in the hands of another teacher to finish out the school year"? She was in so much turmoil and confusion, she said she literally could not think straight. As she looked back on the experience she said, "Now it seems so unreal, like a bad dream. It was like I was a different person at that time in my life."

Those experiences had caused Meagan to lose trust in so many people. Also, she had to deal with authority figures. Her own father had been controlling. He had been a strong authority figure in her life, so in dealing with strong authority figures elsewhere, she realized she was also dealing with her own authoritarian father. In counseling, Meagan began to understand more about trust and respect for authority.

Meagan began to realize that "It is not always what happens to me, but what is important is what I have learned from the experiences that will make me a better person." Through a bad experience, she learned a lot about herself, about people in general, and just how vulnerable she could become under stress. She had allowed others to cause her to feel she was a bad person. The one thing of which I assured her was that she was not a bad person. Relieved, she then began to itemize some things she had learned during our sessions.

In dealing with anger, she learned how to deal with it in more constructive ways. She dealt with the issues of grief, her need to please, how to ask for what she needed, and how to remain open in order to receive advice and direction from those who could help her. Meagan is a person who gave so much, and now she was learning how to receive graciously. "Even Jesus allowed Mary to wash his feet and wipe them with her hair." She began to learn to become more interdependent rather than being independent or too dependent. In other words, she learned how to receive as well as to give.

Meagan was one MK who tended to take on more than she could adequately handle. Now she was learning to pick and choose what was more important and, thus, become relieved from so much stress and tension. She became aware of her strengths as well as her weaknesses. She began to get in touch with her own humanity and the need to say "no" for the sake of her health. She also learned that others, particularly missionaries, are not as perfect as they may present themselves to be or as the people in the churches see them.

I loved the way Meagan was so open, honest, and willing to be vulnerable and show her true feelings. She is a lovely, capable, and caring human being. She now saw herself as a stronger, better person. As she said, "I now know there are pitfalls in life, and I feel better equipped to spot them before I fall into them in the future."

In her evaluation of our time together, Meagan wrote, "From the time I arrived, I felt accepted by Dr. Walters. At first, I was puzzled by what I thought was a lack of 'God talk,' and I came to understand that she was not going to try to 'fix' me. She loved me and showed her compassion. I saw her as truly a representative of God to me. I now believe God sees me as a human being with needs, and He accepts me as I am. I know I am one of God's daughters." She went on to say that her counselor had affirmed and reaffirmed her and encouraged her to not look back. Meagan went on to say, "Doris told me to not allow my mistakes and being sent home to hurt my self-esteem. You've given me back my self-esteem. You have given me back my self-confidence. Thank you."

Meagan shared with me a poem entitled "The Road of Life" (author unknown) that somewhat describes Meagan's journey.

THE ROAD OF LIFE
(author unknown)

At first I saw God as my observer
my judge, keeping track of the things I did wrong
so as to know whether I merited heaven
or hell when I die.
He was out there sort of like a president.
I recognized his picture when I saw it,
But I really didn't know Him.
But later on when I met Christ,
It seemed as though life was rather like a bike ride,
but it was a tandem bike,
and I noticed that Christ
was in the back helping me pedal.
I don't know when it was
that he suggested we change places,
but life has not been the same since.
When I had control, I knew the way.
It was rather boring, but predictable.
It was the shortest distance between two points.
But when He took the lead,
He knew delightful long cuts,
up mountains, and through rocky places
at breakneck speeds,
it was all I could do to hang on!

Even though it looked like madness,
He said, "Pedal!"
I worried and was anxious and asked,
"Where are you taking me?"
He laughed and did not answer,
and I started to learn to trust.
I forgot my boring life
and entered into the adventure.
And when I'd say, "I'm scared,"
He'd lean back and touch my hand.
He took me to people with gifts that I needed,
gifts of healing,
acceptance,
and joy.
They gave me gifts to take on my journey,
my Lord's and mine.
And we were off again.
He said, "Give the gifts away;
they're extra baggage, too much weight."
So I did,
to the people we met,
and I found that in giving I received,
and still our burden was light.
I did not trust Him,
at first,
in control of my life.
I thought He would wreck it;
but he knows bike secrets,
knows how to make it bend to take sharp corners,
knows how to jump to clear high rocks,
knows how to fly to shorten scary passages.
And I am learning to shut up

>   and pedal
>   in the strangest places,
>   and I'm beginning to enjoy the view
>   and the cool breeze on my face
>   with my delightful constant companion, Jesus Christ.
>   And when I'm sure I just can't do anymore,
>   He just smiles and says ... "Pedal!"

Meagan is beginning to enjoy the view and the cool breeze on her face!

Not Totally American

Celia was a sophomore in college and had grown up in a country on the continent of Africa. It had been several years since she left her country and returned to the States to enter college. As one might imagine, there in Africa, at least where she lived, there were no shopping malls, roller skating rinks, nearby pools, or zoos. Celia and her MK friends were forced to use their own imaginations to entertain themselves. These MKs were in good physical shape, perhaps because they spent so much of their time outdoors. They jumped on a trampoline, swung on a special rope, and rode their bikes down cow trails. They played tag and hide-and-go-seek, and they climbed trees. They loved being outside from daylight until dark. They ran around barefoot, sat in sand piles, made mud pies, and even built whole villages with rivers and dams.

Celia remembers that up until she was about five years old, there were lots of white children, MKs, but then various families went home on furlough or had resigned from their mission work. Then Celia had only one white friend her own age with whom to play. She went to an African nursery school where she made many little African friends. She never felt she really quite fit with the group. Celia, at times, wished she were black like the other children so that she could meld into the group and be one of them. Even in nursery school, Celia learned a lot of the native language.

During her first five years of school, she studied what was called a correspondence course. Mothers of MKs served as her teachers. Then, from fifth grade through high school, Celia had to go away to a boarding school that was seven hundred miles away from her parents. She did have her best friend go to the same school at the same time she did. Now that she was living with the big kids, she refused to cry when she was homesick because she feared the big kids would call her a crybaby. She would stifle her pain and, "put on a fake happy face and a brave smile." The first year away from her parents was particularly hard. However, after that first year, Celia became involved in many activities and made many good friends. She said, "The kids in my dorm became my family, and therefore, I didn't miss my parents so much." She and her classmates were really "tight" because they knew the hurt and pain that each was experiencing. Although they didn't really talk about it, they knew at the time that they were the only family they had.

Before going to boarding school, Celia's correspondence course work had been fairly easy, and she had little homework. But now, at the boarding school she felt overwhelmed at times because of the amount of homework she was expected to do. Their housemother did try to mother the girls in her dorm, but there were so many that there wasn't enough of her to go around. Celia missed being able to share her good and her bad times with her parents. Even though Celia had one older sibling at the school, he was often too busy with his friends to pay much attention to his little sister. She clearly stated one of her regrets: "Mom and Dad were cut off from that part of my life, and they would never know what my world was like."

Even though Celia could spend Christmas and summer vacation time with her parents, it was never enough time to catch them up on her life experiences when she had been away from them. When one of her favorite teachers had taken time off to return to the States, it broke her heart and she cried a lot. In these boarding schools, MKs have many different teachers, some short-term while others may stay for years. It seemed to the MKs that they were always saying hello or goodbye.

At one point, Celia had a boyfriend, which grew into a deep relationship. She said, "He was the source of love and care that I missed from my family." This was an international school, but Celia felt that from the sixth to the ninth grade, her spiritual life went on "a downhill slide." Worst of all, she said, no one seemed to notice or care except her closest friends, who seemed to "slide downhill with me." At the boarding school, they did have church and Sunday school classes, but what it had to offer never seemed to meet Celia's needs. By the time she was a freshman in high school, she did seem to find her way back and got back on track spiritually. She said it was a long, hard struggle. Some of her classmates dealt with their painful struggles by turning to alcohol, drugs, and sex. At the same time, Celia had, what she described, as a very "legalistic relationship with God in which I felt pretty miserable." Even in junior high school, Celia's boyfriend became her escape and sole security. She said that their physical closeness, which sometimes got "out of hand," seemed to replace that which she had missed from not having her family. Then the day came when her boyfriend left Africa, and she said, "I hit rock bottom." Her best friend left about the same time. Now, her security was gone, and in this great loss, she cried out to God for His help. At that time, Celia said, "In this experience I came to what I considered to be my first true pilgrimage of faith in Jesus Christ."

Celia described her stateside furloughs as being "traumatic." She was uprooted from everything familiar, and worst of all, she said, "I lost my home." Everything in America was different, from the place she slept to the school she attended. She said, "As much as we MKs were separated from other Americans by our common heritage, there is still a world of difference between MKs and their parents in America. This was home for my parents, but Africa was my home." She, like so many others, did not feel American. On one furlough, Celia felt totally unaccepted at her school. However, after making a few friends, she had little trouble with the other American kids. She said that as early as the third grade, she was proud to get up, introduce herself, and tell them she was from

Africa. She was not even ashamed to tell her friends that she had gotten some hand-me-down clothes over the weekend at some church.

When Celia was in the States for seventh grade, she described it as being the worst year of her life. She did not have a clue about what music was popular with the young people. She didn't know about the latest styles in clothing. She was confused by the strange ways of the kids. She said that American kids couldn't care less that she had come from Africa. It pained her to see their ignorance about Africa and the world, and their lack of understanding of her. She knew she was the one who would have to change or conform if she was to be accepted. She always felt as if she were the outcast and loner. She was the girl who didn't know what songs were playing on the radio or what television shows were popular. Celia cried a lot and was so happy to get back to Africa where her friends understood her. She was aware of the fact that the way her parents viewed the African people and the way she viewed them were quite different. She said, "Since I was raised by one particular African woman, it was easy for me to look at those people and see mothers, fathers, sisters, and brothers. In my eyes there was no color, at least until I got back to America. Yet I know I share the same roots with my parents."

When Celia left Africa for the last time to come to the States for college, she suffered from a lot of culture shock. One of the first things that hit her right away was the prejudice of Americans, both white and black. For the first time she began to notice different skin colors and different social positions. She felt rejected by blacks. She felt the white kids looked down on her for being friends with some blacks. She was also caught up in the materialism of Americans. It seemed that every student had to be dating somebody, and if you were not dating, then you were a "nobody."

One thing Celia really liked about America, though, was the great variety of foods. She said, "It was much better than what we had been used to eating." She was amazed that everywhere she turned she heard the girls talking about dieting. Everybody seemed to be either too thin or too fat. She found herself caught up in the obsession and became bulimic herself. Every day for a year she subjected herself to throwing up what she had eaten.

Celia sees herself now as a mixture of African and American cultures. She had lived fifteen years of her life in Africa and had been back in the States for only four years. She still says, "I don't totally fit into the African culture nor am I totally American. My roots are in Africa, but my family and extended family are in America." She is quick to say that America is a beautiful country, with lots of beautiful culture that she would have to learn about with the passing of time. One sad note that Celia sounded was the fact that too many missionary parents get so caught up in their work on the mission field that they seem to forget about their kids. Many MKs feel that their parents do not see them as being their first responsibility; thus, the MKs have to be satisfied with taking second place in their parents' priority list. Yes, furloughs can be traumatic for MKs who do not view America as their home. Rather, when they return to the States, they feel like the foreigners.

A Heart Divided

In the other MK stories in this book, I have used fictitious names and countries, except for the Mary Boyles story, on Octogenarian. However, one very special male MK who is now in his eighties has given me permission to use his name, the name of his country, and the privilege of using a story he had written about a childhood experience. His name is John A. Tumblin Jr., and he grew up in Brazil.

I had the opportunity of meeting John and his wife Alice in February 2001. We had arranged a meeting at my office and would be joined by some other friends to go to lunch. Before this visit, I had sent John a copy of my book, *Missionary Children Caught between Cultures*. He read it in its entirety before coming to see me.

When I met John and Alice, I felt as if I had known them for a long,

long time. John, even before he sat down, said to me, "You gave me a sleepless, restless night last night." He went on to explain how he had finished reading my book about the issues MKs face upon returning to the States to live after growing up in another culture. He told me that so many feelings had been stirred up in his mind from early childhood. Within the first 10 minutes, John was in tears as he talked about his childhood. He was also weeping over the loss of his home in Brazil. John said to me, "Doris, I thought I had worked through all those feelings a long time ago, but I guess I had only repressed them." Later, in a letter to me, he said, "What a treat it was to be with you yesterday! I can't recall when, if ever, 'I opened up' so quickly to a new friend." I, personally, count it an honor to know John and Alice. In hearing John's story with his struggles and his sacrifices, he became a real inspiration to me. As you read the story of his early childhood, I believe you will be inspired as well.

Later, I asked John and Alice to participate in an MK Retreat held at Kure Beach, North Carolina. John would facilitate discussion in three sessions. There were other MKs of all ages, from Brazil and other countries as well, who came to meet with what seemed like family to them. We were all in tears during those sessions. So many raw feelings were expressed. During that weekend I was able to spend more quality time with John and hear more about his life and his work.

John Tumblin had been a professor of anthropology at Agnes Scott College near Atlanta. He had recently retired and had moved to North Carolina to a retirement home near Burlington, North Carolina. Before that, John had gone back to Brazil where he worked on some special projects for two terms. More recently he and Alice took their children and went back to Brazil for a family vacation for two to three weeks. All the children and grandchildren were on this trip. They, along with their children, visited old stomping grounds and familiar places, and met old friends. What a thrill it was for me to see the pure joy that John exuded as he shared with me the fact that he could go "home" again.

In a Dean's Lecture one year at Agnes Scott, John presented a lecture on "Celebrating Bridges." He had come to a time in his life that he was celebrating the bridge of retirement. He said, "It then came to me, a time with a flood of relief, instead of regret, that I am no longer young. It is in the younger years that anxiety about impressing audiences with formal presentations rightly belongs, or so I told myself. At least for some of us, the older years should be a time for occasionally taking advantage of opportunities to sit with a granddaughter on one's lap, or to join with a group of friends and tell stories that illustrate an insight one might find more awkward to convey directly."

As a part of that lecture, John shared a portion of his early life of wonder. It is so beautiful, and written by John himself. With his permission I share it with you:

> In a faraway place, a long, long time ago, lived a child whose friends called him Dondino because they could not pronounce words like John Jr. in the strange language of his parents. Dondino's parents were foreigners to that land. They lived two days' travel into the interior in the village of Jaguaquara (which means jaguar's den), and directed a primary school which kept them very, very busy. Though his parents loved and were loved in return by the people of Jaguaquara, they spoke the language of the country with a strong accent, which sometimes embarrassed the boy, and they always looked a bit strange and out of place next to the local people. Dondino, like his parents, looked strange too, but at least he spoke Portuguese with no noticeable accent. When he tried to speak his parents' English, though, his pronunciation was heavily flawed, and he didn't know enough words to express adequately what he thought. This was one of the reasons the boy always felt a bit out of place wherever he went. He felt that among his friends, he sounded alright but looked alien, and among U.S. Americans he looked alright but sounded strange. Sometimes he thought about this, felt lonely, and sighed.

Life in Jaguaquara was in many ways pleasant. Instead of automobile traffic there were mile-long cattle drives which raised clouds of dust as they passed through the village on the way to a distant market. There were no airplanes overhead, but each day a wood-burning locomotive blew its melodious whistle as it chugged farther inland pulling a train of passenger and freight cars. His parents never owned an automobile, but there were lethargic donkeys, sure-footed mules, and high-strung horses to be ridden. Dondino had a pet parrot named Louro, a favorite dog named Tigre, and a special friend named Silar Vilar, but he had no brothers or sisters at that time. Sometimes, more interesting than any of these, there were adult visitors who stayed in the home, maybe for days, as there were no hotels in town. He was very shy about actually talking with these sophisticated people from large cities and faraway states, but he liked to sit inconspicuously in the big parlor and listen to their grown-up talk. They knew so many facts! They had experienced so many things! They were so free to express strong, definite opinions about so many topics!

Sometimes Dondino wished very hard that he could stop being a child and start being an adult, and he would decide to begin practicing what he thought were adult ways. While "being an adult" he was impatient with his friends when they cried and mortified when it came his turn to cry. He started to memorize facts: how many cubic centimeters in a liter, how many kilometers between Jaguaquara and Nazare, how many hours there are in a week, who is the president of Brazil... things like that. Above all, he felt, an adult is contemptuous of anyone who claims the reality of anything that cannot be seen, touched, heard, or smelled with the exception of God and the Devil, of course. If you doubted either one of these something scary would pounce on you and devour you when you least expected it, just like the moths who got swallowed up by the lizards who patrolled the white-washed walls of the church at night.

One category of adults who visited in the home evoked a special feeling. They were women who were not busy with children of their own... women like Aunt Alma, Aunt Ruth, and Aunt Vivian... not literally aunts but almost like members of the family... who would separate themselves from the other adults and pay special attention to the boy. They had ways of breaking through his reserve and engaging him in conversations that were a delicious mixture of adult objectivity and the exciting fantasy of stories they sometimes recited, sometimes read to him from books. A problem, though, was that their friendly openness sometimes left him wondering whether to approach them through the formal privileges of a fellow adult or through the permissiveness and uncritical acceptance of a child.

One day when he was in his adult mood, Aunt Alma, who was visiting for a few days, invited Dondino to hear a fairy story, and he blurted out, with the gruffness that often masked his ambivalence, "I don't believe in fairies anymore!" She did not insist on telling the story, which secretly disappointed him, but must have thought that six years old was too soon to give up the rewards of free and freeing imaginings. "How do you know there are no fairies?" she gently inquired. "Haven't you ever seen a fairy tree?"

"A fairy tree?" The boy had never even heard of such a thing, and looked carefully at Aunt Alma's face to see if she were teasing him. Her face was composed, relaxed, and communicated confidence. "Of course," she said. "Early in the morning when the dew is still on the leaves, you can find trees... sometimes... where the fairies have left gifts for girls and boys who believe in them. Maybe you haven't been at the right place at the right time, or maybe you stopped believing with all your heart before you had a chance to see one. Besides, you know, after the sun comes up and dries the dew, fairy trees always disappear."

Still unsure whether she were saying a Truth or not, Dondino hesitantly asked, "Could you show me a fairy tree?"

"I'm not sure," she replied, "for this depends in part on you. Let's keep it a secret, and tomorrow morning I will wake you before the sun starts to rise, and together we will look for evidence of fairies."

The rest of the day, which seemed to have enough hours for a week, eventually dragged itself into night. Dondino carefully laid out his next day's clothes on the chair by the bed so he could quickly dress, pulled up the sheet, and lay there thinking he would never get to sleep. But the next thing he knew a hand touched his shoulder and became an index finger in front of pursed lips on a smiling face that whispered, "Shhh...don't wake the grown-ups." The boy could hardly contain his excitement.

Aunt Alma only held Dondino's hand while they tiptoed through the still darkened house, but did not try to guide him or contain him as they swung across the campus toward the golden center from which the sun was only beginning to emerge. His ears were filled with songbird sounds and the swishing of feet on damp grass. Dewdrops sparkled as the sky grew brighter. A lizard waddled sluggishly onto the east side of a boulder to warm his scaly skin. Trees and bushes were still, as no wind yet stirred their branches.

And suddenly, there it was: the fairy tree! Lit from behind by the full sun on the horizon, its leaves alive with shimmering droplets, the small tree emerged from an indistinct background dead ahead of them. On its branches there were cellophane-wrapped pieces of candy, oranges, and the rarest of all in the tropics, three bright red apples. "It's there, Aunt Alma! A fairy tree is right over there!" cried the boy in awe.

For a shining moment they walked together toward the place where a special gift was occurring. The gift was the removal of the barrier between child and adult, between the possible and the impossible, between perceived and apperceived, between the operation of the left and the right hemispheres of the brain, between fact and significance and deeper meanings that are never fully understood.

For sixty years I have drawn strength from that early morning gift from a woman whose real name is long since lost from memory, but whose care for a child's growth and whose lesson about the possibility of the impossible are a major debt of gratitude I hope to repay, some day, in an impossible, anticipated, life after life.

John Tumblin has contributed so much to the world through his teachings, his warm personality, his giving, his humble spirit. This came from a very precocious young lad who grew up in a faraway land called Brazil. To all who know him, he is a special person and a great MK. This man learned early in his life what it meant to have a divided heart. On June 12, 1968, John gave the commencement address for the seniors at the American School in Recife. These were MK seniors who were graduating from high school. Now, they would all go their separate ways, and many would never see each other again. He knew what it was like to return to the States and face all the reentry issues. He had been through it all, and now he was able to speak as one MK to other MKs about their hearts that would soon know what it meant when he spoke about "With a Divided Heart." His speech, which follows, is, just as relevant to any MK returning to the States for college even today as it was to those seniors graduating in 1968.

With a Heart Divided: Commencement Address to the American School in Recife, June 12, 1968

JOHN A. TUMBLIN JR.

Introduction

Which do you like best...the end or the beginning? Each has its advantages and disadvantages. When one combines the end and the beginning at a single time, however, the good and the bad, the joys and the sorrows may become jumbled and confused.

Graduation is that sort of hodgepodge, but for you the blend of ending and beginning is especially complex. This ceremony symbolizes more than the honorable conclusion of one phase in academic life and the initiation of another; it is also a beginning and an end of relationships with friends, parents, cultures, and countries. And as the meanings of this sink through your mind and body you react with happiness and dread, anticipation and sadness, adrenalin, a lump in the throat, and at least two hidden tears. Why? Because you, more than most high school graduates, have started living with a heart divided.

Like it or not, whether you chose it or not, you are part Brazilian now...and part American. You are what Robert E. Park called a marginal man. Such a person, he said in the language of a man born in the last century, is "one whom fate has condemned to live in two, not merely different, but antagonistic cultures."[1] Marginal Man feels himself not completely accepted in either culture, unwilling completely to commit himself to one or the other, yet ready to defend the views of each against attack by the other. Marginality occurs in persons who have absorbed the values and behaviors of two religions, two cultures, two racial groups, two generations, or whatever. Always there results a sense of double-consciousness. A classic statement describing this was made by the American mulatto revolutionary, W. E. B. DuBois, sixty-five years ago. He wrote: "It is a peculiar sensation, this double consciousness, this sense of always looking at one's self through the eyes of others, of measuring one's soul by the tape of a world that looks on in amused...pity. One feels his two-ness...an American, a Negro, two souls, two thoughts, two unresolved strivings; two warring ideals in one...body, whose dogged strength alone keeps it from being torn asunder."[2] In your case, the problem is less intense...but you are doomed to living with a heart divided nevertheless. Like most conditions of the human experience it is not all bad, nor all good; a lot depends on what you make of it. If you sort out those experiences, resolving some of the contradictions and learning to live with others, you will be stronger than most of those who have had a "regular," routine upbringing.

You have had a variety of experiences, rich and diverse to an extent that is seldom achieved in a lifetime by most adults of even the more developed nations. And of those fortunate adults, those who have had the privilege of such variety, many will not have had the personal adaptability, the flexibility, the freshness and the open-eyed wonder that you have, much less the support of intelligent parents, so as to absorb such experiences in a particularly meaningful fashion. As you well know, this experience did not come to you, and will not remain with you, without cost. May I play prophet, predict some of its advantages and disadvantages, and conclude with some suggestions which I hope will prove of some use.

Advantages and Disadvantages

It is obvious that you have benefited from many formal and informal learning opportunities in your travels and in your contacts; and thus, you have accumulated a great deal of information. More important, however, are personal experiences you have had which should enable you to be more understanding of others for the rest of your life.

Having lived as a member of a minority group, albeit a privileged minority, has given you some ability to identify with those whose unchosen "differences" are enough to make them the object of either envy or scorn. You have felt deep inside you the discomfort, and at times the exaggerated pride, of being bracketed as a member of a category, a nationality, a special group, instead of being recognized for what you are: an individual, a unique personality unlike any other that ever was. You will remember this in the United States and as you travel abroad again, and you will be helped to treat members of other and frequently less privileged groups with the sort of individual acceptance, respect, and consideration for which you longed at times while living overseas.

Having experienced the complexities of communication through the barriers of language, custom, and culture... and the blessings of being able to cut through these barriers more quickly than your parents could... you will be better prepared not only to accept but to feel the fact that much disagreement, individual and collective, is a result of not being able to grasp the other fellow's point of view. You know from experience that a Brazilian who is speaking with animation about any subject sounds to a recently arrived North American as though he were angry and hostile when he is not, at all. You know that the casual and smile-less nodding of the head with which an American greets a Brazilian acquaintance is frequently interpreted as being coldness and aloofness and disinterested when it is not meant to be. You have seen your parents take up business when you knew they should first have taken up a "cafézinho" instead.[3] You have experienced occasions in which your own attempt at friendliness was so misunderstood that the reply you received was totally out of keeping with your motive. You will be more tolerant and forgiving than most of the freshmen you will meet in the States, I hope.

You have had the experience of being rich—really rich from the standpoint of many of the people who look at you with mixed admiration, envy, and hostility. In the United States most of you will not be rich. You will be just another middle-class American student who occasionally wires home for twenty-five dollars in order to survive the next weekend of highly demanding social activities. And you may postpone half-soling a pair of shoes in order to do so. Ideally, your experience of being rich, for once, should make you more aware of the relativity of financial resources. It will help you at times to balance off those who see in all who have wealth the ugly oppressors and ill-users of the less fortunate. Under other circumstances, recalling that to some extent you made your own adjustment by blocking out awareness of suffering and hunger all around you, you will defend the need of controlled, imposed, collective efforts to distribute some of the benefits of wealth and to make possible many kinds of public assistance in and out of your country.

You have had the experience of living in a degree of social isolation, and a good deal of temporariness in living arrangements. Most of you have grown roots in one place, at the most, for three years at a time. You have seen the strains of such rootlessness on your parents, felt it in your relations with them, seen it in their relations with others, and reflected in the pleasures and trials of your friendships here at school. You will remember, as you face four more years of temporary living arrangements, nine months and three months at a time, that you have been able to "take it" in the past and are quite able to do it again. After your senior year of college perhaps you will begin a more stable life, at times boring and pedestrian by contrast, and you will recall how it felt when you were rootless, be able to draw from it strength and stability for yourself and sympathy with others who are just beginning the experience. If you then choose to go overseas you will face culture shock, as your parents did, but it will be milder. You know something of what it is like.

You have lived as a participant in some of the many ways by which men rank themselves in order to apportion privilege and opportunity. In the United States you have known that the badge of color is used as a device for ranking people in order to receive privileges, under some circumstances, while merit, performance, and personal accomplishment are enough in other circumstances. You have also seen strong barriers of class separating people and rendering unequal rewards for equal amounts of effort. You have seen hereditary wealth, membership in political in-groups, near and remote family connections, the boundaries of friendship circles, and other devices used to bind and separate people. You know from experience that the words "we," "ours," "us" are at once the most inclusive and exclusive in any language. You, having known what it feels like to be "them," will be somewhat suspicious of whatever is used to rank people in ways that create a self-perpetuating fallacy or a self-fulfilling prophecy.

What I'm saying, in short, is that there are difficult experiences in your past from which you should be able, through remembering the errors made, and being reassured by the experience of surviving, to become a tougher person. You will need some of that toughness. You will spend two or three or four years at a time without seeing your parents, and the main thing you will miss is just the chance to sit down and talk. But you should be able to "talk" against the background of experiences you have shared living abroad, in a setting where you were drawn closer to each other by having to solve some important problems together. You may have welded yourselves into a more real unit than would have been likely in the fragmentation of interests which so frequently characterizes modern North American urban life.

Practical Suggestions
May I, with hesitation and reticence, conclude by offering a few concrete suggestions as you leave?

Just as you have learned to withhold judgment until you become well acquainted with another country, do the same with your college, the state in which you're going to live, and the customs and culture of the United States at the present time. As surely as it happened here to your parents, you, assuming adult responsibilities in a country which you will know imperfectly, will undergo what Kalervo Oberg called "culture shock" as you settle into life in the United States. At times it will appear too bad to put up with, and at other times too good to be true, and neither is correct. Knowing that you are going to have culture shock, learn what it is, and prepare to live through it as maturely and intelligently as possible.

Expect to do battle with the problem of alienation, and to win. Alienation is a popular word today, although it has been with us for more than one hundred years. It describes a condition which may characterize an epoch, a people, a segment of society, a you. Societies undergoing rapid change are fertile ground for this kind of experience, and individuals whose lives are in the midst of change are especially prone. You will be tempted to become uninvolved, detached, remote, and to reject without assuming the responsibilities of involvement. There are many advantages to this sort of position if it doesn't become a way of life: it gives one a chance to observe, to choose, to judge, to offer suggestions whether they are asked for or not. In the end, however, one's time is too valuable to spend in limbo; one feels that life has meaning only as it is lived within an overall purpose, and few activities are significant unless they are integrated into a purposeful whole. It will be your privilege to be alienated, for a while, from many kinds of activities to which you will be exposed. It is your responsibility, at the same time, to find enough purposeful activities with which to become engaged in the life of the community.

Don't be in a great hurry about it, but do work through to a clear decision on whether you are an American or not. I am speaking especially to those of you who, like me, were born overseas and technically have dual citizenship until you are twenty-one years of age. How did you react to 95 percent of what was written in the local newspapers in the last week [Note: the week following the assassination of Senator Robert Kennedy]? Were you angered? Shamed? Saddened? Made more or less proud of your country? Which country? Ultimately you must be sure in your "viscera" as well as in your mind, and being sure, be willing to accept the costs and the gambles of that citizenship. Among my contemporaries who were born of American parents overseas and lived there long enough to be marginal people, I know of several who are well-satisfied in their choice to be North American, or to be something else. But I know of none who successfully and happily function in a confusion of identity between the two.

Whatever your direction in this choice, don't let your Portuguese get away from you. Use it every chance you get. Use it in college. If there is no course in Portuguese, request permission from your Spanish teacher, your literature professor, your anthropologist friend, to do papers on subjects related to Brazil, papers that will require you to read in the original language. Subscribe to a magazine like *Realidade*, or *Visao*, or even one of the photo-magazines like *Manchete*. Show them to your friends and teachers. Take issue with them when they show stupidity, enlighten them when they are naïve, concerning what is true of countries in which you have lived. This will have multiple benefits; you will educate the teacher and the other students; you will preserve your Portuguese, or other language (who knows when that will be useful); you will open up an area of expertise for yourself which is both unusual and respected in the United States today.

It will be to your advantage, academically and personally, to become an "expert" on something strictly Brazilian. Get to know an author, a man of stature like Jorge Amado, Jose Lins De Rego, Gilberto Freyre, or another. Find out all about him, what he has written, and what relation this has to current Brazil. Do a favor to your classes in history and literature, and to yourself the privilege, of acquaintance with this rich side of Brazilian life. Study a particular set of characteristics of a segment of Brazil. For example, learn all there is to know about the "jangada."[4] A lot has been written about it in the United States and here; it not only makes interesting conversation among amateur sailors and fishermen, but encompasses a wealth of information about history, economics, social change, social problems, politics, and much more. Learn all about a painting style, an art form, a religious tradition, a period of Brazil's history, its relations with a particular other country, or whatever. Become an expert on one thing that is Brazilian.

As a conclusion to what I have to say, remember these words: "nao desprese nada daquilo que voce recebeu aqui."[5] Use it and appreciate it. It will help you not only to survive, but to live a healthier and stronger life... blessed with a heart divided.

NOTES

1. Park, introduction to Stonequist, *The Marginal Man*, page xv, cited in Myrdal, *An American Dilemma*, 1384.
2. Ibid., 1385.
3. *Cafézinho* is Portuguese, meaning "to linger over a cup of coffee."
4. *Jangada* is Portuguese, describing a small fishing boat made of logs bound together. Fishing from this small boat can be hazardous since it is difficult to maneuver.
5. "Nao desprese nada daquilo que voce recebeu aqui" in English means "Do not discredit or reject what you have learned here."

Living in Little America in Asia

Maggie, a twenty-five-year-old female MK, grew up in an Asian country. As she was growing up, the only memories she had were of living in that country. The only house she knew was the house in which she lived until she returned to the United States for college. She had no sense of difference since she had no other country with which to compare it.

Maggie's missionary family lived in an American-style house on a missionary compound, and she went to a school on a military base that was located right there in her city. Thus, the only thing she had to compare with her Asian upbringing was being in a school of all white kids who spoke English. Since she went to that American school, she felt that most of her social life was similar to the American kids, except that it was a smaller American community. She was involved in sports, youth choir at her church, and her class's yearbook.

One thing that was different was that she went with her family to the national church. Since she did not know or speak the language, she did not get involved with the national young people who attended that church. Throughout her time spent in this Asian country, most of her nurturing and support came from her family and members of the other missionary families. Those friendships were developed in the mission "family," which until this day she treasures and refers to them as "precious."

Although Maggie felt some excitement about coming back to the States for one-year furloughs, she was always sad to leave her home and friends in Asia. On the other hand, she wanted to see her relatives residing in the States, whom her parents spoke of often. She admits that she really did not know these people who were referred to as relatives. In America, she enjoyed all the shops in the large malls where she could buy almost anything she wanted if she had the money. In Asia, she was beginning to understand, they just did not have all the items that she was exposed to in America.

Maggie admitted that furloughs did entail a difficult transition for her. Here, she had to establish herself in a new school for one year. The school in the States seemed so huge compared to the school in Asia. She said that she was reluctant to establish or develop new relationships with classmates in America, since she knew she would only have to leave them at the end of their year's furlough. After a short time of adjustment in her new school, Maggie remembers being quite happy. The transition from Asia to America was the hardest part.

In Asia, the school Maggie attended was indeed small, and she was able to be involved in many events and activities. She said that most of the kids were non- Christians. She, however, experienced them as being nice and good friends just like her other Christian friends. There was a cross-section of students, and thus she felt that she had not developed many prejudices like American kids in the States. Maggie did go away to a boarding school only three and one-half hours away when she was a senior in high school. It was like all her MK friends from the American school had transferred, and she knew almost everyone.

The people who influenced her life most were her parents. At that time in her life she adopted her parents' values as her own. Upon completion of high school, she left Asia. She found it very difficult to leave her house as well as her parents and siblings. Leaving her boyfriend was particularly hard for her.

When Maggie entered her American college as a freshman, she had a very difficult time in this new world. At first, she was still trying to live in her known and comfortable world in Asia. She was a foreigner now living in America. Although she had an older sibling in a state college in the same city, they did not see each other often since each had their own friends and activities. Whenever possible her sibling did try to listen, giving understanding and encouragement to her. She struggled with some feelings of inferiority since she was having to make some new adjustments in order to reintegrate herself into this society. Getting used to doing things in a new and different way was not easy and sometimes caused some resentment. She wanted people on her college campus to know, understand, and care about her world in Asia.

Even today, Maggie says she feels equally at home in America and in Asia. When I first spoke with Maggie, she was a senior in college, so after three years on an American college campus she had gained a sense of belonging in America. During her four years of college, she was able to go back to see her family and friends in Asia twice. When she returned she found that none of her friends remained. Many things were different, as progress and development had changed things quickly. "Still," she said, "I feel my roots are not in the States but in my Asian country."

Maggie has been one of the few fortunate MKs who could live with her parents during all the developmental years of her life. In many ways she grew up in "a little America" in Asia since she seemed to have had the best of two worlds. Therefore, I am of the belief that Maggie cannot really identify with those MKs who were less fortunate, and many who spent almost all their developmental years in some boarding school.

The hardest part for Maggie was when she was left in the States, and her parents returned to Asia. As with many MKs, the irony was that Maggie was now living in her parents' country of America, and her parents were living in the land of her birth and the place she still calls "home." When her parents went to Asia they had to go through an adaptive period there while Maggie had to learn to adapt in America, which was actually a foreign country to her.

CHAPTER TEN

Abuse: Sexual and Substance

Images Avoided

Kay, a twenty-three-year-old female MK, came to my office with her parents, who were soon to return to their mission field. Both of the parents were third-generation missionaries, making Kay a fourth-generation MK. The presenting problem was Kay's terrible migraine headaches. She was always either going through one of these headaches or feeling that in a few days she would be plagued by another.

Kay came from a competent, talented family. It was full of achievers, yet no matter what happened, their philosophy was, "That is just life." Her parents' leaving her only compounded her headaches. Kay was under constant pressure and suffered from anxiety. Kay was living with a family friend, so perhaps the parents felt good about this, but Kay was still hearing the words in her mind, "This is just life."

This brilliant young MK had wanted to become a doctor, but various incidents placed roadblocks in the way of her dream. Kay was a good musician and songwriter, and often when her parents were on furlough, the whole family sang in churches where her parents were on deputation.

In the early 1980s Kay was a college student. In that women's college dorm, a terrible experience took place that colored much of her life from that point. She was assaulted one morning early when she went to take her shower. Kay was an early riser and an early-to-bed person. On this particular morning, she seemed to be the only student in her dorm who was out of bed. The silence was eerie. Kay had just put on her robe and stepped out of the shower when a young man surprised her, appearing out of nowhere and asking her where the men's room was. Of course, her first statement was that he was not in the men's dorm, and what was he doing in her dorm? However, he went on down the hallway, perhaps checking out the hallway for other students who might have been on their way to the shower by now. Kay had gone on to the sink and mirrors that lined the wall. It was very bright in there. She was drying her hair with her towel, and when she removed the towel and opened her eyes, the young man was entering the bathroom. She looked at him quizzically. He was smiling. Slowly he reached for her arms. In her innocence, she was still wondering if she could help him find someone or someplace. *MKs are such caregivers*, and no wonder, for they have had two parents as role models for helping people.

In only seconds, this young man had backed Kay up against the cold tile wall. He held her wrists in a vicelike grip. He then began to "close the gap." She had to lift her head to look at his face. His eyes gleamed with intent, and he was no longer smiling. Kay felt completely helpless, accompanied by despair, disbelief, outrage, humiliation, and terror. As she looked out of the sides of her eyes, she could see the doorway about five feet away. She had no memory of how she was able to twist her arms out of his grasp, but fortunately she did. She ran down the hallway toward her room. He ran after her. Her terror mounted when he touched her again. She yelled out, "Stop! Stop it!" He laughed. When she glanced back he was near the exit leading to the stairway. Kay then walked on to her room. When she got inside and felt safe again, she went to look out the window. It was now dawn, and when she looked down below and continued to watch, she saw that young man walk out of the dorm and cross the street. At that moment she felt hate and anger rise up in her. She hated that man who had assaulted her! Shock set in, and Kay sat on her bed and shook for a long time. What a devastating experience! Of all the places in America where she had felt safe, it was in her college dormitory, a women's dorm. She continued to question why this young man was in *her* dorm. She was in a state of shock.

Following this awful, horrible experience, Kay had some bad dreams that continued to haunt her. As we talked about this incident, the worst in her whole life, I asked Kay, in a counseling session, "What would you like to have done to that guy?" At that moment, that old sense of helplessness flooded her mind and gripped her whole being. She wanted him to feel as helpless as he had made her feel at that suspended, piercing moment between disbelief and flight.

Kay said that as she thought about this horrible experience many times later, in fact for years, she had told herself that nothing had really happened. Perhaps this too was "Just life." The bottom line was that Kay was living in denial, denying those feelings, perhaps because she could not deal with them. She had not told anyone, not a family member, or classmate, not a faculty or staff member. When I told her that if it had happened to me, I would want to inflict pain on him that he would never forget, she replied, "But pain holds no terror for me." But then she said, "The threat of pain and humiliation would be sweet revenge for me, indeed." She just wanted him to feel the helplessness she had felt and the feeling of being out of control.

When Kay left the counseling session she told me that throughout the rest of the day, she could see in her imagination "the tiled wall of that bathroom and feel the cold on her back when the guy backed her into that wall." She remembers, instead of telling someone, she went on to classes as usual. She said, "I felt ready for the exam in biology that day." During the past twelve years, Kay had carried the terror and humiliation of that horrible experience. It seemed that sharing it with me had given her some newfound freedom. No wonder Kay was having those horrible migraine headaches.

As I worked with Kay, whom I really came to love, respect, and admire, we talked about ways to deal with pressures and stresses that, by the way, did relieve her from some, but not all, of those mean migraines. Kay worked on many issues, such as family of origin, how to deal with her feelings, how to learn to relax, and how to deal with American culture and its people. Kay actually felt more at home in the country where her parents were missionaries. After all, she had lived there the greater part of her life and felt so comfortable in that culture. Her values were so much nobler than those of her peers. She wanted to see her classmates and peers "walk the walk more than talk the talk." Her expectations of American people were high, and often they disappointed her. Kay's shyness made it somewhat difficult for her to meet and talk to people with any amount of ease, especially people she had never met. She was a strong introvert, so being with extroverted people really made her tired. As I worked with Kay, I saw her grow in self-esteem and self-confidence. She no longer needed the approval of everyone she met. She became more comfortable with herself, and best of all, the migraine headaches became fewer and fewer. She got more direction for her life, and in her words, "began to settle down."

Kay shared with me a poem by Adrian Plass that had meant a lot to her.

> Stranded in the hall of mirrors
> I must struggle to avoid
> Images that cannot show me
> Something long ago destroyed.
> In the darkness, in the distance
> In the corner of my mind
> Stands a puzzled child in silence
> Lonely, lost and far behind.

Kay shared with me some of her thinking in a letter, portions of which follow:

I am learning the past has a way of catching up with one if one treats it like it never happened. If one didn't take the time for the pain as well as the joy, that would not be quite right. Somehow in our culture it is okay to share the joy but we learn to hide the pain. It is easier that way. Easier for others and easier for ourselves. I have gotten *very* good at protecting myself from loss, separation, alienation and culture shock. But I am learning to be human. It is okay to hurt. It is okay to desire not to hurt, as long as my desire not to hurt does not turn into the demand for relief at any cost. At the cost of loving God less deeply—on the plane of I'll do xyz so God will give me health, food, and happiness. At the cost of loving those around me superficially....

When I have a migraine I've learned that if I fight the pain or try to ignore it, the overall pain and tiredness is increased. But if I accept the pain and mentally embrace it, even though all my instincts tell me not to, it becomes easier to bear. I believe, emotionally, this principle is the same. "Shall we accept good gifts from God, and not trouble?" Job asks. And so I struggle to pull both difficult times and pleasant times into a better balance; to live life honestly.... I am learning that acknowledging the past does not change it for the better. It does not transport it away or provide persons or circumstances to explain it away. But it does shape the rubble that before was piled in a heap too high to scale, into an archway, a series of doorways. I have struggled with the fact that I could not "shape the rubble" on my own. In my parents' time people did not go to see counselors to sort out their life, but then, people did not used to have electricity, yet I have no qualms about using as much as I can afford! Part of being human is to need others. Part of MK training is being independent. I search for a better balance somewhere in that dichotomy.

Kay says that the following verse in a book entitled *Two-Part Invention* by L'Engle sums up a journey much like her own.

> In imagination only
> In my single mirror see
> Clear and calm, the one reflection
> Of the person that is me.

Kay said, "Now I am setting out into the unknown. It will take me a long time to work through the (emotions). There are no shortcuts: it has to be gone through.... This is my goal and my journey. May your journeys bring you as much satisfaction."

Innocence Violated

Maxine is a delightful MK with a sparkling personality. She is so energetic. Her eyes sparkle, and her laughter is contagious. However, Maxine has not always portrayed these characteristics. She lost herself and her vivaciousness around the age of eleven. At that age she had been violated by her softball coach who fondled not only her, but also six of her friends.

It happened when she and her missionary family were in the States on a year's furlough. Her former recreation league softball coach was found guilty of molesting several of his young girl students. He was charged and convicted of six counts of taking indecent liberties with the girls under the age of twelve during the mid-1980s. Just days before his trial was set to begin in October 1995, this softball coach decided to plead guilty to the molestation charges. Out of seven counts he pled guilty to five. Two of his victims took the stand as part of the sentencing process. They told the judge about how the molestation had impacted their lives and about the emotional scarring it had caused.

The judge said to the guilty coach, "You are either sick or in need of in-depth treatment, or... not sick and in need of severe punishment. I have a feeling it's a little bit of both." The victims testified and told the court about how the coach had fondled them, and spoke of acts they said severely altered their lives.

Maxine had told me in a counseling session, long before the coach was tried in a court of law, how the coach had fondled her when she was on his girls' softball team at the young age of eleven. Interestingly enough, he took all the girls, one by one, back into his bedroom under the guise of trying on their new softball uniforms for fit. There he fondled them.

Maxine, by this time, was twenty-three years old, and had developed an eating disorder that plummeted her into deep depression. Due to her health problems, the family decided to leave the mission field and return to the States in order for Maxine to get the kind of medical attention she needed, along with counseling and psychiatric attention for her depression.

As I worked with Maxine, I encouraged her to get the other girls along with their parents together, reveal their long-kept secrets, and press charges against the coach. After several years passed, I suppose the coach thought he was going to go scot-free, and the girls had simply forgotten what had happened to them. But now, as young women they finally brought charges. Of course, the coach denied all charges and rejected an offer to plea bargain earlier in the summer of 1995. However, as all the girls' testimonies were identical, it wasn't hard to prove their cases. The coach faced a maximum sentence of fifty years in prison.

When Maxine first revealed her abuse to me, she was experiencing an eating disorder and was depressed. When she began to vividly remember her sexual abuse, she had tried to suppress all of those memories. However, it got to the point that she could no longer suppress what had happened to her. The experience had made her sick. She was very insecure and had many fears.

In 1992, when she first saw the psychiatrist to whom I had referred her, she told him that she would become preoccupied with food for days at a time. At times, she obsessed about food for as many as five hours out of sixteen hours in a waking day. At this time, she was also having trouble concentrating on her college studies. Often she had trouble falling asleep.

After some counseling sessions and meeting with the psychiatrist who placed her on an antidepressant, she began to feel much better. Once they decided to confront the coach and press charges against him, she was feeling much better, and her energy level was improving steadily. Her mood was upbeat. She wasn't feeling so desperate, and her memory improved remarkably. Needless to say, her grades improved rapidly as well. Now she said she could become absorbed in her tasks and feel really good about her accomplishments. But whereas she could be very open with females, she was still having some trouble when it came to male relationships. She felt repulsed by the affection they showed toward her when she was dating. She said that when it came to showing affection she became afraid and would back off. She also had trouble sharing her deeper self.

On first seeing Maxine, her psychiatrist's impression was that she had been suffering from a posttraumatic stress disorder. Of course, once the coach was brought to trial she felt somewhat vindicated. She no longer had problems with anorexia, and her obsessive-compulsive traits disappeared.

From 1992 through 1993, I spent a total of eighteen hours with Maxine. I count it a real privilege to have had the opportunity to watch her work through the abuse and witness what a vivacious person she had become. Her self-esteem is great. She has become a secure, happily married young woman with children. During all this time, her parents were very supportive of her, and she was surrounded by good friends who loved her.

Finally justice was served, and Maxine had become a free human being again. After growing up in another country and culture, she of course had to work through other issues such as separation, the loss of her adopted country and culture, feeling different and having different values from her American peers, culture shock, and feelings of isolation. I would now describe Maxine as a compassionate, energetic, caring, fun-loving, and beautiful young lady. She is a wonderful wife and mother.

Vindicated

Camille is an MK who grew up in Spain. As a twenty-two-year-old female, she was disturbed about many things and was struggling with feelings of anger toward her family, mostly her father. Camille's father had been abusive, physically and verbally. Her mother, perhaps out of fear of her husband, gave the appearance that she stood with her husband instead of taking sides with her children. Both parents were serving as missionaries in the medical area. According to Camille, "Sometimes my father's abusiveness was beyond explanation. People just wouldn't believe it." She said that she was never sexually abused by her father. She and her siblings frequently "froze" with fear of him.

Camille graduated from a small denominational college and began working as a receptionist in the emergency room of a large hospital. This was her first venture outside the Christian community. In the emergency room, each day brought her face-to-face with the results of crime, domestic violence, drunkenness, and drugs. She said, "I worked in the emergency room long enough to know Christians get hurt too, and non-Christian people have good things happen to them." She began to question the faith with which she had known in her growing-up years in Spain. She saw this as a part of forming her own identity.

Camille, at the same time, was agonizing over her relationship with her family back in Spain. It seemed that "their God no longer seemed beyond questioning." For some time, she "threw her Christianity out the window." However, immediately she recognized she had nothing to take its place. She felt it was time to move on from her job in the emergency room, move to another state, and start a new job. She thought it was time for her to make a fresh start.

After her move, upon someone's recommendation she came to see me for therapy. She soon made new friends at her new job. She told me that she was skeptical about these "bolt-of-lightning type of religious experiences." She was ready to learn and grow by taking small steps. Her first priority was to let her parents know how she felt. She voiced her feelings, the whole gamut, in my office in the first therapy sessions. She did not know how to go about working things out with her parents. Before, she had written letters, feeling this would be the safer way. Up to this point her parents' letters were what she called "preachy," and instead of responding to her questions and feelings, their letters were filled with Scripture verses. This was so frustrating. Camille felt she was getting nowhere.

Camille felt all alone. Her sister and brother were living in faraway states. She did begin to make friends at her new job with people who were either missionaries or missionary kids. I assured her that I was there to hear her out. I would be there to encourage her, and she could express her anger without scaring me. She could express her anger as long as she was not destructive. She expressed so much of her anger through tears, even sobbing at times. Before now, she had felt unheard and unloved. Camille needed someone to help her sort out things and also affirm her feelings, and at the same time, help her see her parents' perspective. She needed to talk about how she and her siblings were treated as children, particularly by her father. Her poor relationship with her parents was spilling over into her other relationships with folks here in the States. It was hard enough feeling like a foreigner back here in her parents' country. It was also hard to understand the logic of her parents living in her country (she had been there since age two) and she was now living in the country of her parents' birth. Of course, she had no choice in which country she would live after high school graduation. Missionary kids are programmed to understand that upon their high school graduation, they would indeed return to the United States to receive their college education. There are so many adjustments for MKs to make in order to fit in the country not of their choice. She knew she was American but indeed did not feel American. Having grown up in a Christian fundamentalist missionary family hearing only "Do's and Don'ts" was now taking its toll on Camille. Often she did not know what choices she should make. Life was really hard!

Camille was sent away to boarding school hundreds of miles away from her home at a very early age. Perhaps this is one reason she was as healthy as she was. Had she lived in the abusive environment of home on a regular, long-term basis, who knows what other problems would compound those she was already experiencing?

In our counseling sessions, Camille was able to verbalize all her disappointments, her anger, and all of the feelings, knowing that now, with this counselor who understood missionary kids, she would not be judged. Missionary children, in general, feel that they are judged a lot by parents, other missionaries, and the people in the churches back here in the States. I encouraged her to get all her negative, bitter feelings outside by talking them out. Of course, Camille's parents could easily detect her anger toward them through her letters.

Since Camille felt she was not being heard through her former letters, I encouraged her to sit down and write to them a letter, putting all her thoughts and feelings in writing, not worrying about language, and she did. I then told her that she would not mail them that first letter, but we would keep on refining it until she felt really good about mailing it. Afterwards, each week we looked at her letter. Accusations would not be permitted. She would stick to her own feelings. There would be no blaming. In other words, I expressed to her that we would take anything out of the letter that might put her parents on the defensive. After several weeks, she said, "I am now ready to mail this letter." I, too, felt it was a good letter and ready to be mailed.

Camille's mother was so touched by her daughter's letter that she told her husband that she was going to the States to spend time with her daughter. He was to come on their regular furlough a few weeks later. Camille brought her mother to see me right after her arrival. Her mother told us how her husband had taken advantage of her and even had her believing some of his "stuff." She was often so confused, she didn't know what to do. He was definitely a male chauvinist and did not view women as equal with men. She had been so beaten down, and she had seen no way out of the relationship. After all, they were missionaries. The weeks I spent with Camille and her mother were very productive.

Then Camille's father came home to the States. He came along to counseling with his wife and daughter. After the first session, I was so concerned and disturbed with his lack of hearing, understanding, and processing what was being said by his wife, his daughter, and me. When I asked him to repeat what one of us had said, what he repeated back to us often had nothing to do with what we had just said. I realized this man had really deep problems. I asked him if he would go to a psychiatrist and take some testing. He agreed. The results showed that he was either not willing or not capable of doing any better or changing his behavior. The longer I worked with him, the more I concluded that he just was not capable of changing. He just did not seem to have the mental faculties to process information. He saw no need for him to change his behavior. He was almost out of touch with reality. Some interesting facts were revealed by her father that had helped me to understand his state of mind.

Camille's father had been so arrogant toward his wife and daughter. At one time in Spain, he had actually been jailed for the way he had treated a national colleague. In talking to this man about his own family of origin, I learned that his parents had also been missionaries. He talked about the abuse he had received, along with his siblings, at the hand of his father. He said that when the children, including himself, did something their father disapproved of, he would beat them unmercifully. They would cry and scream so loud (this was on one of their furloughs) that the neighbors called the police, who came to their home. I asked him what happened when the policeman came. I asked if his father stopped beating them after that episode. His reply was, "No, thereafter, before he started to beat us, he would put rags in our mouths so no one could hear us yell." I have found that abuse in families fosters more abuse, from generation to generation. This was certainly true of this family.

Camille's mother told her husband that she was not going back to Spain to live and minister. Of course, he would not be allowed to return to Spain if his wife did not go with him. Camille's mother had tried to work things out with her husband, but there was no way he was going to change. She ended up divorcing him and taking up a new career for herself. She became very self-sufficient.

Working with Camille was a real joy and a challenge. It was so fulfilling to watch her grow and stand on her own two feet. She had met a man, an MK who had grown up in the same country where she had spent the developmental years of her life. She became friends with his family, who invited her to have dinner with them occasionally. I saw them together in therapy many times and came to admire these young people. He had had his share of struggles, and yet they seemed to be able to understand each other as MKs. They fell in love. One day he told her, "Camille, I know you are not ready yet, but someday I am going to ask you to marry me." He was living with his parents, but she had her own apartment. She liked where she lived. She loved looking at the trees behind her apartment building, as well as watching the children playing. She was happy living there.

It seemed that everything was going so well. Then, one night as she was watching television, she thought she heard someone at her door. She punched in 911, and the police came. They did not see anyone around the buildings looking suspicious. She thought, "Oh well, it must have been a false alarm." The officers did warn her that the lock on her back door did not look strong, and it would be easy for someone to break in her apartment. She made a note in her mind that she would have her boyfriend replace it, but she kept forgetting to ask him. Two weeks later, she had come home from work and was relaxing, eating chips, and enjoying a video. She fell asleep. Then she was awakened from a deep sleep. When she opened her eyes, a man was standing in her bedroom. When she lunged for her phone, he grabbed her and put a butcher knife to her neck. At first, he said he only wanted money and her charge card. When she gave him about six dollars and told him she had no charge card, he then told her he was going to rape her. She was terrified, and she began to scream and fight him with all her might. She fought to get back to the telephone, but he stopped her, holding the knife over her. She reached for the knife, slicing her hand on the sharp blade. The man began beating her in the face and on the head, and then he ripped off her clothes and blindfolded her. He told her that if she tried to see his face, she would die. Just before being blindfolded, she remembers seeing the clock, which read 3:30 a.m.

Her attacker forced her into every sex act imaginable. Each time she tried to resist, he would put the knife to her neck. She knew that, after all was said and done, he was going to kill her. She asked to use the bathroom. He led her there, still blindfolded, and let her go in alone. She pushed the door closed and locked it at the same time. She slipped off the blindfold and realized she was naked. Then she heard him going down the stairs. She grabbed a large towel and wrapped it around her. She looked out her bathroom window, second floor, and pushed it up. This seemed to be her only chance to stay alive. When she looked down, he was standing there, staring up at her. She pulled her head back inside, and then heard a crash below. He was coming back inside, and she knew he would be able to break the bathroom door down. In desperation, she plunged out the bathroom window, bouncing off of a storage shed and fell to the concrete patio below. But now she did not know where her attacker was maybe hiding. She looked around, but he was gone. She was hurting so bad, and when she looked at her arm she knew the bone in her elbow was broken. She ran past cars, tripping a car alarm. She headed for a bush beside the apartment building. She thought it was large enough for her to hide. She then headed for a bush close to someone's door. She reached up and rang the doorbell. The door cracked open, the man inside saw her. She told the couple what had happened and they called 911. It was then 5 a.m. Her attacker had abused her for two hours. She knew she had made a very narrow escape. Later, she was told that her telephone line had been cut, and when they checked upstairs they found that her bathroom door was indeed standing open.

I was in my home when a phone call came from my office telling me to call one of Camille's friends. She said something terrible had happened to Camille. I heard the bad news. I was asked if I thought they should call her boyfriend, who had already gone to work. I told her that, by all means, he needed to get to the hospital. He, along with other friends, had gone to the hospital. They were all outraged. She was released from the hospital around noon, eyes swollen, arm broken, and face and legs bruised. As she was being driven to her friend's home, Camille was wondering if her rapist could be following them. As friends dropped in, Camille told her story over and over again. She felt the love and support of her friends and her mother, who was by her side. Her talking about what had happened to her was her first step toward her healing. For her mother, boyfriend, and close friends to hear her describing that horrible event was agony. Friends cleared out her apartment. It was very hard for her fiancée to listen, feeling helpless about her losing her virginity to this rapist. She had saved herself for marriage. Now she was angry at God. Didn't he care? Why had God not prevented this from happening?

Two days after this incident, Camille and her boyfriend came to see me. Again, she went over her story, detail by detail. I believe a lesser person would have folded under the brutality of what had happened. I felt so much pain and sympathy when I saw Camille's condition. She had come so far, and I assured her that she would get through this experience as well.

But who was the rapist? It took several weeks for the police to arrest the man living with his wife next door. The man's wife had awakened in the night and realized he was not there. Camille remembered the day the new couple moved into that apartment. She found out that the woman was trying to get away from her husband, but he always followed her. He was very abusive to her as well. That very first night, Camille thought she had heard him beating his wife. When the attacker returned to his apartment and was asked where he had been, he simply told her not to worry about it. Then, as he turned to go upstairs, she saw a knife in his back pocket. When the man was confronted by the police, he had his own story that did not ring true. His wife just knew in her heart that her husband had done this outrageous thing, so the next day at work, still not completely sure of his guilt, she called the police station and revealed what she could not hold back any longer. On New Year's Eve, the rapist was arrested. There was much circumstantial evidence, one being that he had left a tire iron in her apartment that he had used to pry open her door. The serial number matched the one belonging to his wife's car. She checked with the policeman, and sure enough, her tire iron was missing from her car. The evidence was there: hair and semen samples matched the rapist's DNA. Now Camille had to decide if she wanted to go to court and testify. She would be telling her story to twelve people whom she had never met. After weighing the benefits and the drawbacks, Camille said she indeed did want to go and testify. It was scary, but now Camille was starting to take control of her life. She was feeling stronger and she knew she had the strong support from friends, family, and her counselor. The rapist's wife also testified against him, even after her friends kept saying to her, "Don't do it, don't do it!" She knew in her heart it was the right thing to do.

The judge sentenced the rapist to serve eighty years in prison with no hope of parole. Now, Camille felt vindicated. Knowing he would never be out of prison, the cloud of fear of this man was lifted. Camille had lived a nightmare, but her perpetrator did not destroy her. This

MK who had struggled to find her own identity in America discovered that she had the inner strength to fight back and rebuild her life. Her message is, "There is hope and healing on the other side." I love what she said after everything was settling down: "I think it can be very easy to learn all the theology, but when the rubber hits the road, the price is high." She paid a very heavy price, but her faith was strengthened as she thought about how she could have died that night. She had gained a sense of personal power she didn't know she had. One bit of advice she offered was as follows:

> One thing I dreaded hearing was clichés or pat answers like "God intends all things for the best." Fortunately most of my friends did not say such things. Trying to make sense of a brutal attack is an intensely personal process. What a well-meaning friend finds comforting, the victim may find offensive. Don't try to offer a tidy explanation.

When the rapist was sentenced, she said that the trial had delivered a powerfully healthy message: "You were innocent. He was wrong." After going through such a horrible experience and being vindicated, Camille felt she could stand up to the whole world. She said that as long as she lives, memories of the rape will hurt her, but she will not allow it to control her life.

Camille did marry her boyfriend, and I had the honor of being a part of her wedding. She was a beautiful bride and so happy. They now have three children.

Scars from Child Sexual Abuse

In recent years we have heard and read, more than ever before, about child sexual abuse in America. But who would have ever thought that sexual abuse could take place on the mission fields of our world? I have heard firsthand about dorm staff, dorm parents in boarding schools, "friends" of the family, or even family members taking advantage of the children they have within their charge. When MKs leave their homes and go away to boarding school, most parents would never dream of someone abusing their little children. To be away from family is a terrifying experience in itself, much less feeling unsafe in one's own dormitory.

When I started a counseling ministry for the children of missionaries, I expected to hear stories about the pain of separation and loss, feeling different and having different values, culture shock and feelings of alienation, but never did it cross my mind that I would be dealing with adult MKs, mostly females but also some males, calling me and pouring out their hearts over the telephone, saying, "I was sexually abused on the mission field."

In 1992 I received a call from Rosemary, a female MK from a western state, to ask for my guidance and support. She had entered therapy many years after she was sexually abused at a boarding school for MKs. She had gone away to boarding school at a very early age. She began to tell me not only about her own abuse, but about the abuse of many friends and acquaintances who had attended the same school. Rosemary became courageous enough to broach the subject of her own abuse. She had been contacted by other MKs who had also been abused, asking for her emotional support. At first, they were hesitant and scared to talk about it, but as they trusted Rosemary, they began to open up more and more. As they banded together, they felt obligated to try to do something to stop the predators, one who was still working as a missionary in the school they attended. I can't praise Rosemary enough for her genuine care and concern for these young people. She is a bright, courageous career woman who felt the need and urgency to reach out to those who were hurting just like she was. One of Rosemary's prayers follows.

> Lord, as I journey through my valley of grief, let me recognize the richness and growth produced by co-strugglers in my life.

Let me live my life by impacting the world around me.

Let me touch lives so profoundly that once I am gone, it won't be just a remembrance of my face or my name but a reflection of your love.

A reaching out, a gentleness, and a compassion that "brush-stroked" other's lives. That in me they were able to see past my atrocities and pain.

That I was open enough for them to view the "windows of my soul," and recognize that as deep as the pain had run so also did my depth of love and compassion for those who suffered likewise. A deep blend of your handiwork in my life producing teardrops of gold.

Rosemary, a gutsy woman in her desire to reach out to abused MK women, first started her work by reaching out only to abused females through a newsletter and by sending out packets of encouraging materials to sexually abused MKs. Rosemary established a network system for abused MKs to support each other on their road to recovery. Many individuals, some missionaries and mission boards in particular did their best to derail her efforts and to discredit her, and they tried to stop her in her pursuit to help other MKs, but she refused to give up on this journey that she felt was so important. She put together and distributed a bibliography on sexual abuse. Many of these MKs had suffered not only sexual but also emotional and physical abuse, some even from their parents.

Rosemary gave a number of MKs the opportunity to make statements about their abuse, some graphic and some horrifying. I share with you some of those statements:

Emotional Abuse
- Verbal scolding and reprimands in public
- Constant abusive putdowns

- Nonacceptance of tears, especially at times of separation from families, such as, "If you cry, you can't have your breakfast"
- Being made to wear a dunce cap; sitting on a stool in front of the class
- Dorm parents using their position as surrogate parents vs. their role in mission to intimidate or threaten children in their care
- Dorm parents who lied and said they were keeping our parents informed about our health and emotional status, but our parents were never aware of what was happening.
- Censored letters
- Being confined to our room the entire day as a form of punishment, including missing all three meals.

Physical Abuse
- Teachers hitting our knuckles with a wooden ruler against the desk or chalkboard
- Public spankings
- Beatings with a belt or paddle designed with holes to hurt more
- Beatings with other devices to injure, bruise, welt, and cause bleeding and scars

Sexual Abuse
- Dorm father sneaking into the girl's dorm rooms at *siesta* (rest time), while they were in their underclothing
- Dorm mothers observing teenage boys while they showered naked
- Dorm mothers controlling a key to the closet where hygiene pads were kept—deciding if or when the girls needed them
- Dorm fathers keeping track of the girl's menstrual cycles
- Use of medication/hypnosis by perpetrators to fog or black out the memories of abuse
- Fondling of genitals with finger penetration; fellatio, sodomy, and rape

- Sexually acting out by peers while in dorm settings or at mission meetings
- Parents who sexually abused their children while their children were on vacation or furlough
- Incest by siblings while on vacation or during furlough

Spiritual Abuses

Some MKs may have experienced only one kind of abuse, or a combination of many forms of abuse. In all kinds of abuses, what happened in a matter of minutes may take a lifetime to heal, if it ever does. Spiritual abuse may be the least common or hardest to define, but it is the most devastating of all.

When abused by an adult who is their spiritual leader, the child develops a confusion about who God is. The child may not be able to sort out, with their limited knowledge, that the supposed spiritual leader is indeed a perpetrator, rather than a true representative of God. In the child's eyes, they have been placed in the care of a dorm parent.

One MK told me that when she tried to tell her own parents about her dorm parent's shocking behavior toward her, she was stopped and was told, "Now the dorm parent is your parent away from home, and you are to do what he/she tells you to do." Thus, she accepted the coercion and abuse as God's will, and therefore God must approve. Indeed, God, in her eyes, also became the perpetrator. The concept her little mind could not comprehend was that this was not God's will, nor would God approve of such behavior.

With just this much information, we can readily see how the deepest wounds of many MKs are caused by their spiritual leaders. These children can no longer trust spiritual leaders, who are most often men. Their minds have tried to reason that if God approved of the abuse, then they wanted nothing to do with God. Some sexually abused MKs vow that they are atheists. Many others discount their spiritual guidance, and thus they shy away from the church and religious teachings all together.

Emotions are interwoven with one's spirituality. It is true what someone has said: "Spirituality is the first thing to go out of focus and the last to come back into focus."

Not as much has been shared by male MKs who have been sexually abused as by females who have somehow tried to come to grips with their traumatic experiences. However, it has happened more times than missionaries would ever want to believe.

Once when I was one of the main speakers at an MK retreat, two male MK brothers in their thirties came to me and asked me for a private session and wanted to bring their parents. I agreed, and soon the brothers came back with three other males they had known in their mission school, who also wanted to join the group session.

We gathered in a room, and one of the brothers immediately revealed that he and his brother had been sexually molested by their dorm parent. Suddenly, all three of the other young men sat on the edge of their chairs, eyes wide open, and said, "That happened to you, too?" There in the room were five male MKs who had been sexually molested by one and the same dorm parent, and they were just now able to talk about it. It was as if one man opened the door and four others walked through the door with him.

We all sat in silence for a few minutes, each dealing with our own thoughts, but relieved it was no longer a secret. Perhaps most of all, the missionary parents who sat in that room were most shocked. How could that have happened to five boys in one dorm, and no one knew about it or they simply were afraid to tell?

I vividly remember counseling with two young brothers, ages nine and eleven, who had been sexually abused by a neighbor, a male missionary, on the mission field. The mother was the first to discover this. She told her husband when he came home. The father was furious. This couple called their mission board and was told not to tell anyone about the abuse. They would send someone to the field to talk to them in two weeks. *Two weeks!*

The father of these boys would hardly go outside of his house, for fear that if he met the abuser he would "lose it," and beat him up. They were finally able to share with another missionary couple who kept hounding them saying, "I know something is wrong and I want you to tell me. I want to be here for you and support you."

These parents could not hide their anger, sadness, and disappointment. Their demeanor was revealing. The other missionary finally said to the father point blank, "What is wrong?" The thing that blew my mind was that any mission board would tell them not to talk to anyone about the episode for two whole weeks. That thought still arouses anger in me. Be quiet and let this man continue to abuse other children?

As I talked with these two boys, they were very open with me, telling me things the abuser had done to them that they had never told their parents. The most devastating thing of all was that the abusive missionary was allowed to continue to do his missionary work, while this really great missionary family had to leave. Knowing what they knew, it was impossible for them to go back and interact with the man who was supposed to be a fellow missionary and missionary "uncle" to the boys.

I have noticed several negative coping mechanisms that victims of sexual abuse are prone to implement in their lives. Some are eating disorders; isolation; avoiding intimacy; impulsivity; addiction to food, alcohol, drugs, or sex; self-mutilation; and suicide attempts.

Rosemary was not to be stopped as she reached out to MKs who had been sexually abused. Missionaries called and asked her to stop her work and ministry with MKs, but Rosemary was not to be stopped. She has sponsored conferences and retreats with outstanding professionals leading the discussions.

The number of abused attendees increased with each conference. Here was a group of young men and women, some older, who gathered to share their stories, their pain, their suffering, their guilt, and their compassion for each other.

Mission boards attempted to diminish and deny the facts of abuse in the lives of MKs. Rosemary's organization/ministry caused people to begin to face the facts. Major statistical and theological debates ensued. Rosemary wrote:

> The numbers prove that we have a problem. Yet, conservatives debate that the statistics of abuse are less in the "mission community." Should we not be outraged if even 1 percent of MKs have been abused, or is this also to become a sacrifice? If God counts the very number of hairs on our heads, does he discount 13 percent or more of the MKs who have fallen through the cracks in our Missions' floor boards? "God's will" has been used far too long as a blanket of denial. Our pain has evoked a less than compassionate response that evil happens, but there are sacrifices to be made when serving God. And so are we to accept, as MKs, that one of the greatest services was to be sacrificed in terms of separation, abuse, and finally to be swept under the mission carpet? As one MK so bluntly stated, "God created families first. The Boarding Schools were man made. Surely God must weep for us."

One female MK wrote:

> I am one of the "walking wounded." I have dealt with pain and the discord that the abuse created in my life. I was fortunate enough to be able to share my pain with my parents. They acknowledged my feelings and shared my pain as well, hardly believing such a thing had happened, and they did not know. We grieved together. But, I also know that there are many MKs who will never fully recover but will always carry SCARS. The abandonment and pain for them just won't heal.... Some MKs speak of it quietly mainly because, after all, who wants to hear? Some MKs remain quiet because of the hurt it would cause their parents. Others will remain quiet because for years when they

tried to tell, no one listened or even believed what they were told. This in itself was like being abused all over again.

Another female MK said:

From time to time I have encountered former house parents and teachers. They hugged and kissed me and asked how my life was. A part of me stood back in amazement. "Don't you remember what you did? Have you nothing to say to me?" Part of me wants to confront them and say to them, "Here is the pain. Here is the humiliation. Here is the degradation. It does not belong to me. It belongs to you, and so I am returning it. You may claim it or not. But, it is no longer mine."

One of my male MKs shared his experience with me.

It is with mixed emotions that I write my experiences, frightened and yet confident that I am doing the right thing.... My story begins with my sexual molestation at the hands of a missionary and trusted family friend. On two occasions he fondled my penis while I was sleeping next to him during an overnight visit. I experienced great pleasure during these events, and yet a part of me knew this was wrong. I was seven years old. Even though I told my parents, I was never asked how I felt about it, which sent a clearer signal that it was not to be discussed; it was to be forgotten. Later, I learned that this same missionary had abused others....

The next important event in my life was being sent away to boarding school. I am still angry that I was abandoned—that I was sacrificed to an absolutely evil, abusive situation. The environment was totally abusive: mentally, emotionally, physically and spiritually. Emphasis was placed on living an image, putting on a mask, that everything was okay, while I was dying on the inside. I was not able to openly rebel or even express the way I felt. I was so lonely! This has had a devastating effect on me....

Then, as an adolescent, when we were home on furlough, a pastor attempted to seduce me. I was confused.... But I knew what he was after when he grabbed my crotch and squeezed me. This was not an accidental brushing of his hand against me! I told no one. I internalized it and became ashamed of my arousal. I felt sure that this meant I was a homosexual. Who could I confide in about my fears? From past experiences, I had learned that such things were not to be discussed.... Later, I married.... However, I take full responsibility for what happened next. I began a long series of anonymous sexual encounters with countless numbers of men.... I cut myself off from my immediate and my extended family. Then I got in therapy. My therapist finally extracted my confession. I cannot possibly describe what that was like for me. It was so freeing. I was certainly afraid, ashamed and full of remorse, but I was finally free from my life of pretense and secretiveness.... My life continues to heal, and the healing comes with telling my story. Those who have been abused can work through the pain, and it can lessen its grip to some extent but not be forgotten.

A female MK shared her story of abuse. She said:

When I was in the second grade, I lived in a boarding school. In the morning I would attend classes, and in the afternoons there was lots of playtime. Little did I know how vulnerable I was, and I did not know I was being set up. There was only one other child in my class, so on occasions, he and I would play. The dorm master would invite me to ride on his moped with him. At first, I felt very special. Then it began to happen. We would ride away, and I could recall the direction we would go to a certain location, and then utter blackness surrounded my life. There was pain, an unfamiliar odor, tones of release, shaking, and a wetness. The fear and the ache that enveloped my soul was unspeakable, for my vocabulary did not contain the words to describe the abuse I endured. Returning from those moped rides, I would run and hide at the top of the sliding board on the playground. There, hugging my knees and my body desperately, I needed comfort. My tears would flow and wet my dress, forming a tide pond in my lap.

Dee Miller is now a mental health professional and the wife and daughter of a minister. She was sexually assaulted on the mission field by a fellow missionary. Her book, *How Little We Knew*, leads MKs as well as others through one powerful event after another. Rosemary introduced the book to me. Rosemary condenses its contents below:

It begins with Dee's background, her assault experience and its impact.
The painful confrontations involved denial.
The survivor struggled for growth, healing, the issues of being a secondary victim, and spiritual deterioration.

Rosemary highly recommends this book and says it should be read by church people, missions staff, missionaries, and MKs. She says, "It takes more energy to keep the secret than to share it. She also tells us, from her own experience, that it is time for all to bind together in support of healing the wounds of abuse that perpetrators have brought to mission circles. And, yes, there will always be SCARS."

During the first two years after I started counseling MKs, I received ten different telephone calls from MKs or their mothers expressing grave concern over the number of MKs who had suffered sexual abuse at the hands of someone on the mission field.

As some people read this chapter about the scars left on sexually abused MKs, there is no doubt that some will be in complete denial, saying, "It never happened." Some will say, "Even if it did, it didn't happen often." Some will say that these MKs are simply "wallowing in self-pity." Some will say, "Why don't we forget the past and move on?" And finally some will simply want to kill the messenger.

Marie Fortune, in her book *Is Nothing Sacred?* makes the following statement:

> Shooting the messenger is a common response to the revelation of unethical conduct. When the news is not something the institution or the community wants to hear, its knee-jerk reaction is to turn on the bearer of the news, often with a vengeance. First, the messenger's credibility becomes the issue, and then his or her motivation is suspect. All of this serves to deflect the attention of the church from the real source of the problem, the unethical pastor (perpetrator) and it relieves the church from doing anything about it. (120–21)

On the other hand, MKs, both male and female, who have experienced sexual abuse will perhaps want to praise the messenger for trying to educate the church, individuals, mission boards, and people in general about the problem that continues to exist. These MKs are banding together, giving support and care, seeking to help MKs find hope and healing.

Some ways abused MKs are healing are through group therapy, supportive caregivers, sharing of similar experiences, writing articles and/or books, attending conferences, reading books, listening to tapes, enjoying music, and not least, entering into therapy with qualified counselors who are versed in the area of child abuse, MK issues, and the spiritual ramifications, who can help them work through their massive amount of grief.

Rosemary sums it up by saying, "It's in the 'reflecting pool' of God's

Word and in the darkest part of the valley that I have been able to see my own incompletion of my spiritual growth. God strengthens and molds my character to reflect His Grace and Hope through the very process of Grief." She suggests one Scripture verse that has helped her. Psalm 147:3 assures us that "He heals the broken-hearted, and bandages their wounds." Healing takes time, but the scars shall always remain as reminders of the injury.

Finally, I share with you a poem written by an anonymous MK:

LITTLE TOT

She was just a little tot
With eyes so full of pain:
She yearned for affirmation,
But was scolded once again.
Dad & Mom were busy,
working for the Lord.
They took time for discipline,
time to love they couldn't afford.
Then he made her feel so special,
as he took her on his knee:
She responded to his touch,
starved for love she was, you see.
It wasn't long before she knew
that there was something not quite right.
Pain and guilt—bewilderment
come to haunt her day and night.
So tell me, what could she do?
In fear she looked to Mom & Dad.
But they were too busy in God's work
to see a face grown sad.
They dismissed their doubts,
"It's just a phase she's going through."
They failed to look for answers,

but to God's work they were true.
So she came to fear the God
her parents served so faithfully;
He too seemed to turn away
from her pain and misery.
It was only much later
as she faced her pain so great,
She understood how much God loved her
and "HIS SIN" her God did hate.

A Cocaine Trap

When I arrived at my office that morning, my telephone was ringing. Upon answering it, I heard the voice of a female. It was a missionary mother, who seemed desperate, as she told me about her MK son who was in trouble. She said, "My son, Joe, is facing a real crisis. Would you please help him?" I replied that I would be willing to do whatever I could for her son, but I needed some of the details to understand what the problem entailed.

This mother told me that her son was living in a city about two hours away from my city. He was likely facing a prison sentence. After a few details, I told her to have him call me himself and make an appointment, if he was serious about coming to see me. Within the hour, Joe did call me and made an appointment for the next day.

Upon entering my office, Joe stated clearly that he would, no doubt, be going to prison, having been charged with being a part of a cocaine ring and trafficking drugs. He went on to tell me that he had been living in the States, without his parents, and was feeling very lonely. Some young men had approached and befriended him, and before he knew what was happening, he was involved in a cocaine ring. He went on to tell me how he and an assigned partner had burglarized many places of business. He had even been given a credit card bearing the name of a reputable company and was told to purchase and resell expensive riding lawn mowers. He did as he was told, and had them delivered to the places his boss had designated. Then he received a reward of a couple hundred dollars. Still the drug ring received a large amount of money from the sales. He did this time after time. This cocaine ring included a number of people.

After being in this group for six months, he decided he must get out of this precarious situation, which he saw as a real predicament. He said to me, "All the time I was involved in that group, I realized it was wrong and dangerous, and some way I *had* to get out," but how to get out was the big question. Finally, one day Joe walked into his boss's office and told him he was leaving. As his boss placed a revolver to his head, he said, "No, you are not leaving." Fortunately or unfortunately, Joe was strong enough to face whatever was about to happen. He said, "Well, I will either walk out of here or you will need to carry me out in a black body bag." Miracle of miracles, the gang boss allowed him to walk out.

Upon being free for the first time in six months, Joe went directly to a police station and surrendered to the police, telling them of his predicament. He asked the policeman to drive him around the city because he wanted to show him all the places he had ever burglarized. The policeman obliged him and did just that. Of course, the policeman was shocked to see someone who had been a member of a cocaine ring or any drug group step forward and confess so blatantly. At this time, Joe was arrested but went free on bond. His trial was scheduled to take place only a couple of weeks later, and he was sure that he would be spending some time in prison. He had no idea how long that might be.

I asked Joe to give me the name and address of his attorney. He did, and I wrote a personal letter to his attorney, telling him that Joe was the son of missionaries. He had spent most of his life in another country and culture. He had no sense of belonging in any one place. He had been back in the States less than a year. He felt different and had been very lonely. His family, for the time being, was living on the West Coast, and he had had no money to visit them. Soon, they would be returning to the mission country to which they were assigned. Thus, in this environment and feeling so alone and needy, he had followed the first people who had befriended him. I told the attorney, "I know Joe has done wrong and must be punished, but please go as easy on him as you can. He will never be that naive again, and I believe he has learned a very hard lesson." I also sent him a copy of my book, which deals with the issues and adjustments missionary children must face as they return to America at college age. The biggest issue was how to reintegrate themselves into the American culture. I told him about the support these young people needed from Americans to become a part of this society.

Because of Joe's honesty and because he turned himself in freely, through my support, and my becoming an advocate for Joe, the court had mercy on him, and he did not have to go to prison. Joe was the only one in that whole gang, including the boss, who was not given a prison sentence. In 1996, the rest of that gang was "busted," and that was the end of one cocaine ring. Joe had done an admirable thing by stepping forward and turning himself over to the police, having no idea what the results might be.

Joe had lost everything he owned during that nightmare. He lost his car, his apartment, and all the money he had saved. He was then broke financially and now had to start all over. My aim, as his therapist, was to help him believe in himself again. When I asked him if he knew why he had gotten involved in that group in the first place, he replied, "I did not know then, but I do now. I needed a place to belong, and they befriended me and took me in."

I talked to Joe about how bad things often happen to good people, but what was most important was what he had learned from that bad experience. He acknowledged that he had learned to not allow his emotions take over, and in such a state of mind, to get involved with people he did not know. Never again would he join some group before asking a lot of questions. I wanted him to understand that one mistake should not define who he was. He needed to forgive himself and move on with his life, being the best person he knew how to be. He agreed that he had learned much through the experience that he would never have learned in any other way.

Thanks be to God, Joe was brave enough to step forward and confess his mistake before he had gotten in more deeply with that drug crowd. The marvel of it all is that he was allowed to live and tell his story. The last time I heard from Joe, his mother told me that he was happy, and enjoying being married and fathering a little girl.

A Victim of Alcoholism

On a Tuesday morning, I received a telephone call from missionary parents asking me if they could make an appointment to come to my office with their twenty-five-year-old son. Their son, Bill, was already an alcoholic and was in jail in an adjoining state. He could be released from jail *only* if the parents could assure them that Bill had an appointment with a therapist. We set up some time for the following afternoon. The parents were pleased that I could see them without delay. I had reserved the entire afternoon for them since they were coming from a distant state.

The next day, I met Bill and his parents for the first time. I was able to get an overall picture of his predicament. After time with the family, the parents left the room. Bill and I could then have some quality time together, where we could go to the heart of the matter. I assured him that he could say anything he wished, and if there were things that he preferred his parents not know, I would respect that and keep it confidential. There was one condition. If he had thought of hurting himself or anyone else, then I could not remain quiet on such an issue. He assured me he had no intention of hurting anyone. Bill was so open and was willing for his parents to know everything.

Bill began to tell me his story. He was adopted as an infant. He loved and appreciated his adopted parents. As a very young child he had gone to a mission field in South America with his parents. He claims that culture as his own. He was still trying to determine his own identity after growing up in another culture. Just about the time he had formed his identity in South America, he returned to the States for college. Since his former identity did not fit the demands in the States, he was confused and trying to re-form his identity to fit with the American culture. Sometimes Bill felt he was walking around like a robot, not knowing who he was or where he belonged.

Bill, until now, had never sought or even wanted to find his birth mother. However, lately, he said he often wondered if he had any of his mother's traits or features. He said this as he looked intently at his own hands, saying, "I wonder if my hands are like hers." This was all new to him since he had accepted his adopted family and his life as it was. His parents assured him that if he wanted to find his birth mother, they would do all they could to help him find her. It was clear that Bill had lots of mixed feelings about finding his biological mother, at least for the time being.

In his adopted country, Bill was very popular at his school and among the embassy kids with whom he had formed some tight relationships. He knew that the values of his family differed somewhat from the values of his embassy friends. At the age of twelve, he often spent nights with his friends. One night they went out on the town, and Bill got drunk for his very first time. He had been drinking some before this experience. That night when he became drunk, he passed out behind some large building. He did not know just how long he was behind that building in an unconscious state. From that time, Bill, throughout his high school days, without his parents' knowledge, continued to drink more and more.

Upon graduation from high school, Bill returned to the States for college. He faced many reentry issues and adjustments. He was trying to figure out his identity, and there were so many frustrations. At times like these, Bill drank more and more as a way of seeking relief for his emotional pain. He was very lonely since his parents were so far away. He did not know who he was in America. In other words, he was going through an identity crisis. To reintegrate himself into the American culture seemed to be an impossible task. He was asking questions like: *Who am I? Where do I belong? Why don't my peers understand me? How do I form new friendships in this new culture? How do I ask girls out for a date?* There were so many questions running around in his head.

While living in his adopted country, he was happy. Now he had lost his country, his family, his siblings, his friends, the familiarity of his home, his own room, and all the familiar streets in his community, and even the special foods of that country. In trying to evaluate what was or was not real, he was asking himself pertinent questions like: *Is my behavior helping or hurting me? Is what I am doing helping me get what I want? Is what I am doing hurting my parents? Is what I want realistic or attainable? How committed am I to changing my behavior?* The last question was not a matter of being able to change his own behavior by himself. It was a matter of getting professional help for his alcoholism. He fully realized that, at the age of twenty-five, he was already an alcoholic.

Bill knew he was experiencing culture shock, and he felt the anxiety that naturally results from losing all the familiar signs, cues, and symbols of the community in which he had lived in South America. In America, he was now confronted with new signs, cues, and symbols that were not familiar to him. He believed that the American culture must be bad because it made him feel so badly. There was always that longing to be back in the culture where he had spent the developmental years of his life, where he felt accepted and even highly regarded as a son of missionaries, as well as an American. Now his parents were so far away, and he just needed someone to talk with who could understand him. There was always that longing for home. As we spent several hours together, Bill said to me, "Now, I have finally found someone who understands me. It feels so good."

As Bill and I again met with his parents, he knew, and his parents knew, that he could not overcome his problem with alcohol without some extended help in some rehabilitation center. It would have to be in a place where he would be willing to receive help. We talked about finding a place near his hometown, but they knew of no such place. I left the room and did a little research, and I was able to secure him a place in a rehabilitation center located right there in his home town. When I announced to Bill and his parents that I had found such a place, they were all in agreement for me to contact that rehabilitation center and ask if they could take him immediately for treatment. The answer came back, "Yes, we can have a place for him on Friday morning." Bill and his parents' resounding answer was an enthusiastic "yes." They, nor I, could believe that he could get help so soon, in just two days, and not have to be placed on a waiting list.

Bill really wanted to get well, and he readily committed himself to the facility. He entered on Friday morning, and he was truly pleased to discover that his counselor was a MK. He knew he had found another person who could understand him. After leaving the facility, Bill would also be able to receive outpatient care and counseling until he was strong enough to resist the temptation of drinking alcoholic beverages.

On Saturday morning, I received a telephone call from Bill's parents, who were so relieved and happy to have Bill seriously working on his drinking problem. His mother said, "Guess what? Bill's counselor is an MK himself, and he will know how Bill feels!" We rejoiced together at the wonder of God's providential guidance, care, and love to lead us to the perfect place for Bill's treatment. Bill has moved on with his life, the kind of life for which he had hoped, with a family of his own. His parents, upon retirement, now live in the same town as Bill, which makes him very happy. Bill knows, of course, that once an alcoholic, there is always the danger of falling off the wagon. Now, he does have a strong support system and can truly face each day with courage and hope.

A Family Intervention

Mary, a female MK born in Malaysia, was preparing for her wedding. She came to me with her fiancé Tom for premarital counseling. We scheduled two sessions, which I thought would probably be enough. Those two sessions went very well, but the big difference in personality types kept getting in the way and had to be addressed. For example, Mary was a very organized person who set deadlines for herself and kept them. Tom would get things done, though it may be at the last moment. Besides this, we were dealing with cultural differences, since Mary grew up in Malaysia. Tom's delays created a lot of anxiety in Mary. They were trying to plan their wedding, but Tom kept dragging his feet in compiling his list of guests. By now, six weeks away from the wedding, Mary had her wedding invitations ready to mail. Tom had not addressed even one invitation. She said, "If we can just get through all the plans and the wedding, we will probably be just fine."

After we had met for two sessions they had learned many things about each other that they had not known. Feeling a lot of stress, Mary said, "I feel I need some sessions just for myself." Up to that point I had been thinking, "I believe this is the healthiest MK I have met yet." She just appeared to be so well-adjusted.

Mary, a professional, was still dealing with some family-of-origin issues. She seemed to have a close, warm relationship with her mother. They appeared to me to be best friends. Her mother was a bit formal in her relationship with Mary. Her father, on the other hand, did not seem to be interested in Mary's well-chosen career. Actually, she felt he did not know her. Mary was the only daughter in the family. When she tried to get close to her father, he just seemed cool, and didn't seem to want to interact or converse with her. Of course, Mary felt hurt and angry. Her parents were, at that time, living in Malaysia, but they would be coming to America for Mary's wedding.

Mary was a petite, attractive, and intelligent young woman who was highly respected by her colleagues. Tom was handsome, more than six feet tall, weighing about 230 pounds. He was working with a group of business professionals. Mary was vibrant and full of energy, whereas Tom seemed a bit listless. Mary was organized and creative. She was very analytical. Tom could enjoy spending a lot of time alone, and crowds made him tired. Mary was always on time, whereas Tom was a procrastinator. He tended to be late for appointments.

The wedding took place in a church with lots of family and friends present. Tom's mother, who had died some months before, was missed, but was represented by a beautiful rose on the altar. It was a lovely wedding that went off in good fashion.

About a year into the marriage Tom lost his job, and he did not seem interested in securing another one any time soon. Mary was working very hard. Time passed, and yet Tom had not looked for a job. Mary was becoming more and more concerned. She was getting really anxious since she was now the only one bringing home a salary. Tom just was not "pulling his share of the load."

In the third year of their marriage, Mary became pregnant with their first child, a son. Since Tom came from a rather wealthy family, his father kept bailing him out. In addition to not working, Tom was beginning to drink more and more alcoholic beverages, mostly wine. Tom's father was not a great role model except in his work ethic. When they got married, Mary moved into Tom's already acquired house. Each tended to keep saying, "This is yours, and this is mine." It was not "ours." Mary was feeling more and more uncomfortable living in "Tom's" house. After all, her possessions had been placed in storage. She had none of her familiar things displayed where she would enjoy them. It is so important for MKs to be surrounded by their own familiar things in the States since they have left so much in their country. MKs usually bring back their clothes, some books, some curios, and a few other things of personal choice. She did not feel at home in Tom's place. I could share and understand Mary's need to have familiar things around her. I had returned from Japan a few years earlier to work on my doctorate, and I had expected to return to Japan. However, I began to realize how much MKs need counselors who could understand their backgrounds, their growing up in another culture, and then being transplanted into the American culture.

I resigned from my mission assignment in 1989. I did go back to Japan to sell some of my household goods and pack up my prized possessions to have them shipped back to the States. I spent two weeks in Japan. I found it difficult to say goodbye to my many Japanese friends whom I had made over a period of twenty years. I returned to the States and started my new counseling work with MKs and their family members. I had bought a new condominium and had also bought practically all new furniture. I knew I was beginning a new life. My shipment from Japan took a month to arrive. In the meantime, I found myself staying later and later at the office each evening. What I finally realized was that my condominium did not feel like home since I had none of my familiar things around me. However, when my shipment arrived, and I unpacked and placed those familiar possessions in my rooms, I could finally say, "I am home."

Mary was still missing her country of Malaysia. She missed her family, although they were far from being the perfect family. They were the only family she had, and they were so far away. She had observed that her father didn't really respect her mother, and this bothered her. He never apologized. He never listened to what Mary had to say, and he never consulted the family in making decisions that would affect the whole family. She said, "He never committed himself, and I am tired of his noncommittal stuff." Mary was really angry at her mother for allowing her father to take away her spirit of enthusiasm.

Little by little, Mary realized that Tom was becoming an alcoholic. He was a fifth-generation alcoholic. He was living in denial and was not following through on anything he started. His lack of involvement with their son bothered her. He was taking advantage of Mary's good nature. She realized now that they did not share the same values. He spent his money on alcohol while she paid the household bills.

As Tom continued to imbibe more and more, he would stay up very late at night, drinking. Then he would want to sleep all day. She was now afraid to leave their son with Tom during the day while she went to work. Mary was becoming more and more discouraged. She felt out of control. She even began to question her own judgment. She was full of self-doubt and saw herself as becoming more and more negative. She did not like the change she saw in herself, and she began to ask herself, *Why didn't I make better choices?*

Since Mary had no idea what her father felt about her, she took time out and went back to Malaysia to visit her parents with one goal in mind: "to ask her father what he thought of her." She was pretty anxious and a bit fearful to confront her father with her big question. She waited for the most opportune time to confront him. Then one evening, when her mother was out, her father was sitting on the sofa alone watching television. Mary went in, sat down beside him, and she asked, "Dad, I have a question for you. What do you think of me as your daughter and my accomplishments?" To her complete surprise and astonishment, her dad threw his head back, roared with laughter, and said, "That's the dumbest question I've ever heard." When I asked Mary how she felt at that moment, she said, "I felt discounted and completely rejected." He could see how hurt she was. He then said, "I am sorry *if* I hurt you." Mary left Malaysia to return to the States feeling dejected, helpless, and angry at her father. She could see that her own mother was becoming more impatient with her father as well.

A second child was born to Tom and Mary. Tom was still drinking too much. It was well put when someone said, "Tom is drinking himself to death." Later, when her parents came home for furlough, they were quite upset and concerned about Tom's condition but mostly about their own daughter's health. They just did not know what to do.

Mary, like her mother, never complained to her parents. It was clear that Mary was at her wit's end. Then Mary began coming to see me for more counsel on a regular basis. She had begun to doubt her own thoughts and rationale. She did not ever feel good, was exhausted, and felt she should be a stronger person. Her priorities were not what they should be. She was depressed. One thing she knew, she could not go on living with Tom unless he was willing to get help for his alcoholism. Then she began to bring her parents with her to counseling. They came willingly, but they did not know what to do to help the situation. After much discussion, I suggested implementing a family intervention, which meant confronting Tom and letting him know how his behavior was affecting the whole family. After explaining what an intervention would involve, I asked Mary if she would be willing to agree to an intervention and confront Tom in their home. This would mean that several family members would go with her to confront him. Mary was really scared. For two or three weeks she said she could not do it. She still loved Tom, but she knew that something had to change. I explained to Mary that neither she nor Tom could continue going down this path that would destroy both of them. Finally, I said to Mary, "What is going to happen to Tom if we don't get him help?" She fell apart and said, "He is going to die." At that moment Mary agreed for us to plan an intervention. We would have his parents, her parents and brother, and his uncle to be a part of this intervention.

Mary realized that her house was burning and if she did not get out, she was going to burn up with it. When asked by a family member, "Suppose Tom had a broken leg. Would you not take him to a physician?" Her family and Tom's family assured Mary that she did not have to do all the confronting, but she must take the first step and they would be there to carry her through. The time of decision had come.

An intervention was now set in motion. They had chosen certain family members to participate, and go together to confront Tom. Each member would make a speech telling Tom what he or she had been experiencing with him, how he was destroying himself and his family. He would not be allowed to speak until every family member present had made their speeches. Each had written out their speeches and later met in my office to rehearse them. The following week, just before confronting Tom, they all met in my office one more time to discuss or ask questions. I had chosen another therapist to go with the family to do the actual confrontation since I was already not only a counselor but a friend of both Mary and Tom. They left my office and went to do the most difficult part of the intervention. If Tom agreed to seek help, preparations had already been made about where he would go and how he would get there. If he refused, then Mary must be ready to say, "Then I must take the boys and leave you." When the family arrived at the house, of course, Tom was taken by surprise. They gathered in the living room, made their heart-rending speeches through tears. At first, Tom said, "No," but when Mary told him that she would then have to leave him, he reconsidered. Immediately following the intervention he was accompanied by his uncle who flew with him to an out-of-state facility. After three full weeks in the rehabilitation center, Tom returned home clean and proud of himself. Mary is a much stronger person now, with confidence and hope for their future.

Family interventions do work!

Healing the Hurts of Missionary Kids While Acknowledging the Scars

After Jesus was resurrected from the dead, Peter and a friend were going to a village called Emmaus, a short distance from Jerusalem. As they walked, they discussed Jesus' death, not able to reconcile themselves to all that had happened. Jesus drew near them, but they did not recognize him. No doubt, in their depression they told Jesus how they expected this man to redeem Israel. They had gone to the grave, but they could not find his body. This man stopped in the home of one of the two men.

He ate with them and then vanished from their sight. Then they went out to find the eleven disciples and told them about their experience. As they did this, Jesus suddenly stood in their midst saying, "Peace be unto you." They were terrified. Jesus continued to speak, "Why are you troubled?" Then he said to them, "Behold my hands and my feet.... Touch me and see." Jesus asked the disciples to literally touch him. They did, and this gave them hope (Luke 24). In John 20:27, Thomas stands before Jesus doubting that this was really Jesus. Jesus told Thomas to feel the scars in his hands and touch his side, which gave Thomas hope as he said to Jesus, "My Lord and my God." The scars were evidence of his own healing. The message to us is the same. Scars are the evidence that healing has taken place.

Most MKs are scarred. Missionary Kids are not proud of their scars, but neither are they ashamed of them. However, some have open wounds, they hurt, and they need a "doctor" to help to start the healing process. The Christian counselor may be the doctor. Some day we have the hope that those wounds will only be scars, the evidence of healing.

The counselor sees the scars and leads the MK to see that those scars will always be there and will always be a reminder of the pain they have experienced. The scars are evidence of healing and hope. As they run their fingers over those scars, they still need a caring community, offering encouragement and support. They also need a caring, empathic counselor to help bring healing to those wounds that have not yet healed. One person who has great compassion for MKs has said, "It is important that qualified counselors be identified and made available to MKs."

Not long ago, while talking with Mr. F., a ninety-year-old MK who grew up in Argentina, I heard him say, "I have struggled since I returned to the States on a ship, all alone and deaf, at the age of fifteen, with issues I didn't understand myself. How I wish there had been a good, qualified, understanding counselor there for me seventy-five years ago. As a ninety-year-old MK, I still feel the need for your help." So many

MKs have said, "Where were the counselors when I was hurting so badly, when I desperately needed them—five, ten, twenty, thirty, forty, fifty, sixty, seventy-five years ago?"

A caring community including the church and Christian counselors are crucial for the successful transition and recovery of MKs. They need our love, our care, our time, our support and encouragement. They need someone to walk with them through their feelings of isolation, anxiety, grief, emotional instability, and their loss of status. One MK, now a wife and mother, said to me, "Now, instead of open wounds, today I can praise the Lord for his love, faithfulness, and emotional healing in my life. It took many years to feel healed within, but I know I will always carry the scars." Scars are the evidence of the MK's healing. She says, "I know the Lord used those experiences to grow me in faith, trust, maturity, compassion, and endurance."

> MKs need a caring community and qualified counselors to help them through
> > bewilderment
> > confusion
> > loneliness
> > fears
> > disappointments
> > grief and anxiety

CHAPTER ELEVEN

The Uniqueness of MK Marriage

Caroline and Ben

Introduction

The children of missionaries are a unique group of people who have experienced living in at least one other culture than that of their parents in the United States. MKs are often referred to as "third-culture kids." Therefore, it is reasonable for Americans who have never lived abroad to experience these young people as being "different," for indeed they are different. At the same time, when MKs reenter the States, they also see Americans as being different compared to the people whom they have known in their host country. Just as Americans may see MKs as different and odd, these MKs see Americans as loud, boisterous, selfish, materialistic, and spoiled. This does not mean that MKs do not also recognize Americans' good qualities like kindness, generosity, and caring.

While living in another country and culture, MKs have had their own worldviews expanded. They have had opportunities to travel the world over. They have been exposed to peoples of the world and understand their needs, struggles, dreams, and achievements. Yes, they see the world through very clear glasses. They not only can empathize with people of another culture but also can be realistic about the things they do not like about that culture. After living in a different culture, you might imagine how confusing it can be for these MKs when they return to the States.

For example, I lived and worked in Japan for twenty years. I found Japan, its culture, and its people to be most interesting. I also found that Japanese often do things just the opposite from Americans. They bow instead of shake hands. They eat with chopsticks while Americans eat with silverware. They sleep on mats on the floor. Men go first while women hold the door open for them. Women even help the men put on their coats. They drive their cars on the left side of the road while the steering wheel is on the right side of the car. When introducing someone, they speak the last name first. They say "white and black" while we say "black and white." They needle a thread while we Americans say, "thread a needle." The number thirteen is a lucky number while the number four is an unlucky number. Why? The number four has the same word pronunciation as the word for death, "shi." When you visit someone for dinner, you carry gifts of flowers or fruit, but you must take odd numbers of pieces such as three, five, seven, or nine.

The Japanese schools are different. Students wear uniforms, and attend school six days a week. Many go to prep school after school to help them in some of their most difficult subjects. They must take entrance examinations to enter junior high school, high school, and college. The two main religions of Japan are Shinto and Buddhism. The priests of these two religions made an agreement long, long ago that the Shinto priest would perform the wedding ceremonies and the Buddhist priest would officiate at the funerals. Perhaps this brief explanation can help Americans understand why the children of missionaries and other young people who grow up in another culture can be so confused upon entering the American culture. They have so many issues to confront and so many adjustments to make in order to fit into the American society. You see, when they come back to the States they feel like foreigners here. Thus, it takes time to get used to

America. When I returned to the States to live permanently in 1986, I experienced some of the same issues that MKs do.

We can readily see why there might be a large number of divorces among MKs who marry someone who has never been out of their state much less outside of America. The real question for us to ask is, "What would these two people have in common?" Their backgrounds are so completely different. Their ways of doing things are so different. Therefore, neither can understand their spouse's feelings about certain things. When MKs hear of other peoples of the world who are hungry or mistreated, they can readily empathize. It is very hard for MKs to understand how America can go to war with nations so readily without leaders trying to understand the other's culture, religions, and ideologies. It seems so much easier for America to use force rather than friendship to solve the problems of the world. The fact is that America is seen by many countries in the world as the "big bully."

MKs feel disconnected and confused when they return to the States, and how can Americans begin to understand or even begin to identify with their experiences? MKs, fresh from the culture in which they have lived during the developmental years of their lives, are very lonely, and they seek a place to belong. My personal belief is that many MKs marry in haste in order to have a place to belong, but some have told me that what they found was not the answer to their need to belong. Then when their problems lead to divorce, they are filled with regrets, guilt, and sadness.

On the other hand, when an MK marries another MK, there is an immediate understanding of their backgrounds. It does not seem to matter that they might have grown up in two different foreign cultures, but just being a MK, they find their experiences are so similar. Even then, some carry excess baggage that they cannot blame on another culture. When MKs experience dissolution of their marriages, it is easy for parents to blame one spouse or the other for the failure. They don't seem to have a clue what it was like to be married to someone so completely different in the emotional, physical, mental, spiritual, and cultural realm of their lives.

At this point I will share with you the lives and some of the experiences of two MKs who unfortunately experienced divorces from their first spouses, and ended up marrying each other. This does not mean that they do not have problems in their second marriage, but yet their understanding of each other somehow helps them to resolve those problems.

Caroline's Story
Caroline was born in America while her parents were in the States for their first furlough. She was only three months old when she went with her parents to a mission country. Her earliest memories were of their house that was surrounded by bamboo and a little stream nearby. She also remembered the now outdated furnace that was installed with the grill in the floor, and how she ran across it barefooted while trying not to burn her feet on the hot grill.

After five years in their host mission country, living with dark-skinned people, they returned to the States for a year's furlough. Can you imagine how shocking it was for Caroline to see all white faces and hearing only the English language spoken? This big change caused Caroline to be very shy in the American kindergarten. However, since her parents decided to remain in the States for another year, she began to make friends. She remembers hearing her parents say that "those were lean years" for the family since they did not have enough money to afford the extras in life. Nevertheless, neither she nor her siblings were aware of those lean years. She does remember an elderly couple who gave her what they called "a kissy doll" which Caroline cherished. She said that if she put the dolls' hands together it would kiss her. This was one of her most cherished memories as a child.

After two years in the States, she had just begun to adjust when they returned to their mission country. Now, even their mission country seemed to have become strange to her. She attended an international school where her mother happened to be her teacher. She went there through the sixth grade. She learned the language quickly and felt at home in her adopted country. Even as a young child she did not hesitate to go out in their community and talk with and make friends with the nationals. She would even go shopping for her mother since her language ability was better than her mother's was. She said that the joke at their house between her siblings and their parents was that if someone came into the community looking for a member of her family, they just had to ask, "Where does Caroline live?" and they would immediately be given directions to their house. Caroline could take a bus or train and go anywhere she wanted to go by the time she was nine years old without any fear of being accosted.

Occasionally, Caroline spent nights with her national girlfriends, and at such a time they would go to the community public bath. Caroline felt a bit modest going to the public bath with all the nationals. She remembered going to her friend's house and using the toilet, which was simply a hole in the floor with a cover over it. Once when using that toilet, she dropped her watch into the hole. Her parents offered to try to retrieve it when the "honey bucket truck" came to pump it out each week. She politely told them "no."

In the sixth grade, Caroline found herself back in the States, in an English-speaking school. She said, "That was the most miserable year of my life." She and her siblings were noticeably different in the way they dressed and the way they spoke. She remembers her classmates ridiculing them, and they were called unbecoming names. Somehow she realized that her classmates made fun of her simply because she was different.

This time when they returned to their mission country, she attended an American school on an army base along with one of her brothers. The three older brothers were already away in boarding schools. As a teenager, she remembered going through the regular teenage crushes and breakups with some of the American guys at her school. One guy she dated was named Berger, and classmates nicknamed him "Cheeseburger." Another guy she dated was named Beverage. Her classmates teased her about dating boys with such fascinating names.

When she was a senior in high school, her parents returned to the States, which made it very difficult for Caroline since she wanted so much to graduate with her classmates there. This time, she knew she would not be returning to her mission country. This made her feel very sad. However, she did finish her senior year of high school in the States. It was hard to fit in at a new school when she was a senior. She felt a lot of anger.

After graduation she moved into an apartment with a high school friend and worked at a local hospital. She described her housemate as very strange. Her housemate's father had died when she was quite young, and her mother was an alcoholic. Caroline started dating a young man who also worked at the hospital. After a few months, feeling a need to belong, she married.

She remembers how she and her boyfriend had been in a car accident a few days before the wedding, and she had two hundred stitches in her head. It did not take long for Caroline to discover that the man she had married was "not nice at all." He had been married once before marrying Caroline. She realized that she had felt sorry for him, and she thought that with her love and care she could change him. She stayed in a very abusive marriage for twenty-one years. They had a son, and she felt trapped and at the mercy of her husband. She knew one thing; he was a male chauvinist with anger issues. One of his outrageous expectations of Caroline was to live in a less than adequately warmed house. In fact they had a wood-burning heater in the living room where they spent all their time. He slept on the sofa, and Caroline slept on an air mattress on the floor. She was expected to feed the stove with wood all night to keep the room warm. She even had the task of cutting the wood and stacking it on their porch. She had to run his bath water and lay out his clothes for the next day. Caroline said, "This man did not know how to be a father."

Her son lived a rather secluded life until he started to school. He was a good student, and she proudly saw him graduate from high school and go away to college. By this time, her husband had become more and more abusive, verbally and physically, breaking doors off their hinges and wrecking things. She could not go anywhere without her husband's permission. She could not even use the telephone when he was at home. Caroline's son had been the light of her life, but now she did not have to think about him and his safety anymore.

About this time, Caroline was diagnosed with skin cancer and told she could live for only six months. After her surgery she decided it was time to leave her husband and start a new life for herself. The good news was that she had been misdiagnosed and her life was not limited to six months. She realized, however, that life was too short to live the way she had for twenty years. She found a good lawyer who became her advocate as well. He got her a good settlement and even found her a house to rent. Caroline called friends who helped her move while her husband was on a twenty-four-hour work shift. The friends were eager to help because they had witnessed her abuse. They showed up one morning with two trucks. Her husband came looking for her, but her friend's husband would not let him come into their house. Caroline simply went to the door and told him, "Under no circumstances will I ever come back."

Caroline said, "My son is the only reason I do not regret marrying that man." When she told her son she had left his father, the son's reply was, "Well, Mom, it is about time." Caroline moved to another state and found a good job, using her second language. She also did volunteer work at a children's hospital. There she made many new friends and became involved in a good church.

Ben's Story

Like Caroline, Ben first went to their mission country when he was only three months old. Even though both he and Caroline went to the same country at the age of three months it does not mean that they were the same age. However, it does mean they knew each other and each other's families all of their lives. Ben's parents lived and worked in their chosen mission country for more than forty years. He was the youngest of six boys. Ben has only scant memories about his kindergarten years, but he has more vivid memories of being in the first grade since they were back in the States for furlough. He spoke his first word in the language of his adopted country rather than his parent's language, English.

Ben's family had a nanny who helped take care of the boys. He remembers, more often than not, taking his ripped clothing or a lost button to the nanny to repair. If he needed someone to talk to, he often went to the nanny. Ben became very good in the language. All of his friends were nationals. He would invite those children into his home. They came for lunch and dinner and sleepovers occasionally.

Eventually, Ben and his brothers all went away to boarding schools. He remembers being expelled from school the last year of his elementary school education for smoking cigarettes on the school grounds. Some of his "cronies," along with Ben, were sent to the principal's office for the same offense. The principal got so animated in scolding the boys that he slammed his fist down on his desk and broke the glass on top of the desk. All the boys burst out in laughter. The principal was so angry that he called their parents to his office and announced to them that their boys were expelled for the rest of the school year. For that part of the year, Ben was homeschooled. The next year he was able to go to an American school right there in their city. In those days, he was always eager to arrive home from school since he would always find his friends waiting for him to get off the school bus so they could play and hang out together.

Ben always looked forward to the annual mission meeting when all the missionaries in their country got together for business and fellowship. The best part was riding the overnight train. He said he loved the "clickety-clack" sound of the train on the rails. Since it was an overnight train, he enjoyed watching the men fold down the seats that became bunk beds. He still remembers the comforting sound that lulled him to sleep on the train.

At age fourteen, Ben remembers returning to the States for furlough as a "goofy, pimply, awkward boy." At that time, Ben was the only son still living with his parents. That year he attended a predominantly black school, a new experience for Ben. It was on that furlough when he "began to understand a little bit about racism, prejudice, and ignorance."

Upon returning to their mission country, Ben went away from home for his high school education. Even though it was a Christian school, Ben said it should have been named, "Sheltered living in a bubble for missionary children." The boarding students lived in a dormitory which Ben refers to as a commune. He spent lots of time playing his music and practicing sports. Occasionally he would go on camping trips with some of his friends. In his senior year of high school, Ben described himself as a pompous, conceited, spoiled, and selfish human being. Although he was popular, he was not happy.

Ben looked forward to high school graduation. He thought, at that time, that he was "on top of the world." After hitchhiking across the country he returned home to pack his clothes and some other items. Then he would be leaving his country and traveling to the States accompanied by his mother. He and his mother would visit other brothers already living in the States. After a day or two with a brother in a northern state, he set out for a southern state where he would enter college. His mother stayed on for a longer visit with her other son. Upon arrival he was to take a Greyhound bus to the small town where the college was located. He did not know where the bus station was, but by the time he found it, the last bus had already left. He had no idea how to get in touch with anyone. He also admitted that he did not even know the telephone system, and how to use one. He had no idea what to look for in the phone book to seek help. Most critical of all was that he had only sixty dollars to last him for one month. Ben said, "I was petrified."

Ben described that little town as "a place you see in the movies, with the courthouse in the center of town, and the streets would run around it, and it was known as 'The Town Square.' Besides the money Ben had in his pocket, he had a backpack, a guitar, and a camera. Finally he found a taxi, but when he found out from the driver that it would cost him eighty-five dollars to take him to the college town, Ben was horrified. Finally, he was able to talk the driver into taking him for forty dollars. When they arrived the taxi driver dropped him off at a bus stop, only to find out that it was no longer a bus stop. What would he do now? Since he did have directions, he started out walking to his uncle's house. Ben had come from a large city in his host country where buses ran every ten to fifteen minutes. Now he was in this "prairie" town where he had not seen a bus at all.

Ben stayed with his uncle and his family for three weeks before school started. These relatives were more like strangers than family. They had no idea what Ben's life had been like prior to arriving in the States. Therefore, they did not even know the right questions to ask him.

In Ben's host mission country he was known as a "foreigner," but in this small town where he looked like everyone else, he said, "I was nothing. Less than nothing, actually." Finally the day came when he signed up for his classes and found the dormitory where he was to be living. He said, "I was terrified. I was lonely and scared." To make things worse he had a roommate who insisted on playing only one album, and as loud as the volume would go. Ben put up with this all semester until exam time came. He could not study in that type of atmosphere. He finally told his roommate that if he played that album one more time, he would throw it with the whole stereo system out the window, and he would toss him out as well. They lived on the third floor. The fellow did not believe Ben would do what he said he would do. Sure enough, he did it again and sneered at Ben. Ben opened the window, removed the screen and tossed the album, the turntable and the whole system out the window. Then he grabbed his roommate and was ready to toss him out but was restrained by an Iranian student who calmed Ben. The second semester, Ben moved and had a new roommate, and they got along just fine. Since he enjoyed drama, he joined the theatre troupe. He had new friends and began to party and drink a lot of alcoholic beverages. His attitude by now was, "I just don't care anymore!"

When hitchhiking to his grandparents for Christmas holidays, he got a ride on a eighteen-wheeler truck. He was amused. He had never seen a truck like this. The driver even taught him how to drive it. The down side was that the driver introduced him to marijuana and cocaine. When he returned to school after the holidays, all he wanted to do was go home. Somehow he did make it through that school year and was able to return home for the summer. When he arrived home he was proud to show his parents his new driver's license, and announced to them that he was going to tour the country on a motorbike. He had a great time meeting and being with old friends. He described it as a "terrific summer."

Ben said that the best part of the summer was riding his motorbike, stopping at inns, and speaking the language fluently with the innkeepers and others whom he met along the way. He realized the drive was both beautiful and inspiring. At the same time he felt sad because he knew he would never be able to do that again. Leaving his country was so traumatic that he doesn't seem to remember much about actually leaving or arriving in the States.

Instead of returning to college Ben decided to take a year off and work with one of his brothers in construction work. The work was hard, and he earned only a small salary. He watched the other construction workers and was a fast learner. However, he spent most of his money on drugs. He said, "I worked, got high, either on pot or whatever drug was available, and drank for the whole weekend. Then the cycle began all over again." He was offered a job by a cousin that paid more money, and he took it. He realized that what he was doing was using drugs and alcohol to escape his struggles and ease his anguish and pain. By now, he was growing tired of this kind of life.

His grandfather who lived on the East Coast was able to convince Ben that going to college was the best thing he could do with his life. His grandfather spent a lot of time talking to him. Ben could see how happy his grandfather was when he spent time with him. He enjoyed hearing his grandfather's stories of the Great Depression and how he had started his own jewelry business. However, after twelve robberies in nine years, Ben's grandfather, after being severely beaten, was convinced it was time for him to retire. Ben was now living with his grandparents.

In his grandfather's last years Ben became his constant companion. His grandmother suffered from diabetes, and in a short time his grandfather suffered from cancer, but Ben did not know about his grandfather's terminal disease. He kept telling Ben how much he needed to get a good education. Ben agreed and registered at the community college. He became completely involved in theatre, building sets, learning about the lighting, and even did some acting himself. He learned all about the technical aspects of theatre productions. For the first time since returning to the States to live, Ben felt he belonged somewhere again. He had friends and family and especially his grandfather. Together they did some vegetable gardening, and what they could not eat, they canned or preserved. Those two years Ben had with his grandparents were the best. They proved to actually be his salvation.

As Ben watched, he could see that his grandfather's health was declining. This was hard for Ben, and he could not entertain the thought of his dying anytime soon, much less in only four more weeks. One day when Ben returned home, he heard his grandfather calling his name. He went to the stairs that led down to the basement and saw his grandfather standing at the bottom of the steps. He told Ben he couldn't get up the steps on his own. Ben helped him up the steps and placed him in his recliner, and gave him a glass of water. Then he called his aunt, who told Ben not to worry, his grandfather would be all right. He then called his brother and heard the same thing from him. Looking for someone to hear him, he called his father in his mission country. His dad said he would call Ben's aunt, his sister. Ben tried to convince his father that he needed to come to the States and spend some time with his father before he died. His dad either refused to believe and heed Ben's plea, or he was in denial that his own father could be that sick. They were to come to the States on furlough soon, and evidently he believed his father would still be there.

In the meantime, Ben's grandfather grew progressively worse. On a Sunday, some of the family members had come for a family picnic and had gone home. Ben had a growing fear that his grandfather would die that night. He didn't want to be alone and watch him die. Even though Ben had pleaded with some of the family members to stay, they all said they had to go home. That night after going to sleep in his recliner he awakened Ben, who was still in the room. He needed help to go to the bathroom and then put him to bed. After getting him in bed he asked Ben to go and get his grandmother and come back. He said to Ben, "It is almost time." He told his wife, "I love you, and I will be waiting for you." Then he looked at Ben and said, "Son, take care of your grandmother, okay?" Ben promised he would. Then, Ben asked him if he was "going." His reply was, "Yes, son, I am. I love you and am proud of you. Don't give up, okay?" Then he closed his eyes, took a deep breath, exhaled and became still. Ben said, "I watched his spirit leave his body." He stood there, having no idea just how long. Then he became very scared and ran to call 911. When the emergency personnel arrived, they pronounced him dead and put him in an ambulance.

Ben went back into the house to call his aunt and his brother. Then he left the house. When he returned he started screaming at his brother for not staying with him. He called his father and remembers screaming at him for not listening to him and not coming home to be with his father. Ben said, "This was the first time I had dealt with death. I had not even talked about death, nor even given any thought about death until that night."

When Ben's father arrived home for the funeral, he did apologize to

Ben for not hearing him when he was told he needed to come home and be with his father. Ben was so hurt, he could not accept his apology at that time. He told his father, "My grandfather was the only one who made me feel like I really mattered and that I was worth something." Ben now felt so alone. His grandmother went to live with his aunt while Ben continued to live in their house. He became completely immersed in his studies at the community college, especially theatre. Sad to say, Ben began to get involved in taking drugs and drinking again. He had a couple of girlfriends. He said, "Sex was just another way of dulling my pain, along with drugs and booze." This is the way his life continued for the next three years until his parents retired from their mission work and returned to the States. At that time, he still did not have a clue as to what he wanted to do with his life.

At the end of three years after his grandfather's death, Ben's parents moved back to the States into the home place where his grandparents had lived. Ben was in school and involved in theatre. His grandfather's influence continued to urge Ben to "get an education so you can have a better life."

Church attendance was the last thing on Ben's list of things to do. As he was about to finish his college work, he was continuing to party, date, and deal drugs. He met a young lady who was hopelessly hooked on drugs. He described her as "a spoiled rich kid" who knew how to use people. On one hand, Ben appeared to be "smooth" and "having it all together." However, he said, "I knew that inside, I was screaming." He felt no one really cared about him, who he was, or from where he came. He just wanted to be "somebody."

Ben got more and more involved with the spoiled, rich girl and provided her with drugs as well. When her parents kicked her out of the house, she moved in with Ben. Soon she discovered she was pregnant. Upon discovering this she completely stopped taking drugs. After their son was born, she became "very strange." She went back to live with her parents, but within a couple of months she had "a raging argument" with her mother and moved back into Ben's apartment.

Ben and this young lady got married. He now realized what a great responsibility he had caring for a family, but his partying continued. His feelings for his wife were waning. Ben had begun to settle down, but his wife's partying continued until she discovered she was pregnant a second time. During that pregnancy she stopped taking drugs but resumed taking them after her delivery. Then there was a third pregnancy, but she did not stop taking drugs that time. Ben worked hard to provide for his family. He was working in construction and was very good at it. His wife demeaned him by telling him that even a "trained monkey" could do his kind of menial work. She wanted him to get "a real job." In their fourth year of marriage, their sex life was practically nonexistent. Ben said, "After she had crushed my spirit, I was crushed in almost every other area of my life."

Following the birth of their third child, the marriage crumbled completely. One night she and a male friend returned home completely drunk. Ben was awakened to a loud crash at the front door. When he opened the door she and her friend were "dead drunk, lying on the front stoop, laughing like wild hyenas." She was truly an alcoholic as well as a drug addict. Ben lost his temper and manhandled his wife. She called the police, and Ben spent the night in jail. The next day his parents bailed him out. When he went to court, the charges against him were dropped, and he was released. He now saw his wife as "a hopeless victim of an alcoholic insanity." He had been lured by her beauty and their mutual interest in doing drugs. Ben strived to be the "typical good father." He was determined he was not going to "totally leave my children in the clutches of this alcoholic and drug addict."

During this stressful time, Ben's mother died of a pulmonary embolism. Ben was devastated. He said, "My only advocate and best friend, the one who always loved me, no matter what, and who would listen to me, was gone." In order to dull the pain he started drinking again. He finally divorced his wife in 1996. He continued caring for the needs of his children, calling them if not seeing them every day. It grieved him to know that his children had been exposed to his former wife's seven different boyfriends who would spend the night with her on a regular basis.

Up to this point, Ben and his father did not have a good relationship. According to Ben, "We didn't really know each other." His mother who had given them their common ground was now gone. Ben felt like a lost little boy.

In October after his mother's death in May, Ben went to a gathering of missionaries, all from the country in which he had grown up. It was a kind of reunion that had been taking place for about twenty years. There, they had a memorial service for his mother and other missionaries who had died the year since they had last met. Before his mother's death she had asked a local pastor to visit Ben. He did, but he did not talk about church. In fact, they talked about everything but religion, Christianity, and the church. This really puzzled Ben for he had expected the minister to reprimand him for not attending church. He saw the minister was interested in him as a person, and for that reason he did go back to church, the first time in fourteen years.

At this gathering of missionaries at the memorial service, Ben was the only one in his family who attempted to speak about his mother. The other brothers and his father were just too emotional to try to speak. It was very emotional for Ben as well. As he spoke about his mother he said, "All my past came flooding my mind, that part of my life I had completely shut down." At that gathering he heard about a group of men planning to go to his country and build a house for a missionary. When he returned home he called one of the men and volunteered to go with them, but they already had their team and didn't really need him. This rejection almost "drove him over the edge." He came very close to taking his life, but his love for his children stopped him.

Ben called me in Winston-Salem, and we talked for a long time. I suggested that he come to my city and we would spend hours in intensive counseling, which he did. It was January and we had one of the biggest snowstorms on record. After driving eight hours in the snowstorm, he arrived at his hotel and actually walked to my house two blocks away. We talked until late Friday night and started again on Saturday morning and continued until late Saturday night. He dealt with so many issues, and he would process all that information on his way home. I suggested that he call that work team again when he got home because I believed that a trip back to his country was important for him to bring closure to that part of his life. Within thirty minutes after arriving at home, a team member called him, saying they had had a cancellation and asked if he could go.

Returning to his home country was exactly what Ben needed. He said, "I came to know who I truly was, and how I needed to change. I was truly able to put to rest the demons in my mind and heart, about who I was, and where I needed to be." Upon returning to the States, he had a great "homecoming" with his family. He secured good jobs and could provide well for his children, now his main focus. Ben was living with his dad, who by this time had remarried. His dad and his new wife lived part-time there but also part-time in her home in another state. A week before his father's sudden death, they had a good talk and said a lot of things that both needed to say to each other. His father said, "Well, I feel much better knowing that all my sons can now take care of themselves in their own businesses." Ben said, "The day my father died was the day I truly grew up." He had now watched his grandfather and his own father die right before his eyes.

The missionaries had honored his mother the year before, and now it was time for Ben and his brothers to go once again to the missionary gathering to honor his father's life and death. Up to this time in his life, Ben had been only once. Now, Ben felt he needed his missionary family more than ever before. At this reunion Ben had a lot of fun meeting other MK friends, and experienced some much-needed healing. He loved remembering and truly communicating with people who truly understood him. There was one particular family who had been friends with his family through the years in the mission field. Ben remembered Caroline, the only girl in that family with four brothers.

The following year, Ben again attended the missionary gathering or reunion for his third time. There, he met Caroline again. Ben said, "She had been through hell and a nasty divorce a few years earlier from a domineering pig of a man." Ben found himself following Caroline and talking to her every chance he had. Ben said, "The best time at the reunion was when we MKs gathered around the fire, and we sang songs, told our stories, laughed, cried, listened, and sometimes prayed together." In short, they shared their life experiences, the good and the bad, which was a real catharsis for most of the MKs. Ben said, "We grew up in a poor, desolate country and left it as a world power, rebuilt and reborn, and it was our home. And we were forced to leave. And we came home to a foreign land, the United States of America. But most of us have adapted and survived." Most of them, at one time or another, felt lost, but these reunions helped them realize that they were not alone in their suffering.

Ben and Caroline spent a great deal of time walking and talking at that reunion. After they returned home they talked online day and night. After a few months they realized that "God had put us together at this particular time." Ben asked Caroline to marry him, and she said "yes." They realized they had so much in common. After all they had both gone to the same country when each was three months old. Caroline had one grown son, now married, while Ben had three children, all still school age. She said, "Ben is a good man, and we are happy together."

Caroline and Ben in Marriage

What makes a marriage of two MKs so special? First and foremost, MKs grow up in countries different from that of their parents. In the case of Caroline and Ben, they just happened to grow up in the same country. Nevertheless, just being an MK makes it easy to understand other MKs, no matter what country in which they may have spent their developmental years. They all speak a second language. They have a common understanding of what it is like to relate to different people. They have a broader world experience, and they somehow develop a sense of caring for them. They are empathic and sensitive to world needs. They feel "odd" in both countries, but they understand this as they relate to each other. They always feel they are in transition and always will be. They appreciate the simple things in life, particularly the beauty found in nature. They are accepting of other people. They enjoy the foods from other countries and can appreciate their customs. When families of two MKs grow up together in the same country, they and their family members can speak to each other in that same foreign language.

MKs understand the needs, struggles, dreams, and achievements of each other, unlike their counterparts in the States. They claim a worldview. They maintain a sense of relationship to at least two cultures while not having full ownership in either. Their sense of belonging is limited to relationships to others who have their similar experiences. They readily identify with each other, unlike the way they may try to identify with the young people in America.

MKs married to non-MKs often feel lonely, shy, socially inferior, fearful, anxious, rejected, and misunderstood. No matter how much they may try, communication often breaks down between them, more so than in non-MK marriages. The MK's multiple cultural experiences add new dimensions to a task and create and aggravate ambiguities and ambivalence toward themselves but much more toward their non-MK spouses. It is very difficult for the non-MK spouse to identify with all kinds of feelings MKs face such as homesickness, loneliness, fear, isolation, alienation, anger, inferiority, and looking for warm personal relationships. Being separated from parents and siblings and friends from their country creates all these feelings and more.

Caroline and Ben discussed with me how their MK sensitivity can be good and bad at the same time. Being too sensitive can open oneself up for disappointment and pain, whereas not being sensitive may cause pain for someone else. They readily told me about how they felt pain when their non-MK spouses did not have a clue about why they were hurt. They felt the pain and then the anger toward their ex-spouses. Yet, they tended to keep those feelings inside. MKs married to MKs feel more accepted for who they are. They feel loved, appreciated, and respected for who they are. They find that they have similar problems, experiences, goals, interests, and lifestyles.

One of the main issues that MKs married to each other with blended families encounter is their respective children's acceptance of a stepparent. Girls, in particular, often feel threatened by a stepmother, seeing her as the intruder who might steal away all their father's love. Ben's two girls have dealt with jealousy and possessiveness. Sometimes they have even bodily tried to get between them. Ben's son loves and respects Caroline. The younger daughter shares a lot about her life and school activities with Caroline. She knows Caroline loves her and wants the best for her. At times, she becomes very clingy toward her father. Ben and Caroline are working through the various issues with which blended families must deal.

To my knowledge, there are not a great many MKs who marry MKs who have had previous failed marriages. Unfortunately there are not that many MKs who might be available in second marriages or in first marriages as far as that is concerned. I have often had MKs say to me, "If I ever get married a second time, it is going to be to an MK who can understand me." Some have said, "If only I could have married an MK the first time around, perhaps I would not be facing a divorce."

In the end, we know that both spouses in any marriage have issues and struggles. The uniqueness of MKs and marriage is that they are indeed different from other American young people who have never lived anywhere outside the continental United States. An MK married to a non-MK often feels like a stranger in his or her own home. However, perhaps the biggest problem with broken marriages is that the partners are not willing to accept each other as they are. Too many just do not have the patience it takes to work out their problems and remain together.

CONCLUSION

Implications

As you have read the stories of MKs in this book, let me emphasize that they do not want your pity. They only would like to have you try to understand and support them. Most of the MKs I have known are proud to have lived in a different culture and country. In fact, I have had only one MK say to me, "I wish I had never been a MK. I would have preferred to have grown up in the United States of America." Regardless of all their reentry issues, the struggles of being different and feeling different, they still are appreciative of their backgrounds. When an MK is born in another country or has gone there as a young child, and then spends all the developmental years of their lives in that culture, that country is the only "home" they have ever known. Until they return to the States for their college education, they have not had another culture to compare with the one in which they have spent the first seventeen or eighteen years of their lives. However, upon their return to the States, knowing they will not be going back, they begin to feel really different.

Of course, on furlough they have been confronted with the differences between themselves and their peers, and even the differences in culture and customs, but they knew they would return to their "home" country. When their year of furlough is ended, they are always eager to get back to their country, their homes, their rooms, their pets, their friends, their schools, and their everyday life in that country. Thus, being a MK can, at the same time, be a blessing and a curse.

I will point out here some of the implications of being a MK. Webster defines "implication" as "to fold and twist together." MKs have actually experienced the folding and twisting of two cultures until they become what is often referred to as "third-culture kids." MKs are a mixture of two cultures all wrapped up in one personality. MKs adapt to local customs, learn the local language, and are able to expand their worldviews as they live in a different culture. In most cases they love and identify with that culture and its people. They develop a relationship to at least two cultures while not having full ownership in either culture. They incorporate components from two cultures into their lives, but their sense of belonging is limited somewhat to relationships to others who have had similar experiences. Their personalities are developed in the midst of two societies. Just about the time they have formed their self-identities in their "home" country, they return to the States for their higher education. They, to their amazement, realize that some of their cultural baggage does not fit in American society. Thus, they have the task of re-forming their identities, which can, at times, become confusing and painful, and yes, it sometimes makes them feel angry. As they suffer from culture shock and try to find a place to fit in, they find they are in a constant process of unfolding and untwisting and trying to make sense of what is happening to them. It may take years before they actually feel at home in the States.

I have identified five implications of being a product of two different societies and cultures. The first implication is the question: *Where is home?* When people in the States say to MKs, "You must be happy to be back home," referring to the States, MKs are appalled, and their first thoughts are, *But I am not at home. My other country is my home.* Then they ask themselves, *What will my reply be to this question?* Their mother may be from Georgia, and their father may be from Texas, but they have no state they can claim for their own. For example, one MK may say, "I am from Africa. Africa is my home," and their peers give them this look of surprise, and may then ask questions like, "Well, then, you must have lived in a grass hut and eaten bugs. Did you ever meet Tarzan?" You see, young people in the States know very little about other countries of the world. MKs would rather avoid answering the question, "Where are you from?"

I remember once meeting a young female missionary doctor at the airport in my city. Since she was going to be there for a few weeks, she needed to rent a car. I went with her to the rental-car counter. She was giving the clerk answers to the regular questions. She had flown in from the state of Washington, but she had spent her most recent years as a doctor in Gaza, and I had secured living quarters for her in Winston-Salem. When the man asked her for her address, she looked at me and asked, "What address should I give him?" To simplify things I told her to give them my personal address.

Trying to explain where home is can be a time of trying to unfold and untwist in order to give a satisfactory answer to the question "Where is home?" It does take time to figure out what the answer will be.

A second implication is: *Who am I?* Again, MKs must unfold and untwist the cultural differences to come up with an acceptable response. MKs have said to me, "I know I have the American face, but I do not feel American." The truth is, they are third-culture people with a good mixture of both cultures. In their "home" country, they have grown up with American parents in an American home, but, at the same time, they are greatly influenced by the people and culture they encounter every day of their lives in the community, the church, the school, where they shop, the observance of holidays there and in the home of their parents. When they visit in the homes of the nationals, they eat their food and observe their etiquette. For example, in many countries of the world, people eat with a fork in the right hand and a knife in the left hand. In the States, that would look odd to most Americans, and may be considered rude or unacceptable as good manners. In Japan, when the nationals eat rice or a salad, they hold the bowl in their left hand near their mouths. These may seem like small things to the average person, but to the MK it may be disturbing as they seek to adapt to the proper etiquette in the States. It takes time to unfold and untwist the proper thing to do at certain times.

A third implication is: *How Resilient am I?* Just how resilient are MKs as they seek to reintegrate themselves into the American culture? I believe MKs have learned to be pretty flexible, pliable, adaptable, and yielding, although in doing so, they may feel a lot of anxiety and frustration. Often MKs return to the States alone on an airplane, and most often they do not have a "safety net" in the form of a support group, someone to meet their plane and give them a warm welcome. Even relatives who perhaps meet them upon their arrival are pretty much strangers. On the mission field, other missionaries have been their family—aunts, uncles, cousins, and grandparents. There seems to be no way MKs can recapture such a family or community in the States. One missionary father attended a counseling session with his daughter who talked about her struggles and pain upon being left by her parents who returned to the mission field. She expressed how she felt so alone and abandoned by her parents. Then her father responded empathically saying, "I am just now realizing that when my daughter returned to the States, she did not have a safety net like her mother and I always had when we returned for furlough." He went on to say, "We had friends whom we had known over many years, and we knew all our family members who came to the airport to warmly welcome us home with their hugs and greetings." As MKs unfold and untwist and know the effect of one culture and suddenly try to get used to American culture, I believe MKs are pretty resilient people.

A fourth implication is: *Who is my family?* MKs go to another country with their parents or are born there. Some live with their parents during their entire time in that country, while others may live with their parents until they enter the first grade, and if lucky until they enter the fifth grade. Then they are sent away to some boarding school. They know their parents are truly their parents. However, at boarding school there are a headmaster, teachers, staff, and dorm parents. They may not see their parents more than two or three times a year. Suddenly, they have lost home and parents, and now the school staff and school mates become their family. With this group of children, they eat, sleep, study, and play. Now they have a larger "family." At first, it can be very difficult. They feel sad and lonely. Many have told me that they cried a lot into their pillows, not wanting others to see their tears. Somehow, after some time, they come to accept that this is their plight. They will be with most of these classmates in elementary, junior high, and high school. They are disciplined, not by their biological parents, but by school staff and dorm parents. In the meantime, they and their parents have missed out on the growth and development of each family member. Once MKs go to boarding school, they never again go back home to live with their parents permanently. MKs sometimes come to feel more at home and a part of their boarding school family than they do with their own biological families. One middle-aged male MK who had been sent away to boarding school at a young age said, "My parents have now retired, but when I go to visit them, we have nothing in common to talk about." He went on to say, "Both my parents and I feel somewhat awkward." It takes a lot of unfolding and untwisting for MKs to figure out who their real families are.

A fifth implication is: *How do I deal with my grief?* One day the MK is at "home" in his host country, and the next day he finds himself in the States. In a matter of hours, his life totally changes. Many who have gone away to boarding school already know what separation and loss are all about. They have somewhat accepted the fact that they will never live with their parents, for they are destined to leave their country and go away to the States to enter some college or university. Yet they are not ready for that complete break with their families, their country, and their friends. Suddenly, they have lost all the things that are familiar. One morning they wake up, wondering if they are here or there. The loss is more than the average American can imagine. The grief, at times, seems insurmountable. Who can they turn to for comfort and understanding? They dream of being back "home," and the dream is almost like being there even if for the short period of a dream. They realize they are now separated from all they have known. In short, it is like a death experience. One MK perhaps speaks for many when he says, "When I left my country, I felt I was experiencing a thousand deaths at once, including my own. When I left my country, I had really left everything except my body in my 'home' country." Can anyone who has not had this experience begin to fathom the huge amount of grief MKs face? I don't think so.

In order to deal with their grief, some MKs seek a good counselor, one who can help them deal with their grief. Some find a friend or friends with whom they can share the pain of their grief. However, I fear that far too many suffer in silence, with their grief held inside. They may want to appear strong, but inside they are hurting so bad, knowing it is taking its toll on their health and self-esteem. Many MKs become depressed. Anger is always a part of grief. Often, no matter how irrational it may seem, we ordinary people become angry at a dear person who dies and leaves us. MKs often feel abandoned, and they wonder, "How in the world could my parents do this to me?" Then they feel angry at their parents, but since they are "doing God's work" the MK may then feel guilty for feeling that anger. What do they do with their anger? They turn the anger inside and then become depressed. I have known some who became depressed and could not get better until they began taking an antidepressant each day. I am grateful for a wonderful psychiatrist in Winston-Salem, Dr. Robert Gibson, who has helped numerous MKs and missionaries through their periods of depression. At such a time, it takes a lot of unfolding and untwisting for MKs to get through their grief and find their real selves.

Empathy goes a long way. This is what they need from folks in America—relatives, college classmates, professors, and the people in our churches. Many people in the States don't know that the MK needs help, because the MK wants to appear strong and have it all together. From reading this book, Americans, I hope, will become sensitized to the needs of MKs and ask them, "What can I do?"

Once an MK, he or she never stops being an MK. It is a lifetime experience. Many have lived through the folds and twists and then reach out to others who are still working through the impact of the folds and twists in their lives. MKs are perhaps the most resilient people I know. Janice Patterson, Ph.D., who is an assistant professor of curriculum and instruction at the University of Alabama, Birmingham, and coauthor of the book *Bouncing Back*, says that a resilient child is one who can withstand hardships and bounce back. Many MKs find the courage and strength to bounce back and move on to bigger and better things. However, I am sad to say that some seem to fall through the cracks. These are the ones who really need our love, understanding, and support.

APPENDIX

WHO AM I?

When I was growing up, adults always asked me what I was going to be, but there came a time when what I was going to be wasn't as important as who I was. Everyone questions who they are and MKs are no exception. Who is an MK.

I am   a combination of two cultures. I am neither and I am both. I am the brat who throws a temper tantrum and refuses to dress native for the American church.

I am   the six-year old who can't wait to go away to school and I am the six-year old who cries herself to sleep the first two weeks of school.

I am   the one who complained about eating oatmeal every day of my life, and I am the one who orders oatmeal at the restaurant for old time's sake.

I am   the one who desperately worries about fitting in, and I am the one who wears my native wrap around the college dorm and doesn't care what anyone thinks.

I am   the one who has lived under strict school rules, and I am the one who returns to America and questions what my real values are.

I am   the one the churches make a saint out of, and the one other people pity and laugh at.

I am   the one who traveled halfway around the world before I was four, and I am the one who has no home.

I am   the one who promises to write, but never does because it's too difficult to deal with the reality of separation.

I am   the one who has seen the devil dancers, and I am the one who has seen the rock concerts.

I am   the one who knows and understands world missions, life and death, heaven and hell. I am the one who has seen God work miracles.

I am   the one who knows prayer works, and I am the one who sometimes finds it difficult to pray.

I am   the one who has learned to live with a politically unstable government, and I am the one who waits impatiently by the phone for news that everything is safe.

I am   the one who has spent only three months a year at home. Yet I know, beyond question, that my parents are the best in the whole world.

I am   the one who speaks two languages, but can't spell either. I am the one who has devotions from a French Bible.

I am   the one who wears a thousand masks, one for each day and time.

I am   the one who learned to be all that I'm expected to be, but still not sure of who I really am.

I am   the one who chooses my college by where my friends are, because nobody understands and MK like another MK.

I am   the one who laughs and cries, sings and prays, gets angry and doubts, fears and questions, expects and receives, hopes and dreams.
But I am one who cares!

I am a MK and I am proud of it!

—Anonymous Missionary Kid

BIBLIOGRAPHY

Cowley, Malcolm. *Exiles Return.* New York: Viking Press, 1991.
Ekman, Paul. *Why Kids Lie.* New York: Scribner, 1989.
Fortune, Marie. *Is Nothing Sacred?* Cleveland: United Church Press, 1999.
Miller, Dee. *How Little We Knew.* Lafayette, LA: Prescott Press, 1993.

Doris L. Walters, B.A., M.R.E., M.A., D. Min. is a retired therapist who organized and developed Missionary Family Counseling Services, Inc., Winston-Salem, North Carolina. As a missionary to Japan herself for over twenty years, Dr. Walters has been keenly aware of the stresses and challenges faced by missionary children and their families. This, combined with her extensive training and experience in pastoral counseling and program development has made Dr. Walters uniquely qualified to establish and lead this innovative counseling program which continues to exist today in Winston-Salem. Dr. Walters was selected as Alumnus of the Year by Gardner-Webb University in 1992, Who's Who of American Women in 1993, Who's Who in the World in 1995, Who's Who in Executives and Professionals 1996, and American Registry of Outstanding Professionals in 2001. She is a certified diplomate in The American Psychotherapy Association.